THE CAMBRIDGE COM
RILKE

Often regarded as the greatest German poet Maria Rilke (1875–1926) remains one of the n.... influential figures of .... pean modernism. In this *Companion*, leading scholars offer informative and thought-provoking essays on his life and social context, his correspondence, all his major collections of poetry including most famously the *Duino Elegies* and *The Sonnets to Orpheus*, and his seminal novel of modernist anxiety, *The Notebooks of Malte Laurids Brigge*. Rilke's critical contexts are explored in detail: his relationship with philosophy and the visual arts; his place within modernism and his relationship to European literature; and his reception in Europe and beyond. With its invaluable guide to further reading and a chronology of Rilke's life and work, this *Companion* will provide an accessible, engaging account of this extraordinary poet, his enduring legacy and far-reaching influence.

KAREN LEEDER is Professor of Modern German Literature at the University of Oxford and a fellow of New College.

ROBERT VILAIN is Professor of German and Comparative Literature at Royal Holloway, University of London.

*A complete list of books in the series is at the back of this book*

# THE CAMBRIDGE
# COMPANION TO
# RILKE

EDITED BY
## KAREN LEEDER

*and*

## ROBERT VILAIN

CAMBRIDGE
UNIVERSITY PRESS

CAMBRIDGE UNIVERSITY PRESS
Cambridge, New York, Melbourne, Madrid, Cape Town, Singapore,
São Paulo, Delhi, Dubai, Tokyo

Cambridge University Press
The Edinburgh Building, Cambridge CB2 8RU, UK

Published in the United States of America by Cambridge University Press, New York

www.cambridge.org
Information on this title: www.cambridge.org/9780521705080

First published 2010

Printed in the United Kingdom at the University Press, Cambridge

*A catalogue record for this publication is available from the British Library*

*Library of Congress Cataloguing in Publication data*
The Cambridge companion to Rilke / edited by Karen Leeder and Robert Vilain.
p.   cm. – (Cambridge companions to literature)
Includes index.
ISBN 978-0-521-87943-9
1. Rilke, Rainer Maria, 1875–1926 – Criticism and interpretation.   I. Leeder, Karen J.
II. Vilain, Robert.   III. Title.   IV. Series.
PT2635.I65Z654   2009
831′.912 – dc22       2009040947

ISBN 978-0-521-87943-9 Hardback
ISBN 978-0-521-70508-0 Paperback

# CONTENTS

CONTENTS

# ACKNOWLEDGEMENTS

The editors would like to acknowledge the assistance of the staff of the Taylor Institution Library in Oxford, and the Deutsches Literaturarchiv in Marbach am Neckar. Research for this volume was made possible by the generosity of New College, Oxford, and Royal Holloway, University of London. We are deeply indebted to all our contributors whose enthusiasm for and commitment to the volume have made it a truly collaborative endeavour. We are also grateful to Lara Elder for editorial assistance in the early stages and to Maartje Scheltens and Linda Bree from Cambridge University Press for their patience and careful advice.

The editors would like to acknowledge the kind permission of the following to cite Rilke's poems in translation: excerpt from 'The Swan' from *New Poems [1907]* by Rainer Maria Rilke, a bilingual edition translated by Edward Snow. Translation © by Edward Snow, reprinted by permission of North Point Press, a division of Farrar, Straus and Giroux; various of *The Sonnets to Orpheus* from Rainer Maria Rilke, *'Sonnets to Orpheus' with 'Letters to a Young Poet'*, trans. Stephen Cohn (Manchester: Carcanet, 2000) and 'The Tower', in Rainer Maria Rilke, *New Poems*, trans. Stephen Cohn (Manchester: Carcanet, 1992) © Carcanet Press Ltd.

The editors are also grateful for kind permission to cite the following original poems: Tom Paulin, 'The Swan', in Tom Paulin, *The Road to Inver: Translations, Versions, Imitations, 1975–2003* (London: Faber and Faber, 2004) © Faber and Faber; Don Paterson, 'Anemone', in Don Paterson, *Orpheus. A Version of Rilke's 'Die Sonette an Orpheus'* (London: Faber and Faber, 2006) © Faber and Faber; Jo Shapcott, 'Dinner with Rilke', in Jo Shapcott, *Tender Taxes* (London: Faber and Faber, 2001) © Faber and Faber; Robin Robertson and Pan Macmillan for 'Fall' in Robin Robertson, *Slow Air* (London: Picador, 2002) © Robin Robertson 2002.

# NOTES ON CONTRIBUTORS

ULRICH BAER is Professor of German and Comparative Literature and Vice Provost for Globalization and Multicultural Affairs at New York University. He is the author of *Remnants of Song: Trauma and the Experience of Modernity in Charles Baudelaire and Paul Celan* (2000), *Spectral Evidence: The Photography of Trauma* (2002) and *Das Rilke-Alphabet* (2006); editor of *110 Stories: New York Writes After September 11* (2002); editor and translator of *The Poet's Guide to Life: The Wisdom of Rainer Maria Rilke* (2005).

PAUL BISHOP is Professor of German at the University of Glasgow. His research interests include all aspects of European modernism, with a particular emphasis on the history of psychoanalysis and its relationship to literature. He has published on a variety of figures, including Goethe, Schiller, Nietzsche, C. G. Jung, Ludwig Klages, Thomas Mann and Rilke.

HELEN BRIDGE is Senior Lecturer in German at the University of Exeter. Her publications include *Women's Writing and Historiography in the GDR* (2002) and articles on Rilke and on GDR literature. She is currently working on a study of Rilke and visual art.

RÜDIGER GÖRNER is Professor of German Literature and Director of the Centre for Anglo-German Cultural Relations at Queen Mary, University of London. Monographs since 2000 include: *Nietzsches Kunst: Annäherungen an einen Denkartisten* (2000); *Grenzen, Schwellen, Übergänge: Zur Poetik des Transitorischen* (2001); *Rainer Maria Rilke – Im Herzwerk der Sprache* (2004); *Thomas Mann – Der Zauber des Letzten* (2005); *Das Zeitalter des Fraktalen: Ein kulturkritischer Versuch* (2007); *Wenn Götzen dämmern: Formen ästhetischen Denkens bei Nietzsche* (2008).

ANDREAS HUYSSEN is the Villard Professor of German and Comparative Literature at Columbia University. He was founding director of Columbia's Center for Comparative Literature and Society (1998–2003) and one of the founding editors of *New German Critique* (since 1974). His books include *Drama des Sturm und*

*Drang* (1980), *After the Great Divide: Modernism, Mass Culture, Postmodernism* (1986), *Postmoderne – Zeichen eines kulturellen Wandels*, co-edited with Klaus Scherpe (1986), *Twilight Memories: Marking Time in a Culture of Amnesia* (1995) and *Present Pasts: Urban Palimpsests and the Politics of Memory* (2003). Editor of *Other Cities, Other Worlds: Urban Imaginaries in a Globalizing Age* (2008). His work has been translated into many languages.

ANDREAS KRAMER is Reader in German and Comparative Literature at Goldsmiths, University of London. His research interests include early twentieth-century German literature, in particular its international contexts; the European avant-garde; and literature and film. He has published widely on these topics and his most recent book is *Regionalismus und Moderne: Studien zur deutschen Literatur, 1900–1933* (2006).

KATHLEEN L. KOMAR is Professor of Comparative Literature and German at the University of California at Los Angeles. She has published on a variety of topics from Romanticism to the present in American and German literature, including on authors such as Hermann Broch, Rainer Maria Rilke, Alfred Döblin, Christa Wolf and Ingeborg Bachmann, among others. Her books include *Reclaiming Klytemnestra: Revenge or Reconciliation* (2003), *Transcending Angels: Rainer Maria Rilke's "Duino Elegies"* (1987), *Pattern and Chaos: Multilinear Novels by Dos Passos, Faulkner, Döblin, and Koeppen* (1983) and the collection *Lyrical Symbols and Narrative Transformations*, co-edited with Ross Shideler (1998). She was elected President of the American Comparative Literature Association 2005–7.

KAREN LEEDER is Professor of Modern German Literature at the University of Oxford, and Fellow and Tutor in German at New College, Oxford. She has published widely on modern German literature, especially poetry, and has translated work by a number of German writers into English: most recently: *After Brecht: A Celebration* (2006). An edited volume, *Schaltstelle. Neue deutsche Lyrik im Dialog*, appeared in 2007 as did a special edition of *German Life and Letters*: 'Flaschenpost': German Poetry and the Long Twentieth Century. A collection of essays, *The New German Poetry*, is due out in 2009 as is the volume, edited with Robert Vilain, *Nach Duino: Studien zu Rainer Maria Rilkes späten Gedichten* (2009).

CHARLIE LOUTH is Lecturer in German at Oxford University and a Fellow of The Queen's College. He has published *Hölderlin and the Dynamics of Translation* (1998), as well as essays on German poetry from Goethe to Celan.

THOMAS MARTINEC read German, English and Philosophy in Mainz and New York (NYU). After he finished his PhD with a book on Lessing's theory of tragedy's effect (2003), he became DAAD-Fellow in German Studies at Lincoln College,

Oxford. He is now Lecturer in German Literature at the University of Regensburg, where he is working on a book on modernist poetry and music.

ANTHONY PHELAN is Fellow of Keble College and Professor of German Romantic Literature at Oxford. He has published a student guide to Rilke's *Neue Gedichte* and edited *The Weimar Dilemma: Intellectuals in the Weimar Republic*; *Reading Heinrich Heine* appeared in 2007. His main area of interest is the relation between philosophical critique and literature in modernity: Jena aesthetics and German Romantic fiction provide one current focus, the relationship between Walter Benjamin and Brecht another.

ROBERT VILAIN is Professor of German and Comparative Literature at Royal Holloway, University of London, and Lecturer in German at Christ Church, Oxford. He specialises in German, Austrian, French and Comparative Literature in the late nineteenth and early twentieth centuries, with a special interest in lyric poetry. He has published widely on authors such as Hofmannsthal, George, Rilke, Yvan and Claire Goll, Thomas Mann, on Franco-German literary relations, detective fiction and the relationship of literature and music. He has been joint editor of the journal *Austrian Studies* since 2003.

WILLIAM WATERS is Chair of the Department of Modern Languages and Comparative Literature and Associate Professor of German and Comparative Literature at Boston University. He is the author of *Poetry's Touch: On Lyric Address* (2003).

# CHRONOLOGY

1875    4 December: birth of René Karl Wilhelm Josef Maria Rilke in Prague. Parents Josef Rilke and Sophie (Phia), formerly Entz, belong to the German-speaking minority of what was then the Austrian principality of Bohemia. Their first child was a girl who had died at birth; Rilke is dressed in girls' clothes until he starts school.

1882    School in Prague.

1885    Separation of parents.

1886    Military Academy in St Pölten, Lower Austria.

1890–1  Military Academy Märisch-Weißkirchen (Hranice), remembered by Rilke as a time of persecution, until he is able to engineer his departure.

1891–2  School for Trade and Commerce in Linz

1892    Return to Prague and the start of private tuition for the 'Abitur' (school leaving exams). Death of his Uncle Jaroslav Rilke, Ritter von Rülicken, with whom he was staying, who leaves a legacy to allow him to study.

1894    *Lives and Songs* with the support of his friend Valerie von David-Rhonfeld.

1895    University in Prague. At the end of his first semester he publishes *Offerings to the Lares*, dedicated to Prague, and works on a number of literary magazines.

1896    Leaves Prague and follows his friend, the painter Emil Orlik, to Munich to study there.

1897 Meets the German Russian writer Lou Andreas-Salomé, fourteen years his senior, and spends June–August in Wolfratshausen near Munich as part of her circle. Changes his name to Rainer. In October he follows her back to Berlin and finds quarters near her and her husband. Dedicates himself to writing and publishes the collection *Dream-Crowned*.

1898 Returns to Berlin-Schmargendorf. Spends April–May in Florence and Tuscany with Lou and writes 'Florentine Diary', dedicated to her, though not published until 1942. Publishes *Advent*.

1899 In Vienna meets Arthur Schnitzler and Hugo von Hofmannsthal. April–June first Russian travels with the Andreas couple. Visit to Leonid Pasternak and Leo Tolstoy in Moscow. In autumn he writes the first version of the poems (he calls them prayers) that will become 'The Book of Monastic Life' and the first part of the *Book of Hours* (1905) as well as the first version of *The Lay of the Love and Death of the Cornet Christoph Rilke*. Publishes *Two Tales from Prague*, the collection *In Celebration of Myself* and writes an essay on 'Russian Art' which will be published in 1901.

1900 Intensive study of Russian literature and poetry. Second Russian journey with Lou Andreas-Salomé from May to the end of August. Visits and cements friendship with writers and critics. In September accepts an invitation from the painter Heinrich Vogeler to visit the artists' colony in Worpswede; there he is inspired by the landscape but also by the artists he meets: the painter Paula Becker, the sculptor Clara Westhoff and the visiting writer Carl Hauptmann. His impressions are contained in his so-called 'Worpswede Diary' but also in the poems that will become the collection *The Book of Images* (1902). *Stories of the Dear Lord* is published. Paula Becker becomes engaged to Otto Modersohn and Rilke leaves abruptly to return to Berlin.

1901 Separates from Lou, breaks off his studies. Marriage to Clara Westhoff on 28 April. The young couple move to Westerwede, near Worpswede. Their daughter Ruth is born on 12 December. Première of the drama *Everyday Life* in Berlin at the Residenztheater is a failure.

1902 Financial crisis drives Rilke to work as a critic for the newspaper *Das Bremer Tagblatt*. He is commissioned to write a monograph on the artists' colony at Worpswede, and also one on Rodin. The collection *The Book of Images* appears. At the end of August Rilke moves to Paris and visits Rodin for the first time. Clara follows him; their daughter is left behind with grandparents in Bremen. Inspired by the relationship with the sculptor, but made anxious by the city, Rilke writes the poem 'The Panther' probably in November. This will become one of the most famous of the *New Poems*.

1903    The monograph *Auguste Rodin* appears. Spends April in Viareggio to recover from his city sojourn, and finishes what will become the *Book of Hours*. Begins correspondence with Lou Andreas-Salomé which allows him to process his experiences in Paris. Many of the passages will find their way into his novel of 1910 *The Notebooks of Malte Laurids Brigge*. From September spends time in Rome with Clara until June 1904. Letter writing becomes important. Correspondence with Ellen Key and *Letters to a Young Poet* (to Franz Xaver Kappus), which will be published in 1929, date from this time.

1904    Rilke journeys to Sweden on the invitation of Ellen Key to stay at Lund with Hanna Larsson and the painter Ernst Norlind.

1905    Travels in Germany. July–September in Friedelheim, also with Clara, on occasion, and gets to know the banker and writer Karl von Heydt. In the autumn returns to France to Rodin. Spends winter in Rodin's house in Meudon-Val-Fleury where Rodin asks him to stay on as his private secretary. *The Book of Hours*, which has been finished since 1903, appears with the Insel publishing house. His first lecture tour on Rodin in Dresden and Prague.

1906    Meudon and then to Paris. His father's death in Prague on 14 March interrupts Rilke's second lecture tour. In Paris he gets to know Amélie Nádherný von Borutin and her daughter Sidonie and the poet Emile Verhaeren. Rupture with Rodin. Work on the *New Poems*. In the summer he journeys to Belgium and in December to Capri, where he will stay until May 1907, as the guest of Alice Faehndrich who assists him with his translations of Elizabeth Barrett Browning's *Sonnets from the Portuguese* (1908). *The Book of Images* appears, and *The Lay of the Love and Death of the Cornet Christoph Rilke*, which becomes a bestseller.

1907    June–October in Paris, finishing the *New Poems*, which will be published later the same year. Inspired by the Cézanne exhibition in the Salon d'Automne. Visits almost daily and records his impression in letters to Clara which will be published posthumously as *Letters on Cézanne*. November: his third lecture tour. Correspondence with Sidonie which will continue for the rest of his life. In Vienna meets Rudolf Kassner, Hugo von Hofmannsthal, Richard Beer-Hofmann. Holiday in Venice which will inspire two of the last of the *New Poems*. On 20 November Paula Modersohn-Becker dies in childbirth. In December Rilke returns to Germany with Clara.

1908    Stays with Alice Faehndich on Capri again and then, after successful negotiations with Insel secure him an income, he moves straight back to Paris to finish the *New Poems: The Other Part*, dedicated to Rodin. Moves to attic room of Palais Hôtel Biron with Clara to work on his novel. The anniversary of the death of Paula Modersohn-Becker prompts his poem 'Requiem for a Friend' and a few days later another poem 'Requiem for Wolf Count of Kalckreuth', a young Munich poet of Rilke's acquaintance who had committed suicide.

1909    Concentrated work in Paris on reissues of earlier poems. On 13 December meets Princess Marie von Thurn und Taxis-Hohenlohe in Paris.

1910    Visits Anton and Katharina Kippenberg, the publishers, in Leipzig to dictate the last parts of his novel *The Notebooks of Malte Laurids Brigge* to them, which then appears at the end of May. A period of restlessness follows after publication of the novel. Guest of Princess Marie von Thurn und Taxis-Hohenlohe in Castle Duino, near Triest; followed by a stay at Castle Lautschin in Bohemia in August, then with the Nádherný sisters in Janowitz. Persuaded by Jenny Oltersdorf to embark on a journey with companions at the end of November to North Africa, Algiers, Tunis and the holy city of Kairouan and thence to Egypt.

1911    Returns to Paris in April. Still without orientation after the publication of *Malte*, he embarks on various translations (the strong impressions from Egypt will find their way into the *Duino Elegies*). Agrees to a divorce from Clara which, because of the religious cast of the Austrian laws, does not take place. Visits Castle Duino on the Adriatic coast from October until May 1912. Aesthetic crisis.

1912    Mid-January he writes the first lines of what will become the *Duino Elegies* 'Who, if I cried out, would hear me – among the angelic orders?'. He completes two *Elegies* and some fragments, but keeps them back. Summer spent in Venice in the company of the ageing actress Eleanora Duse. Departs for Spain in October first visiting Toledo, and then moving down to the South, to Ronda.

1913    Returns to Paris in February to work on poems which will become the cycle 'Poems to the Night'. Spends the summer travelling in Germany. Meets the Expressionist Franz Werfel, and reads the poetry of Georg Heym, leading him to write an essay 'About the Young Poet'. In September he visits a psychoanalytic congress with Lou and meets Freud. From mid-October in Paris. Publishes *The Life of the Virgin Mary*, written early during his Duino visit.

1914    Receives letter from divorced pianist Magda von Hattingberg, which initiates a correspondence in which Rilke believes he has discovered his soul mate, his 'Benvenuta' (welcome one), but a meeting ends in disappointment. After a period of self-analysis he writes the poem 'Turning-Point' on 20 June, which signals a fresh energy and a new aesthetic beginning. Reads Georg Trakl, Franz Kafka and Friedrich Hölderlin. Outbreak of War. Writes his 'Five Songs' under the influence of the first days of war, but only a few weeks later does not want to see them reproduced. Meets the painter Lou Albert-Lasard, who seems to be a kindred spirit in a very nationalistic time. Alongside poems of existential lament such as 'Exposed on the Mountains of the Heart', he writes love poems to her ('Lulu'), with whom he will maintain a relationship until Autumn 1916. In dire financial straits, moves into the lodgings where she is staying. December in Berlin and thence to Munich where he will remain until 1919. Meets the painter Paul Klee and many writers including the wealthy writer and patron Hertha König, who buys him Pablo Picasso's painting *The Acrobats* (*Les Saltimbanques*), to remind him of the atmosphere of Paris.

1915    Summer and autumn as the guest of Hertha König. In Autumn he writes the fourth *Elegy*. The 40-year-old Rilke receives his 'call up' on 24 November, and, despite the intervention of many friends on his behalf, is sent to a barracks in Vienna, where he suffers during training and is soon moved to the Austrian war archive.

1916    Meetings with Rudolf Kassner, Stefan Zweig, Karl Kraus, Oskar Kokoschka. May–June in Rodaun as Hofmannsthal's neighbour, where Lou Albert-Lasard paints her famous portrait of him. On 9 June released from the army. Returns to Munich in July.

1917    Munich from May to June. October revolution. Translates from the Renaissance French poet: *The Twenty Four Sonnets of Louise Labé*.

1918    Munich. Meets Ernst Toller, Oskar Maria Graf, Alfred Wolfenstein. Watches the events of the November Revolution with great approval.

1919    Deeply shocked by murder of the Socialist leader Kurt Eisner, First Minister President of the Free State of Bavaria. Flees the 'White Terror' leaving Munich and Germany for the last time. Journey to Switzerland where he renews his acquaintance with the painter Baladine Klossowska ('Merline') and her sons. Embarks on reading tour, and writes the speculative essay 'Primal Sound'. Meets Nanny Wunderly-Volkart, who becomes a close friend and correspondent. Surrenders his old Austrian passport for a Czech one, which allows him to visit Marie von Thurn und Taxis in Venice. Begins love affair with Merline, with whom he visits the Swiss canton of Valais.

1921    Journey through Switzerland. Preface to *Mitsou*, drawings by the young Balthusz Klossowski (later Balthus), Merline's son. Writes 'The Testament' (published 1974), a document of (self-)recrimination about the demands of art and the need for companionship. Still unable to work on the *Elegies*, he turns to translation of Paul Valéry's poem 'The Graveyard by the Sea' ('Le cimetière marin'). Corresponds in French with Merline who has been in Berlin and on her return they hunt for lodgings and discover the run-down Château de Muzot near the town of Sierre in the Rhône Valley of northern Switzerland, which he will buy in 1922. Merline returns to Berlin in November having rendered it habitable for him.

1922    In February, with a 'hurricane in the spirit', he finishes the *Duino Elegies*, which had been begun in winter 1911/12 in Duino, and writes *The Sonnets to Orpheus*, dedicated to Wera Ockama Knoop, a young dancer from Munich whom Rilke had known as a child but who had died, also the fictive 'Letter from the Young Worker'. His daughter Ruth marries Carl Sieber on 12 May.

1923　Travels in Switzerland. Translations of Valéry. Reads Proust. Merline returns to Switzerland. Symptoms of illness appear which, despite some respites, will trouble him until his death. In December visits the sanatorium in Valmont. *Duino Elegies* and *The Sonnets to Orpheus* appear.

1924　Sojourns in the clinic at Valmont at the beginning and end of the year. Poems in French, culminating in the collections *Orchards* and *The Valaisian Quatrains*. Late poems in German too such as 'Early Spring', 'A Walk', 'Gong'. Begins a correspondence of poems and letters with the young poet Erika Mitterer (which will appear as *Correspondence in Poems* in 1950) and which will continue until the year of his death. Many visitors, including Paul Valéry and a last visit from Clara Rilke.

1925　January–August in Paris meeting many writers, including Paul Valéry and André Gide. On returning to Muzot Rilke writes his will in October including his famous 'Epitaph'. His translation of Valéry appears. In December he returns to the Valmont sanatorium.

1926　Spends January–May in the sanatorium. Important correspondence with the Russian poet Boris Pasternak, who is in exile in Paris, and also with the Russian poet Marina Zwetajewa-Efron, the dedicatee of his last elegy. His French collections appear in Paris to good reviews. Summer travelling and visiting friends. Last meeting with Valéry in September. On his return he does not remain in Muzot, having also injured himself on the thorn of a rose in his garden. On 30 November he returns to Valmont. Mid-December writes his last poem 'Come you, you last one . . .' in his notebook. Dies of leukaemia on 29 December.

1927　2 January: funeral in Raron (Valais).

The following abbreviations have been used throughout this volume to refer to works and letters by Rilke and a standard reference work:

KA         Manfred Engel, Ulrich Fülleborn, Dorothea Lauterbach, Horst Nalewski, August Stahl (eds.), Rainer Maria Rilke, *Werke: Kommentierte Ausgabe in vier Bänden mit einem Supplementband* (Frankfurt am Main and Leipzig: Insel, 1996)

SW         Rainer Maria Rilke, *Sämtliche Werke*, ed. Ernst Zinn, 7 vols. (Frankfurt am Main: Insel, 1987–97)

B          Rainer Maria Rilke, *Briefe in zwei Bänden*, ed. Horst Nalewski (Frankfurt am Main and Leipzig: Insel, 1991)

*RHB*      Manfred Engel (ed.), *Rilke-Handbuch: Leben – Werk – Wirkung* (Stuttgart, Weimar: Metzler, 2004)

*Notebooks*  Rainer Maria Rilke, *The Notebooks of Malte Laurids Brigge*, trans. Stephen Mitchell (New York: Vintage, 1985).

References to these volumes will be given in the form: KA i, 49; SW iii, 11; B i, 251; *RHB*, p. 2; *Notebooks*, p. 56. References to other bibliographical items will be provided in full in a note on the first mention, and in abbreviated form thereafter.

Quotations are generally given only in English, except where a particular linguistic or formal point is being made, or when a reader who has German might particularly benefit from having the original. In these cases the translation usually precedes the original but from time to time the order is reversed for the sake of clarity or precision. The translations used for *The Notebooks of Malte Laurids Brigge* are those of Stephen Mitchell (see above). There is no standard edition of Rilke in English. Contributors have therefore used a range of different English translations of the other works, depending on the individual poems cited, and in order to best represent the particular point being made. These, and any adaptations to them, are all acknowledged in the notes to the individual contributions. Some contributors have provided new translations. Unless otherwise specified, all other translations are by the author of the contribution. Rilke's own frequent use of ellipsis will be reproduced as it appears in his work; an ellipsis with square brackets [ . . . ] indicates an editorial omission.

KAREN LEEDER AND ROBERT VILAIN

# Introduction

Glücklich, die wissen, daß hinter allen
Sprachen das Unsägliche steht

Happy are those who know that behind
every language there stands the Unsayable

Rainer Maria Rilke (1875–1926) is one the leading poets of European modernism, comparable in importance and influence with American-born T. S. Eliot and the French poet Paul Valéry. Arguably the greatest German poet of the twentieth century, his influence nevertheless extends far beyond poetry and far beyond Germany. His work has been important in philosophy, religion and the visual arts. Despite being famously 'difficult', his work continues to attract new readerships and is regularly translated and re-translated, into Japanese, Chinese and Arabic as well as the European languages.

He features regularly as a source or an inspiration in a variety of creative literatures from across the world and has motivated a host of visual artists; he has often been set to music (classical and rock) and is a staple of television and Hollywood film. Today he even enjoys a reception as a guru of queer studies and New Age thinking. The fact is that Rilke developed tropes of style and attitude that have proved essential for the cultural life of the twentieth century and beyond. To speak of Rilke is to speak of world literature. It is almost impossible to grasp the key elements in the development of modern culture without reference to him.

Rilke was the author of some twenty volumes published between 1894 and 1927, mostly verse (in German and latterly in French), but including a unique prose work *The Notebooks of Malte Laurids Brigge*, often described as the first truly post-realist novel of international stature. Rilke's poetry might be said to encapsulate many of the dilemmas of the twentieth century and beyond: the loss of belief in a divinely sponsored universe, the struggle with industrialisation, a preoccupation with war and death and the atomisation of society. However, his canonical published collections, like the *New Poems* or the *Duino Elegies*, represent less than half of the prodigious volume of poetry he produced. There is a vast body of what the translator Stephen Mitchell has called 'uncollected' poetry that includes some of his most important and often-cited individual poems: 'Turning-Point', 'Exposed on the Mountains of the Heart' or 'Gong'.

Rilke was, however, also an author of dramas in the Naturalist and Symbolist modes, and an accomplished translator, whose versions of poems by Paul Valéry and of Elizabeth Barrett Browning's *Sonnets from the Portuguese* are still widely admired and read in their own right. Indeed he is one of only a handful of writers able to publish original work successfully in more than one language. His late poetry, written in French after his move to Muzot in the Valais in 1921, has still not gained the critical attention it deserves, but allows an insight into how creative processes move across traditions and languages. Moreover, his critical essays are rich in reflections on the ambitions and diversions of an age, fuelled as they are by an engagement with the traditions of the past and the thinkers of the moment (Nietzsche and Freud, for example).

But they also offer a perspective on his own aesthetic convictions and practice. For example, his acclaimed letters on the painter Paul Cézanne or his monograph on the sculptor Auguste Rodin still have much to tell us about their subjects' vision, but they testify also to Rilke's own developing aesthetic. Equally, there is a considerable (in part still unpublished) correspondence: both private, with his many sponsors, colleagues and lovers, but also more public, as he was acquainted with many of the prominent writers, artists and thinkers of his age. Throughout his life Rilke wrote letters as an almost daily custom in which he explored circumstances or ideas that were concerning him at any given moment. Philosophical explorations rub shoulders with frank insights into the messy reality of his relationships or descriptions that will find their way into his published poetry barely revised. The letters are a seedbed for his published work; but they are also in many ways continuous with it. They shed a very significant light on the writer and the age in which he lived, as well as continuing to inspire in their directness and intensity of address – as in his famous and often reprinted *Letters to a Young Poet*.

But it must finally be as a poet that Rilke is read. His early poetry, a densely textured and imagistic form of subjectivism, was redolent of the mystic neo-Romantic turn of the declining years of the nineteenth century. His *New Poems* (1907 and 1908) heralded the cleaner, clearer saying of the new century in their concentration on 'things', but also extended the poetic lexicon and the possibilities of verse – especially through his manipulation of the fixed form of the sonnet. The novel, *The Notebooks of Malte Laurids Brigge*, started in 1904 and completed in January 1910, is a sustained reflection on death, but also documents the phantasmagorical breakdown of reality, the degradation of urban modernity in the shape of Paris, the atomisation of narrative and encroaching psychosis, which for many mark the archetypal confrontation with the modern. It was death in the terrible reality of the First World War that contributed to Rilke's long creative crisis and effective silence between 1910 and 1922. When this was broken with the publication of the *Duino Elegies* and *The Sonnets to Orpheus* it was in the context of a changed world. The *Elegies*, in particular, chime with T. S. Eliot or Wallace Stevens to speak of a world after God, after catastrophe, and after any sense of coherent wholeness has been lost. The only place it can be regained is in the work of art itself. This is reflected in the way Rilke's poetic language stretches the boundaries of the sayable by drawing on traditional forms but pressing them into new and often radical coinages in the white heat of intense bursts of creativity. It is here that Rilke's true legacy can be identified: in the injunction to an orphic celebration of the here and now which will lift life out of mortality and transform it in into the sanctity of art.

It is not surprising if that mission has sometimes been misunderstood or rejected by later generations. Some have found Rilke's view of the world unpalatable and, especially after 1945, his elitism and otherworldliness was met with profound scepticism. Rilke found himself rejected by left-wing critics in the west and in the socialist regimes in the east including the German Democratic Republic. The scathing allegories of modern life; the praise for a self-negating kind of intransitive love (which did not preclude treating some of his many female admirers notably badly); the brooding on death; the aristocratic insistence on the magisterial role of the poet: all these seem precisely to devalue the ordinary human reality upon which the poems claim to insist. There is some truth in all of these charges. However, for all that Rilke seems to offer an aesthetic solution, one fit only for the poet, he in fact insists that all human beings share the ability to translate the world. 'You must change your life' was the credo of 1908 that ends the poem 'Archaic Torso of Apollo' and, at its profoundest level, Rilke's work is about an experience of being which includes, indeed privileges, but is by no means limited to, the experience of art. It is perhaps this vivid exposure of being, together with all its vulnerabilities and celebrations, that has allowed his work to transcend the boundaries of culture and language and has secured his reputation right up to the present day.

In any case despite a decided 'Rilke abstinence', as Manfred Engel nicely puts it (*RHB*, p. 11), especially on the part of German critics after the War, Rilke's influence on modern literature is both well documented and inescapable and reads like a roll-call of the greats of the twentieth century. His poetry has inspired translators and other poets from Auden to Heaney. It has been set to music by a range of composers as diverse as Paul Hindemith and Arnold Schoenberg, Darius Milhaud and Dmitri Shostakovich, Harrison Birtwistle and Oliver Knussen, and has inspired a number of contemporary Indie rock bands. Artists who have sought to interpret him include Cy Twombly and he has been quoted on TV by representatives of the popular mainstream such as Oprah Winfrey. He is cited in work by authors including J. D. Salinger, James Merrill, Adrienne Rich, Milan Kundera, Amitav Ghosh and Philip Roth as well as contemporary authors from as far afield as Iran and Cuba; he even features in crime fiction, most persuasively in Ken Bruen's *Rilke on Black* (1996). He has also been subjected to a large range of cultural analyses by important critics such as Martin Heiddeger, Paul de Man, Maurice Blanchot and Giorgio Agamben. Despite his aversion to the paraphernalia of the modern, he has fascinated many in the cinema: both auteurs, who have set out to come to terms with his legacy, such as Wim Wenders in his *Wings of Desire* (1987), but also in Hollywood, where he pops up in a plethora of often unlikely places from Woody Allen's *Another Woman* (1988) to *Sister Act 2* (1993). Most recently he has furnished texts for CDs and sell-out tours of twenty-four cities across Germany, as part of the 'Rilke Project' (2005).

Rilke's own cultural roots go well back into the past: drawing sustenance from the great writers of antiquity, including Ovid and the ancient Egyptians, from thinkers and from artists. Thus while his voice is unique and instantly recognisable, his work draws together many disparate strands of thought and aesthetics. One of the goals of this volume has been to take full advantage of the challenging variety of his work and to elucidate precisely this richness. Thus a familiar text-by-text approach has been supplemented by a structure that highlights the variety and interdisciplinary nature of his work. As has been mentioned, Rilke's difficulty is a prominent feature in his reception and can be daunting, especially for those readers coming to him for the first time. This volume aims, like all the *Cambridge Companions*, to give the reader some sense of the character of his work, some impression of his achievement and some orientation within the critical debates that have raged over some aspects of his work and status, combining information and critical evaluation in a sophisticated yet approachable manner. The contributors have in general been sparing in their use of traditional critical apparatus (especially when discussing a single work) but their essays are designed to bring readers up to date with the fruits of recent as well as older scholarship.

In addition to an introductory survey of his life and a study of his social context, the volume therefore includes an essay on his correspondence (Rilke articulated some of his key poetic principles in letters, and indeed 'correspondence' is itself a vital poetic term for him) and a chapter on the early Rilke and his transition from the poetic legacy of the nineteenth century into a poet with his own original voice. Readers can then progress to a discussion of individual works, including all his major collections of poetry, and his seminal novel of modernist anxiety, *The Notebooks of Malte Laurids Brigge*. Each of the chapters on single major works or collections contextualises those works, most notably with reference to the large number of free-standing, uncollected poems that often crucially articulate Rilke's developing poetics. A second section focuses on six of the key frameworks that help situate Rilke culturally. Four chapters situate Rilke in his own context: the first offers a sustained examination of Rilke's place in modernism, the defining cultural development of the early twentieth century; the second analyses Rilke's reception of (and debt to) a large and eclectic range of literature in German and from elsewhere; the third considers Rilke's vital engagement with the visual and plastic arts; and the fourth examines Rilke's reception of significant trends in European philosophy, including the spiritual, religious and mystical dimensions of thought. Two final pieces situate Rilke from a later perspective: the first examines developments in Rilke's treatment by successive waves or styles of criticism, for many of which he was almost exemplary; and finally Rilke is read through the many significant poets from the English-speaking world who have engaged with him and his legacy. With its invaluable guide to further reading and a chronology of Rilke's life and work, it is hoped that this *Companion* will provide students and scholars of the nineteenth and twentieth centuries with an accessible, engaging account of this extraordinary poet, his enduring legacy and far-reaching influence.

## PART I

# Life

# I

RÜDIGER GÖRNER

# Rilke: a biographical exploration

Among the stunning array of German-speaking writers and intellectuals around 1900 the poet Rainer Maria Rilke was perhaps the most cosmopolitan, only matched in his worldliness by his friend and compatriot, Stefan Zweig. Even though Rilke's actual knowledge of the world was mainly confined to continental Europe, except for his journey to North Africa in 1910–11, and firmly excluded the Anglo-Saxon sphere, of whose blunt materialism he remained suspicious until the end of his life, the poet's outlook was decidedly international and anti-chauvinistic, and he remained open-minded towards other cultures until the end of his life. His horizon as traveller and reader stretched from Bohemia to Russia, France to Scandinavia, Italy to Egypt, and from Spain to Switzerland and their respective literatures. He was a migrant and a belated troubadour, at times a vagrant revered, if not idolised, by aristocrats, industrialists, fellow artists and artisans alike, and eventually recognised by anyone able to appreciate German poetry as probably its most sublime master after – or even alongside – Goethe, Hölderlin and Heine.

There was something anachronistic about this poetic artist even though his art was quintessentially modernist in style and poetic approach without ever disregarding, or disowning, tradition. Bach, Beethoven and Nietzsche influenced him as much as Rodin, Cézanne, Klee and Picasso. He studied eclectically, if not erratically, and liked to read the Grimm brothers' German dictionary like a novel. His life was full of rich experiences that were without exception intimately connected with art. His creed was that life and art should serve each other.

Towards the end of the nineteenth century the concept of 'life' had become a buzzword among artists and intellectuals in Europe. 'Life' deserved a realistic, if not naturalistic, treatment in the arts; it challenged scientists and ideologues alike who investigated the forces in, and behind, 'life' or distorted them in the shape of a precarious biology, or rather biologism, which was prone to turn into racist ideology. Undercurrents of nationalistic conflict

9

became increasingly difficult to contain, particularly in multi-ethnic states, such as the Austro-Hungarian empire, in whose core province, Bohemia, and her capital Prague, Rainer Maria Rilke lived until the age of ten. Those undercurrents surfaced as folkloristic versions of 'life' in the arts (for example in the music of the Czech composers Dvořák and Smetana) and politics, eventually striving for proper political, social and cultural recognition, or released in open aggression. 'Life' was deemed a drive worth dying for – at least this is how ideologues later indoctrinated and mobilised the young to enter the First World War triumphantly, only to find that the triumph of 'life' ended in carnage. But art, too, mirrored this attitude. It is telling, for instance, that Cavaradossi, the artist in Puccini's opera *Tosca* (1900), should end on his heart-rendering confession that, in real terms, he had but loved 'life' by itself. This belief in 'life' was perceived as the main legacy of Nietzsche's Zarathustrian vision of perfecting oneself,[1] which was perpetuated by Stefan George and his circle as well as the poets Richard Dehmel, Franz Werfel and many others.[2] 'Life' was also the object of aesthetic refinement as demonstrated by the young Hugo von Hofmannsthal, whilst others (most notably the early Thomas Mann) showed that the artist was unable to attain 'life' and live it to the full. 'Life' was at the time in competition, so to speak, with the experience of 'decadence', half-heartedly deplored by Nietzsche, but unequivocally advocated by Oscar Wilde; a sentiment that led writers such as Gottfried Benn, in his early career, to focus on dissecting the decay of life.

By the 1890s 'life' determined a new understanding of art. Biographies began to flourish and be turned into a popular genre. The suggestion was to regard the arts as graphics of 'life'. Nietzsche, or what was thought to be the essence of his philosophising, turned into the main inspiration for this tendency to establish the sacred trinity of 'life', 'will' (preferably to an initially rather undefined 'power') and the 'aesthetic justification of Being'. This is the intellectual setting against which Rainer Maria Rilke's cultural socialisation developed.

### 'An anxious, heavy childhood'

These are the words with which Rilke once characterised his early years in Prague, in an exchange with Ellen Key, the great Swedish educationalist whose study *The Century of the Child* Rilke praised in a review (1902; KA IV, 262–8) as a breakthrough in the understanding of childhood and the principles of a humane education. René Karl Wilhelm Johann Josef Maria Rilke was born, two months prematurely, on 4 December 1875. His parents, Josef and Sophie Rilke, married in 1873, suffered from unfulfilled ambitions for themselves. Josef had hoped for a major military career but had to confine his hopes to advancing within the offices of the North Bohemia railway, and Sophie – or Phia as she was known – dressed for ever in black, as if perpetually mourning her lot. She had dreams of a life in high society but instead had to put up with her husband's stifling conventionality and at times uncouth behaviour. All their frustrated aspirations were projected onto René who was even dressed as a girl to compensate for the loss of their daughter who had died only a few days old. Estrangement between René's parents was always in the air and led to their separation in 1885.[3]

The weight of this 'anxious childhood' in Prague, where the Rilkes belonged to the German-speaking minority, was increased rather than shed when René was taken to the military academy of St Pölten in Lower Austria in 1886. He loathed life there and later admitted that it had traumatised him, but this experience taught him to cope with adverse conditions and to 'persist'; 'persistence' was to become one of his most frequently cited notions. One of his first major expressions of self-assertion was to insist on being discharged from this academy only to find that the family council back in Prague had determined that he would attend the school for trade and commerce in Linz, which he did, albeit only for half a year (1891–2). Afterwards he returned to Prague where he found in his uncle, Jaroslav Rilke, a relative who was most sympathetic to his intellectual needs.[4] He provided the means for René to complete his Abitur (school leaving certificate) and later to study literature, art, history and even one semester of law, but in 1896 René left Prague for Munich without a degree although accompanied by his artist friend, the painter Emil Orlik (1870–1932).

It was whilst he was still in Prague that Rilke published his first two volumes of poetry, *Lives and Songs* (1894) and *Offerings to the Lares* (1896), inspired both by his first real love, Valerie von David-Rhonfeld, and by the atmosphere of Prague, which also informed most of his early prose. *Offerings to the Lares* in particular displays a profound sympathy for Czech tradition and culture, striking for someone who belonged to the German-speaking community that on the whole segregated itself at the time quite demonstratively from the Czechs. Not so early René Rilke, who turned this segregation into the subject of many a story and poem.

Equally, however, Rilke needed distance from his home town, which seemed increasingly oppressive to him, in order to find himself and his own voice for writing about the darker and sinister side of this strangely fascinating jewel on the river Moldau. During his time in Munich and, from 1898 until 1901, in Berlin, Rilke explored his memories of Prague in numerous, at times haunting novellas, poems and short plays. Symptomatically, he called one collection *Am Leben hin* (1898), suggesting an existence just 'alongside life' without being in the midst of the 'élan vital'; and one stage piece is titled *Everyday Life* (1900; KA III, 743–76), implying that one first needs to deal with the ordinary before indulging in the Dionysian ecstasy of life for life's sake. In his play one of the protagonists speculates about a cynical desire to have 'many a life', which is glossed by his female counterpart with the words, 'That would be the art of modern man' (KA III, 771). Rilke's actual object at the time was to match every experience with a 'new' life. The play was completed at Easter 1900, was first performed in December 1901 in Berlin, and published one year later. When writing this play, it must indeed have seemed to Rilke that, by then, at least two such 'experiences' had supplied him with more than one life: first, his encounter with the Russian-born writer Lou Andreas-Salomé in Munich in the spring of 1897, and second, his reading of Nietzsche and his subsequent journey to Florence.

## Transformations in life – for the arts

Under the influence, if not the tutelage of Lou Andreas-Salomé, whose books *Female Figures in Ibsen's Plays* (1892), *Friedrich Nietzsche* (1894) and an essay entitled 'Jesus the Jew' (1896) had impressed the young poet, Rilke experienced a fundamental change: he turned his effeminate first name 'René' into 'Rainer'. Later on he was even to change his style of handwriting in an attempt to abandon any traces of playful ornamentation. It was Lou, once for a short while Nietzsche's closest friend, who communicated to her young admirer, and lover to be, the essence of Nietzscheanism, and in his 'Florentine Diary', which he kept for Lou, Rilke attempted to see art from the perspective of Nietzsche's Zarathustra and engage in reflections on the meaning of art and the existential condition of the artist: 'Every artist is born abroad, as it were; and his home is nowhere but within himself.'[5]

Similarly, the 'Schmargendorf Diary' assembles Rilke's attempts to gain insight into the working of the artistic mind and to acquire utmost precision in describing 'life'. It was in Berlin that he met the revered playwright Gerhart Hauptmann to whom he was to dedicate the first edition of his collection of poems, the *Book of Images* (1902). Moreover, Berlin brought Rilke into contact with the sociologist Georg Simmel whose student he became for a short while and who taught him to perceive objects as meaningful entities containing not only matter but shape and time. In Berlin-Schmargendorf Rilke worked on what was to become the only 'best-seller' during his lifetime, his dramatic prose poem *The Lay of the Love and Death of the Cornet Christoph Rilke* (1899; subsequent versions 1904 and 1906) and on the first part of his major early poetry composition *The Book of Hours* (1899–1903; first published 1905). Whilst the 'Cornet' takes the reader back to the world of the war against the Turks in the mid-seventeenth century, the first part of *The Book of Hours* celebrates the monk-like existence of the poet whose inspired and inspiring company consists of words only. In the 'Florentine Diary' Rilke had already referred to artistic creation as a quasi-clerical order that connects the artist with the sacred. It is indeed one of the subtle paradoxes in Rilke's development that when he had reached the threshold of modernism in writing he sought to receive his main inspiration from medieval, in parts clerical sources and most importantly from the pre-modern, even archaic world of Russia. In those years (spring 1899 and summer 1900) and after intensive language studies, he travelled through Russia twice, first with Lou Andreas-Salomé and her husband, the orientalist Friedrich Carl Andreas, and for the second time with Lou alone. Even in the last year of his life Rilke was to call Russia 'the most decisive' experience in his development in view of her 'unheard-of spatial dimensions', the sheer 'brotherhood' of the people and their deep humanity.[6] It was only Russia that he recognised as his spiritual 'Heimat' or homeland; she opened up immeasurable horizons for him and introduced him to what he perceived as uncorrupted civilisation. The archaic world of Russia was a revelation to him and the impressions that he received from encounters with Leo Tolstoy, the painter Leonid Pasternak and the peasant poet Spiridon Dimitrievich Drozhzhin stayed with him for good. The 'Russian circle' came to a symbolic close when the Russian poet, Marina Zwetajewa-Efron, became the last major emotional attachment in his life. Russia had transformed Rilke to the point of a changed appearance, including his habit. Simplicity was now for him the order of the day, but not at the expense of his ever-refining poetic skills that continued to strike a neat balance between sheer verbal virtuosity, experiment with form, sensuality, reflectivity and immediacy of expression.

### From Worpswede to Meudon: the poetics of the visual arts

After his return from Russia Rilke was looking for something similar to the Russian landscape and found this when he revisited the artists' colony at Worpswede near Bremen at the invitation of one of its most important representatives, the painter and illustrator Heinrich Vogeler (who, incidentally, went to live in communist Russia in 1931). Rilke was commissioned by the publisher Velhagen & Klasing to write a monograph on the Worpswede artists, in particular Fritz Overbeck, Fritz Mackensen, Hans am Ende, and Otto Modersohn. Curiously absent from his first major study on Worpswede – his inauguration as an eminent poetic art critic – were two female artists to whom Rilke was closest, clearly too close to be included in a critical appreciation, namely Paula Becker, who married Modersohn in 1901, and her friend, the painter and sculptor Clara Westhoff, who became Rilke's wife in the same year. The introduction to this monograph amounts to an essay on the history and meaning of landscape painting, and in his characterisations of the painters' individual contributions to the specifically Worpswedian rendering of landscape, Rilke shows how all of them had taken the painter Eugène Delacroix's advice literally, namely to take the 'words of painting' from the 'dictionary of nature' (KA IV, 349). *Worpswede* (1902), together with his reflections on Russian art and the Swiss artist Giovanni Segantini, had prepared Rilke for what was to become his major challenge as an art critic, his studies of Auguste Rodin.

In the years 1901–2 Rilke wrote the majority of his reviews and critical appreciations, most notably his detailed review of Thomas Mann's 1901 novel *Buddenbrooks*, which the novelist was to regard in retrospect as the finest comment on his first masterpiece. Although Rilke loathed journalistic work, he was forced to keep it up for some time to maintain his young family (the couple's only child, Ruth, was born in December 1901). In a rare moment of ironic self-observation in his letters, Rilke wrote to Modersohn on 25 June 1902: 'if I write into my beard and hold my left hand in front of it, then, my writings will turn more journalistic' (B I, 117).

Rilke went to Paris first from late summer 1902 until the end of June 1903, later from September 1905 until July 1906 and from May until the end of October 1907 – shorter stays were to follow in 1911 and 1913, and his extended final visit was in 1925. Initially, the main reason for his journey was to study, like Clara had done before him, the art and ethos of Rodin, but also to appreciate the reality of life in this hub of artistic creativity and to find himself, meaning his very own vocation in life and art. Yet, at first Paris appeared to him 'alien' and 'hostile' and it was not before he had come to Paris for the third time that he almost felt at one with the city. His monograph on Rodin (which had already appeared in spring 1903) is the most concise and penetrating study on this artist to date and did much to introduce Rodin to a wider public at the time. But he needed distance from Paris, which he found in subsequent stays in Viareggio and Rome, to reflect on this extraordinary urban experience and transform it poetically, mainly in his *Book of Hours* and the first versions of what became his only novel, *The Notebooks of Malte Laurids Brigge*.

However critical Rilke was about Paris, the metropolis on the Seine never ceased to fascinate him. It helped him to reshape his life, albeit at the expense of his family, for Rilke and Clara decided to live separate lives (but were never divorced) for the sake of fostering their respective artistic careers. Experiencing Paris turned out at first to be unsettling for Rilke in the literal sense of the word: after having lived there twice it became virtually impossible for the poet to settle anywhere for a longer period of time, except during his last years in the castle tower of Muzot. During his second stay in Paris (1905–6), Rilke acted for some nine months as Rodin's private secretary. Such was the artist's confidence in the young poet that he asked Rilke to take over most of his correspondence and stay in one of the studios on his estate at Meudon where he confided to him his innermost thoughts on art and the vocation of the artist. It was at Meudon that Rilke met the Irish playwright George Bernard Shaw and the highly cultured Bohemian aristocrat Sidonie Nádherný von Borutin, soon to be another of his important female confidantes, and, back in Paris, the Belgian poet Emile Verhaeren who became a close friend. Following on from the success of his Rodin monograph, Rilke prepared a lecture on the artist during his time at Meudon, which he delivered in Dresden, Prague, Berlin and Hamburg in the course of autumn and winter 1905–6.

It was also during this time that his poetic art matured. What he had learnt from Rodin was to perceive objects and to shape them through whatever artistic medium. But the main point was for the artist to do this 'on behalf of the objects'. *Schauen* (which suggests a comprehensive way of looking, or, more literally, 'spectating') and *bilden* (giving shape) became Rilke's aesthetic imperatives that informed the two volumes of his *New Poems* containing his so-called 'poetry of things'. These principles were reinforced when he encountered the works of Cézanne exhibited in the Salon d'automne in October 1907. In Cézanne's paintings Rilke believed he saw a whole assembly of 'vibrating transitions' between spaces and colours; he regarded the painter as a narrator of shapes and shades; and he noted that the one poem that Cézanne had known by heart at the very end of his life was Baudelaire's 'A Carcass' ('Une Charogne'), suggesting that the artist has to be able to engage with the essences of the beautiful and the horrific, thus penetrating perfection and decay.

Now, Rilke wanted even to *see* emotions; letters turned in his eyes into fabrics, even lace. Like Rodin he hoped to become identical with the landscapes he was writing about; likewise, his prose and poetry were to turn into a landscape of words. Between his second and third stay in Paris Rilke experimented with this way of writing, most strikingly in his prose written on Capri where he also worked on a rendering of Elizabeth Barrett Browning's *Sonnets from the Portuguese* into German. During that time Rilke gave shape to the idea of the lonely but 'great loving soul' which he found in letters of a Portuguese nun, again from the seventeenth century, but also in the Renaissance poet Gaspara Stampa as well as in the Romantic writer Bettina von Arnim. They were to reappear in his novel *Malte Laurids Brigge*, and even later in the *Duino Elegies*. To Rilke, these 'lovers' worship love for love's sake and do not wish to 'possess' their beloved.

### Impressions, encounters, journeys: Rilke in search of foci

Even before Rilke embarked on his major journey to North Africa in November 1910 after completing *Malte*, he found himself travelling almost incessantly. Between autumn 1907 and November 1910 he stayed in Breslau, Vienna, Bremen, Venice, Capri and Paris, Munich and Duino, Lautschin and Janowitz Castle, the latter two located in central Bohemia, as the guest of Princess Marie von Thurn und Taxis-Hohenlohe and Baroness von Borutin. Given this extraordinary talent for travel and experiencing different places in relatively short amounts of time, it is surprising to find that in Rilke's work the spatial element is, comparatively speaking, under-represented. Spaces are more present in Rilke's letters of this period, particularly when he reflects what he had seen in Egypt and, later, in Spain. He speaks of the 'relentlessly huge things' in terms of edifices and landscapes along the Nile (10 February 1911) but transposes this experience onto the task of the intellectual in his age, namely to 'clear' the sky over the landscapes of the mind (2 June 1911). In his correspondence with Marie von Thurn und Taxis he identifies the Austrian cultural philosopher Rudolf Kassner as one such intellectual who was capable of bringing particular concepts, such as dilettantism, 'to their senses', meaning that he clarified their essence (B I, 359).

With hindsight, the frequent disruptions in Rilke's life, his incessant travelling and changes of scene and friends amount to a peculiar form of continuity. There was a logic behind his seemingly erratic way of life; and this logic was intimately connected with Rilke's endeavour to find the ideal conditions for writing and cultivating his oeuvre. It was the logic of a poet who subscribed to the principle first expressed in one of his most famous poems 'Archaic Torso of Apollo' which ended with an imperative but without an exclamation mark: 'Your life you need to alter' (KA I, 513). However, between the completion of *Malte* and the outbreak of the First World War, Rilke was not only looking for the most congenial company and conducive atmosphere for his work; facing a serious creative crisis, he was also searching for the work itself and his own sense of purpose as an artist. Writing confessional letters turned into a substitute for poetic creation. Sometimes he felt compelled to apologise to his correspondents for the sheer quantity of letters he heaped upon them, assuring them at the same time, the Princess Thurn und Taxis for one, that this would not continue for ever (2 June 1911; B I, 358).

Inspiration came from all sides, from El Greco's art and from the landscape around Ronda in Spain, which reminded him of the rocks of Duino on the North Adriatic coast. He read again Baudelaire, Dante and Leopardi and Shakespeare's *The Tempest*, in early 1914 Marcel Proust's *Swann's Way* (*Du côté de chez Swann*), Heinrich von Kleist (mainly his prose), discovered for himself some Japanese poetry, was stunned by what he saw of Georg Trakl's verse as well as of Franz Kafka's first publications. But perhaps most importantly, it was then that Rilke came into contact with Hölderlin's works, which were being rediscovered at the time and which supplied him with the unique combination of elegiac and hymnal poetic structures and rhythms that would characterise his own poetry to come.

Not that Rilke had ceased writing poetry in those years. On the contrary, he wrote the poetic cycle *The Life of the Virgin Mary* in January 1912 in Duino (later set to music by Paul Hindemith), immediately followed by the first of the *Duino Elegies* and drafts of others that he was to revise and complete a decade later. What it is that connects *The Life of the Virgin Mary* with the *Duino Elegies* is a curious but rarely discussed question: perhaps more than anything else it is the reciprocity of 'Klage' (lament) and 'Rühmung' (praise) as well as the notion that the knowledge of the heart outweighs any intellectual pursuits. There was also his 'Spanish Trilogy', poems on the Narcissus-figure that betray Rilke's tentative interest in Freudian mytho-analysis; there were occasional poems that experiment with poetic registers close to Expressionism, including the poem 'Turning-Point', which suggests a move round from 'work of the face' to 'heart-work' (KA II, 102), implying a conscious shift from the pre-eminence of visual perception to the work of innermost feelings. This included a new perceptiveness for music even though it remained tentative, if not ambiguous. Rilke's attitude towards music was conditioned by his fear that it might 'overwhelm' him.[7] As so often, it was a personal relationship that influenced his views on art – in this case his encounter with the pianist and writer Magda von Hattingberg in spring 1914, which resulted in arguably Rilke's finest love-letters and his most intense period of listening to and reflecting on music. Later occasions of 'being exposed to music' (this is how he rated the experience) – for instance in Berlin in 1919 when the Polish pianist Wanda Landowska played for him, or in Muzot with the Australian violinist Alma Moodie – were clearly important to him. But it was the combination of experiencing love and music at the same time that threatened to 'overpower' the poet. Consequently, he backtracked.

There was another reason why he felt uneasy about this relationship. For the first time in his life he accompanied a performing artist on her concert tour and felt, once again, 'exposed' to the commercialisation of art. What was more, the Hungarian composer Casimir von Pászthory had written music for Rilke's *Cornet* and Hattingberg suggested to him in 1915 that they should appear jointly on stage for a good cause (collecting money for the troops). Rilke was incensed, as can be seen from a letter he wrote to his publisher at the time, Anton Kippenberg. The thought of 'Rilke evenings' disgusted him and he refers to the music for *Cornet* as a 'musical manual' that could but cheapen the quality of the poem.[8]

### The politics of a non-political poet: Rilke and the First World War

The intrinsic complexities of Rilke's political attitudes became most apparent during the First World War. Perhaps to his own surprise he saw in the outbreak of the war the uprising of the people's destiny or even fate itself and at least initially he seemed to have welcomed, like so many on both sides, the supposedly 'cleansing' effect of this almighty 'thunderstorm'.[9] Rilke's contribution to the war effort consisted of a five-part poem, 'Five Songs', written in August 1914 and published in the Insel Almanac later that year: here he saw 'pain acting' on its own *and* in the name of 'future blood'; it celebrated the 'unheard of' scale of this acting and the sudden presence of the once remote and only mythical 'war god' (KA II, 106–11). The poem wavers between stunned admiration for the extraordinary and sheer bewilderment at what was happening; it suggests that through this suddenness there is something equally terrific and horrific at work able to mobilise *all* of the people's emotions, almost regardless of what they had previously believed in; and this very much described Rilke's own situation at the time. However one interprets this poem, it confirms that Rilke had, at last, lost his innocence in political matters. This new concern with politics would eventually lead him, the protégé of aristocratic literati, to republican, if not quasi-socialist views in the immediate after-war period and to drafting a 'political speech' that suggested an almost Freudian 'working through' of the experience of loss and pain (KA IV, 705–6).

The war had confined Rilke's space. He could now only travel within German-speaking countries; worse still, he was drafted into the Austro-Hungarian army and underwent a very brief period of military training in January 1916. It was only thanks to the determined intervention of friends like Hugo von Hofmannsthal and Stefan Zweig that he was soon transferred to the exceptionally relaxed service in the military archive in Vienna, which provided him with protection and time for his own work and travels. Even though Rilke eventually enjoyed the maximum of preferential treatment he felt traumatised by this entire experience, for it reminded him of his time in the military academy in Linz. Rilke's poetic production came to a virtual standstill during this period but, as often before, letter-writing and translating poetry (mainly Michelangelo's sonnets) kept him close to the by now only flickering flame of artistic creation.

Rilke spent most of his time in Munich, Berlin, on estates in Westphalia and in Vienna, encountering the art of Picasso, Kokoschka and Klee. After having read Wilhelm Worringer's study on *Abstraction and Empathy* in 1913, Rilke felt challenged by the conception of non-figurative art which fascinated him when he encountered Klee's work. In financial terms his situation had stabilised, mainly due to high sales of the *Cornet* during the war and to a major donation from an anonymous source (which proved to be the philosopher Ludwig Wittgenstein).

In the Munich district of Schwabing, however, Rilke came into close contact with the mysticism of Ludwig Klages and Alfred Schuler whose obscure theories and radically conservative tendencies were in conflict with Rilke's otherwise liberal-minded outlook. His reading of Oswald Spengler's exceedingly pessimistic work on the *Decline of the West* early in 1919 complemented this fascination on Rilke's part with the 'mythische Mensch', meaning both the mythologically oriented man and the myth of man and manhood; the latter was reinforced by his parallel reading of Hans Blüher's *The Function of Eroticism in Male Society*. This partly explains why Rilke expressed strong sympathies with Mussolini's fascist revolution in Italy, mainly in his correspondence with the Duchess Aurelia Gallarati-Scotti between 1923 and 1926.[10]

In one of his few poems written during this period (in April 1916) Rilke speaks of 'cells of hatred' that he sees growing everywhere (KA II, 148). Judging from his letters he became increasingly desperate to strengthen his inner resistance against the cruelty of the war and the hardship of the people. At the same time, he was at odds with an attitude that demanded activism at all costs which would only lead to 'political dilettantism'.[11] Instead, he wrote, people should concentrate on what they really can do. One month after the revolution in Germany, Rilke, who felt increasingly attracted by socialist beliefs, surprised one of his many correspondents with the following definition of 'revolution': 'By the way, to me revolution means the overcoming of fraudulent conditions in favour of the deepest of tradition.' Revolutions occurred, according to Rilke, in the 'most gifted of moments' but after the 'unheard-of achievements [*sic*] and hardship of the war' people appeared to him too exhausted for the new challenges and demands that any revolution presents.[12]

Rilke who had once declared that it was in the powers of the artist to create a time of his own now deplored the sheer acceleration of events and a historical momentum that not only gathered in pace but seemed to spiral out of control. The assassination of Karl Liebknecht and Rosa Luxemburg in January 1919 and, only one month later, of Kurt Eisner – all three figureheads of Germany's radical left – confirmed Rilke's view that people were not really ready for this major transition to democratic republicanism. In fact, Rilke had entertained friendly relations with Eisner who wanted to turn Bavaria into a people's republic. When in May 1919 these attempts were brutally crushed by right-wing forces and intervention from central government in Berlin, Rilke's flat in Munich was searched by police twice, given his close relations with Eisner and the writer Ernst Toller, a radical left-wing writer. Furthermore, the police questioned him about his supposed political involvement, suspecting him of having produced communist propaganda. For Rilke, this was the final straw. In June 1919 he accepted an invitation to give a reading in Zurich and left Germany for good. There he remained, at least for some, a different kind of suspect: in July 1925 a press campaign was launched against him accusing him of excessive Francophilia. It could therefore not have come as a great surprise when in November 1926, one and a half months before he died, Rilke declined membership of Germany's most illustrious cultural club, the Prussian Academy of Arts. He had closed the file labelled 'German affairs'. What remained an ever open and unsettled account to him was his contribution to German culture in terms of its poetic language. His final, and by any standards unique, contribution to that was still to come.

## The Swiss route to Rilke's poetic twin peaks

Switzerland received Rilke well. It appeared to him the most European and cosmopolitan place on the Continent. Swiss neutrality during the war had allowed the country to house European artists and intellectuals who wanted to escape bloody xenophobia. It even provided a platform for the most daring of artistic experiments to take place: the cultivation of nonsense in the shape of the Dada movement in Zurich with its emancipation of spontaneity and celebration of performance for performance's sake; and it was there that Stefan Zweig was able to stage his anti-war play *Jeremiah*. Even though one could not imagine a more fundamental difference than that between Rilke's poetics and Dada's performance-driven aesthetics there is one reference in Rilke's draft of the introduction to his 1919 reading in Zurich that suggests his awareness of new trends. He told his audience that the sequence of the pieces he was going to read was not premeditated but spontaneous. 'Under the influence of your presence and participation I will decide on the spur of the moment which poem to read' (KA IV, 709). It is interesting to find that he refers to his poems as attempts to provide every animal, plant, process or object mentioned in them with their respective 'space of feeling' (KA IV, 708).

To judge from the way in which Rilke was to explore Switzerland in the seven years to come, it seems that he increasingly thought of this country as being his very own 'space of feeling'. The German, French and Italian parts of Switzerland were equally important to him and it appears that Rilke believed that in Switzerland he could experience Europe in a nutshell. During the first two years in his new environment he kept moving from one place to the next, re-establishing for himself a certain travel routine between cultures and languages. But even in the Helvetian Republic he sought the company and protection of aristocratic families, such as the von Salis, the von der Mühlls and the von Wattenwyls who offered him temporary lodgings.[13]

Between 1919 and 1921 Rilke began translating Paul Valéry, completed the description of an unusual experiment ('Ur-Geräusch', 'Primal Sound' or 'Sound of the Origins'), produced in an act of what seemed like 'automatic writing' a poetic cycle called 'From the Literary Remains of Count C. W.'; and wrote a piece of experimental prose called 'The Testament'; which was to document yet another experience of creative crisis. The 'Primal Sound', the poem on Count C. W. and 'The Testament' all reflect Rilke's desire to engage with the hitherto unknown. 'Primal Sound' in particular relates to the quintessentially Romantic (but also Nietzschean) desire to 'poeticise' science. It suggests an experiment through which a person's individual 'sound' should be identified. Rilke proposes a phonographic transposition of the line where the two halves of the skull are grown together, which is as person-specific as a fingerprint. The sound created through this process he called 'arch sound' (KA IV, 699–702). What links this experiment with the world of Dada is the interest in raw sound materials (as in Kurt Schwitter's 'Ursonate' or 'Sonata in Primordial Sounds'). Similarly, 'The Testament' deals with primal experiences, the secrets behind life and art, an assembly of more or less fundamental concepts and the different forces of life and will that meet each other in the author's 'heart'.

It is tempting, but perhaps misleading, to regard all these experiences, including the semi-conscious writing up of 'From the Literary Remains of Count C. W.', as preparations for the two pinnacles of Rilke's poetic achievements, the twin peaks of German poetry in the twentieth century: the *Duino Elegies* and *The Sonnets to Orpheus*. But for that to happen Rilke had to find a reliable domicile. In summer 1921 he discovered it near Sierre, at the beginning of the Rhône Valley, in the shape of the medieval castle tower Muzot, which was bought a year later by his patron Werner Reinhardt of

Winthertur. He allowed the poet to stay there indefinitely as a rent-free sitting tenant. Rilke called the castle walls his 'large animal', which he liked to stroke after completing a day's work.[14] For the first couple of weeks after moving into the tower Rilke could only write letters; 'letter labour', as he liked to call this, was in his view also poetically essential occupation.

Shortly before he discovered Muzot, Rilke recalled a Roman tower in the park of Duino castle, opposite an almost surreal spiral staircase on its own that no longer led to anywhere. But Muzot was different; surrounded by a landscape that seemed to him like a synthesis of all landscapes he had ever seen. Strangely, the entrance to an adjacent chapel bore an ancient swastika. Rilke remarked on it when he could not have known what significance this symbol was soon to adopt.[15]

## The 'Orders of Angels' and the sound of the lyre

Rilke's friend 'Merline', the painter Baladine Klossowska whom he had known from his days in Paris but met again in 1919 in Geneva, helped him to make the castle tower of Muzot properly inhabitable. On New Year's Day 1922 Rilke learnt of the death of a young dancer, Wera Ouckama Knoop; he studied the French poet Paul Valéry's poetic dialogue 'The Soul and the Dance', received a photograph of the Bust of Queen Nefertiti and, as a gift from Merline, a print of Conegliano's pictorial rendering of the Orpheus myth. The combination of these impressions and what had been building up in him during the years of creative hardship triggered, or so it seems, the ensuing outburst of creativity that resulted in the completion of the ten *Duino Elegies*, the 'Letter from the Young Worker' and *The Sonnets to Orpheus*. Whilst the *Elegies* drew on archaic, Jewish and Islamic motifs, the sonnets reconnected Rilke with Greek mythology. It is noteworthy that a fictive letter, that is to say, a piece of prose writing, mediates between the two lyrical compositions. In it a young factory worker writes to a poet whose reading he had attended. In his letter the young man addresses the position of Christian religion, the meaning of its edifices, of cathedrals in particular, and of sacred music. Most importantly, it questions the lasting significance of the cross as the sublime symbol of mankind, for it associates the cross with crossroads, in other words, with a moment of decision but also transition. The young worker, who is mostly dealing with machines and wrestles with questions of faith, argues that the cross should dissolve from within. We should overcome morally restricting notions like 'original sin' and allow man to be emancipated from the punishing side of Christian dogma. The young worker claims that the poetry he had heard during the reading taught him what it means to praise existence or rather 'life' as such. But the upshot of this letter is that, once again, (poetic) art is needed to support this awareness of life and its unrestrained appreciation (KA IV, 735–47). Through this letter Rilke constructed the image of his 'ideal reader and listener' who may just have listened to his *Duino Elegies* and is ready to receive what he was about to compose next, *The Sonnets to Orpheus*. If seen in this way all three works composed within the space of barely one month, amount to a most varied and complex, but coherent, poetic narrative.

Through the figure of Orpheus Rilke was able to show in his sonnets that death was but a complement to life; this thought continued to gain prominence later in his letters.[16] Rilke advocated the emancipation of the senses from bourgeois morality and in so doing supported once again a Nietzschean thought, namely the revaluation of values in perpetuity. The 'orders of angels' he called upon in the *Elegies* was to Rilke not a Christian motif; the angel signified the complete transformation of the visible into the invisible, the latter being a more intense form of reality. Likewise the Orpheus figure functions as an agent of transition and transformation. He is virtually 'standing in music', as the young worker in his letter called a state of being that is conditioned by the full absorption of what was to Rilke a precariously ambiguous medium. On the one hand it epitomises the sublime; on the other hand it can overwhelm the listener to the point of paralysis. Interestingly, the young worker imagines the stones of the cathedral, its pillars and arches as penetrated by all the music that was ever played and caught in it. These stones only keep vibrating but they are not transformed into living entities like those who are touched by the song of Orpheus.

## Towards the shadowlands

'Victory and defeat are but the two sides of one and the same helplessness', Rilke wrote in June 1926.[17] This was as much a political as an existential statement, a general observation and an accurate account of his own situation. He had experienced artistic 'victories' and triumphs, not least through the completion of the *Elegies* and *Sonnets*, but it seemed to him that the 'defeats' were equally profound, previously during periods of creative lows and, since spring 1923, ill health. His rhythm of life was now marked by increasingly longer periods in sanatoria accompanied by long reflections on his state of health. The uncertainty about the nature of his illness – only weeks before he died a particularly painful form of leukaemia was diagnosed – gave space for metaphorical characterisations of the pain he was exposed to. In a letter to Lou Andreas-Salomé in October 1925 he spoke of being encircled by suffering 'like in a Breughel painting of hell'.[18]

Considering his deteriorating state of health, his poetic and epistolary productivity was stunning, not to speak of his social life, which seemed undiminished between 1923 and mid-1925. One of his last visitors was the young actress Elisabeth Bergner. He still received floods of visitors and when he visited Paris in January 1925 he seemed virtually to be holding court. The cream of the French literati came to see him, from André Gide to Paul Valéry (whose reputation in the German-speaking world rested on Rilke's translations), Edmond Jaloux, Jules Supervielle, Jean Cassou, Jean Giraudoux and Charles Du Bos. Later he was to read Jean Cocteau's work on Orpheus with great admiration. In Paris he re-encountered, too, the air of Russian culture as preserved by Russian émigrés, such as his acquaintance of former days, Jelena Woronia, the poet Iwan Bunin and Julia Sazonova's then famous puppet theatre. Later he exchanged letters with the young poet Boris Pasternak, who brought him into contact with Marina Zwetajewa-Efron, his last great love affair, conducted solely through the medium of letters. His deep empathy with things Russian came to a symbolic conclusion in the fact that only three months before he died Rilke employed a multi-lingual Russian as his last secretary.

Rilke's previous experience of a similar sort of epistolary relationship had resulted in an exchange of letter-like poems, amounting to a veritable poetic cycle in the Romantic tradition, with the young Austrian poet Erika Mitterer – incidentally the only example of a fruitful poetic collaboration in Rilke's entire oeuvre. This productive exchange also demonstrated that Rilke had not lost his passionate concern for 'the young poet', who was to him an iconic figure and symbol of creative potential that was, however, in need of constructive guidance. From Franz Xaver Kappus to Alexander Lernet-Holenia, from Regina Ullmann to Claire Studer – Rilke's 'Liliane' (after 1921 married to Yvan Goll) – stretched the line of poetic hopefuls who sought Rilke's tutelage and received an unusual degree of attention, encouragement and, in some cases, emotional affection.

In artistic terms, Rilke's final years are of much interest because he not only connected with modernists in their respective fields (Ernst Křenek in music, for instance, Baladine Klossowska in painting, Kafka and Cocteau in literature) but he also changed his poetic style significantly. He even broke with his firm principle to offer only coherently composed poetic cycles or sequences, for in the last year of his life he compiled a selection of occasional poems: some of them belong to his finest and are published under what was by his previous standards a surprising title, *From Pocket Notebooks and Memory Pads*.

Paradoxically, it is the complex simplicity that appeals in Rilke's last poems and the way in which they engage in existential problems often expressed in surprising metaphors:

> Breath, you invisible poem!
> Steady sheer exchange between the cosmos
> and our being. Counterpoise
> in which I rhythmically become.[19]
>
> *(Sonnets,* II: 1)

Rilke was by then able to transfer this way of poetic expression into French, too, demonstrating that he had accomplished what he had been striving for since his first encounter with Rodin: not only to be able to mediate between cultures but to switch the languages of poetry with ease and to fluctuate between poetic registers in the two languages that mattered to him most whenever the subject matter or moment of inspiration required it.

'Erect no memorial stone', he wrote in one of the *Sonnets to Orpheus*:

> Let the rose
> bloom every year to remind us of him.
> Because it's Orpheus. His metamorphosis
> is in this, and this.     *(Sonnets,* I: 5)

Rilke himself desired to be at one 'with what is song' and 'ahead of all Departure, as if it were / behind you like the winter that's just passed' as he said in the thirteenth Orpheus sonnet of Part Two. Even at the very end of his life he found the strength to document and transform this final experience poetically:

> Now come, the last that I can recognize,
> pain, utter pain, fierce in the body's texture.
>
> (KA II, 412)

In the fabric of Rilke's life the artistic word needed to have the final say; for he knew that only the word would last.

## NOTES

1 See Katja Brunkhorst, *Nietzsche's Presence in Rilke* (Munich: iudicium, 2006).
2 See Bruno Hillebrand, *Nietzsche: Wie ihn die Dichter sahen* (Göttingen: Vandenhoeck & Ruprecht, 2000).
3 Donald Prater, *A Ringing Glass: The Life of Rainer Maria Rilke* (Oxford: Clarendon Press, 1986), pp. 5–11.
4 Joachim W. Storck, 'Rilke. Leben und Persönlichkeit', in *RHB*, pp. 1–2.
5 Rainer Maria Rilke, *Das Florenzer Tagebuch* [1942], ed. Ruth Sieber-Rilke and Carl Sieber (Frankfurt and Leipzig: Insel, 1994), p. 38.

6 Quoted from Horst Nalewski (ed.), *Rilke: Leben, Werk und Zeit in Texten und Bildern* (Frankfurt am Main and Leipzig: Insel, 1992), p. 59 (comment made by Rilke on 17 March 1926 to an unspecified friend).

7 See Rüdiger Görner, 'Musik', in *RHB*, pp. 151–4.

8 Rainer Maria Rilke, *Briefwechsel mit Anton Kippenberg 1906–1926*, ed. Ingeborg Schnack and Renate Scharffenberg, 2 vols. (Frankfurt am Main and Leipzig: Insel, 1995), vol. I, p. 29. See also Rainer Maria Rilke, *Briefwechsel mit Magda von Hattingberg 'Benvenuta'*, ed. Ingeborg Schnack and Renate Scharffenberg (Frankfurt am Main and Leipzig: Insel, 2000).

9 As it happened Rilke wrote a prose poem 'Gewitter, Gewitter' ('Storm, Storm') (KA II, 105) shortly before the outbreak of the war when he was still in Paris. His friend, the Swiss writer Regina Ullmann had told him about experiencing a frightening thunderstorm at Altoetting, a place of pilgrimage in Bavaria, from where she had sent him a black candle 'consecrated' by flashes of lightning as she put it (see KA II, 508).

10 The entire scale of Rilke's political views only became apparent when a comprehensive anthology of his letters on politics was published in 1992: Rainer Maria Rilke, *Briefe zur Politik*, ed. Joachim W. Storck (Frankfurt am Main and Leipzig: Insel, 1992).

11 Rilke, *Briefe zur Politik*, p. 238 (letter to Dorothea Freifrau von Ledebur, 19 December 1918).

12 Ibid., p. 237.

13 The most vivid account of this crucial and final period in his life is, once again, given by his own letters: Rainer Maria Rilke, *Briefe an Schweizer Freunde*, ed. Rätus Luck (Frankfurt am Main and Leipzig: Insel, 1994).

14 Rilke used this phrase frequently with reference to Muzot, most notably in his letter to Anton Kippenberg after completing the *Duino Elegies* (B II, 217).

15 Rilke, *Briefe zur Politik*, p. 393 (letter to Margot Countess Sizzo-Norris-Crouy, 15 July 1922).

16 See for example the letter to Countess Sizzo of 6 January 1923 (B II, 268).

17 Letter to Wilhelm Hausenstein (B II, 444).

18 Rainer Maria Rilke and Lou Andreas-Salomé, *Briefwechsel*, ed. Ernst Pfeiffer (Frankfurt am Main: Insel, 1989), p. 476.

19 Rainer Maria Rilke, *Duino Elegies and the Sonnets to Orpheus*, trans. A. Poulin, Jr. (Boston: Norton, 1977). All subsequent translations are from this edition.

# 2

ULRICH BAER

# The status of the correspondence in Rilke's work

Rainer Maria Rilke's vast correspondence touches upon the full range of topics addressed in his poetry and prose. In what amounts to approximately 17,000 letters (not all of them yet published due to copyright restrictions with addressees), Rilke sometimes abandoned the constraints of German verse, and occasionally syntax, to produce powerful and surprisingly accessible meditations on life, art, death, religion, love and politics. Rilke wrote to housekeepers and politicians, fellow poets and lovers, teenage girls infatuated with his verse and, though rarely, to critics who had engaged with his work. The only criterion for inclusion in Rilke's little black book, where he meticulously kept track of all his correspondence (at the end of his life, it contained several hundred entries with notes on every letter written and received), was that a letter, even from an unknown individual or someone of far lower social standing, 'spoke to him'.[1] Rilke took each word in every letter seriously, as can be gleaned from the immaculate way he covered pages and pages of stationery with his prose. A little over a year before his death in a Swiss sanatorium, Rilke stipulated in October 1925 that his letters ought to be published alongside his other writings: 'Since for now several years I have had the custom to channel part of the productivity of my nature into writing letters, there exist no obstacles to publishing my correspondence [...] (should my publisher Insel Verlag make such a suggestion)' (*Briefe*, II, 1192). Given the profundity of thought expressed in his letters and Rilke's own high estimation of these missives, it is virtually impossible to gain a full understanding of the poet without taking the correspondence into account.

Rilke's will was not honoured. The publication of his letters is still incomplete, and has followed inconsistent standards. It commenced in 1929 when Rilke's widow, daughter and son-in-law released the perennially popular *Letters to a Young Poet*, which Rilke had written to the aspiring poet Franz Xaver Kappus, who was enrolled in the military boarding school where Rilke had been a student a few years previously, between 1903 and 1908.[2] In these ten letters, Rilke offered original and moving advice on how to be an artist, how to love and how to live. A six-volume selection (published between 1930 and 1937) comprises mostly letters written by Rilke about his views on art and about his vocation as an artist.[3] There are also many letters written to his wife that were included in this first edition to improve his public image as a husband and father (Rilke had left his family when his daughter was not quite a year old). These letters are principally concerned with Rilke's impressions on viewing art in Paris, his daily struggle in forcing himself to work and his early doubts about his talent as a poet. But they fail to convey what is found in subsequent collections published over the next few decades by different editors, publishing houses and individuals (including the recipients of his letters). In these later editions, Rilke reveals his remarkable capacity for turning the meticulous description of an object, event, site, person, or experience into an analysis of how our consciousness shapes reality and how the encounter with the world can, in turn, prompt us to transform ourselves.

Several collections are indispensable for an understanding of Rilke as a person and author. In many of these letters Rilke often explains, in great detail and surprisingly clear language, his most profound thoughts. There are passages that clarify and develop at length the complex themes that Rilke would later express in his poems in striking metaphors and thus necessarily in a condensed and sometimes recondite fashion. Since many of these letters are occasioned by encounters with individuals, travels, specific experiences or events, they always remain grounded in Rilke's experiences of everyday life even when they offer reflections on the fleeting nature of our existence and on our unquenchable thirst for experiences of transcendence in a godless age.

Instead of insisting as he does in his poems rather abstractly if movingly, for instance, that death is part of life, Rilke used the existing genre of the condolence letter to develop this notion in very concrete ways. He offers actual advice on the process of mourning to Margot Sizzo in a letter of 6 January, 1923:

> Words... could they be words of consolation? – I am not sure about that, and I don't quite believe that one could console oneself over a loss as sudden and great as the one you just experienced. Even time does not 'console,' as people say superficially, at best it puts things in their place and creates order – and even that only because we so quickly begin to take this order lightly to which time contributes so quietly by finding the proper place for, appeasing, and reconciling everything within the great Whole. Instead of admiring what has been placed there and no longer pains us acutely, we regard it as a result of our forgetfulness and the weakness of our heart. Ah, how little it *forgets*, this heart, – and how strong it would be if we did not deprive it of its tasks before

they had been fully and genuinely achieved! – Our instinct should not be to desire consolation over a loss but rather to develop a deep and painful curiosity to explore this loss completely, to experience the peculiarity, the singularity, and the effects of particularly *this* loss in our life. Indeed, we should develop a kind of noble greed and strive to enrich our inner world with particularly *this* loss and its significance and weight... The more profoundly we are affected by such a loss and the more painfully it concerns us, the more it becomes our *task* to claim as a new, different and definitive possession that which loss now so hopelessly emphasises. *This* amounts to the infinite achievement that instantly overcomes all the negative aspects of pain, all the sluggishness and indulgence that is always a part of pain.[4]

Rilke urges his bereaved friend to acknowledge and explore the loss she has experienced and to recognise to what extent life is always departure and arrival, loss and gain. This does not mean one ought to cherish loss as a challenge: 'It becomes our task not to dissolve pain into consciousness; pain tolerates no interpretation' (*Letters on Life*, p. 102). Rilke suggests staying with the feeling of loss, rather than evading it and pretending that one can run from it, or turn it into something else. Although the passage cannot be marshalled as a guide to reading Rilke's poetry, it aids in understanding some of the enigmatic lines in the *Duino Elegies*, for instance: 'All this was mission. / But could you accomplish it? Weren't you always / distracted by expectation?' (KA II, 202).[5] In the letter to Margot Sizzo Rilke continues to explain our 'task' in life as the challenge to experience all that happens, rather than defending ourselves against certain aspects of the fullness of life – which includes losses and gains. While Rilke develops this thought in the letter patiently and carefully, not least out of respect for the addressee's state of grief, in the poems the inseparability of life and death is presented in more condensed fashion, and consequently more enigmatically.

The recipients of Rilke's correspondence can be broken into four major groups. There are Rilke's letters to professional associates (editors and other artists, including the sculptor Auguste Rodin); to his wife and other family; to close friends, mentors and lovers (including Marie von Thurn und Taxis, Nanny Wunderly-Volkart, Lou Andreas-Salomé and Baladine Klossowska); and to unknown individuals who sought help from a well-known author. Although some letters to close friends and lovers might contain particularly personal information, even Rilke's formal correspondence with professional associates often contains highly revealing passages about Rilke's inner life. Sometimes, the letters function as a substitute for direct personal contact, or they allow Rilke to keep his beloved at bay and preserve the sense of solitude he needed to work, while assuring her of his love.

In many of the letters we gain insight into Rilke's daily concerns and his struggles in outlining various artistic projects. Rilke can be funny, charming, seductive and engaging in these letters, but he is never condescending, nor does he pretend to speak from a place of knowledge. Instead, Rilke's letters all originate in an urgent inquiry into himself, into the world, into other people. 'Do not believe that the person who is trying to offer you solace lives effortlessly under the simple and quiet words that might occasionally do you some good. His life contains much hardship and sadness and remains far behind yours. But if it were otherwise, he could never have found these words' (*Letters on Life*, p. 3).

The chief distinction between fiction and all epistolary prose is the direct effort to communicate with another individual and its often concrete referencing of ordinary circumstances that are not dictated by aesthetic criteria but by the vicissitudes of life. These two features – striving for directness and clarity and the willingness to engage with non-traditional subject matter – ultimately become a central dimension and one of the poetic principles of all of Rilke's work. For this reason, Rilke's ceremonious daily habit of writing letters (which he called his 'ascent into a state of conscious reflection' and a 'coming to his senses' as a poet) can be seen as a way of putting into practice his belief that the phenomenal world can offer us all we would ever wish to experience, understand and know (*Briefe*, I, 567). Especially the letters written before 1921, when Rilke finally moved to Switzerland which he considered a refuge and haven, often convey a strong sense of existential disorientation, artistic hesitation and loss over a world that disappeared in the First World War (Rilke literally lost his country of origin and Austro-Hungarian citizenship when the Habsburg Empire was divided into several states after the war). These letters correspond to the narrative of an author's urgent quest for authentic artistic expression that is chronicled in *The Notebooks of Malte Laurids Brigge*. But in his letters Rilke moves toward a state of mindfulness that is only touched upon occasionally in *Malte Laurids Brigge*. It is a stance of attentive openness toward everything that is available to us in the phenomenal world and the refusal to dismiss perceived reality in favour of an abstract, transcendent realm. In the letters, he does not only explain this stance but he also *enacts* it when he describes the world around him in great detail. Rilke's letters are thus not only reflections on what it means to have an artistic vision of the world, but they are actually the way to achieve such a vision: by patiently, calmly and without any preconceived notions keeping our focus on what surrounds us. This stance of mindfulness characterises Rilke's world view more accurately than anything conveyed in the novel that made his reputation as the harbinger of modernist disillusionment and fragmentation: for in his letters Rilke strives to counter the sense of fragmentation when he insists on paying attention to the entire world around him. Our sense of fragmentation (which we like to consider modern but which is more likely a general human experience) is produced not by too much stimulation but by our inability to rest our eyes and mind on one thing at a time. We hasten from object to object, from experience to experience and from person to person without truly taking in all that is offered to us at any given moment. By focusing on details in his letters, Rilke explores what we may have missed by being preoccupied with presumably more important questions: questions of belief, art, life, love and death. All of these concerns, Rilke insists, can be approached through anything in life: a falling leaf may occasion more profound thoughts on loss than a funeral scene.

To his brother-in-law, Helmut Westhoff, Rilke writes on 12 November 1901:

> Most people do not know at all how beautiful the world is and how much magnificence is revealed in the tiniest things, in some flower, in a stone, in tree bark, or in a birch leaf. Adults, being preoccupied with business and worries and tormenting themselves with all kinds of petty details, gradually lose the very sight for these riches that children, when they are attentive and good, soon notice and love with all their heart. And yet the greatest beauty would be achieved if everyone remained in this regard always like attentive and good children, naïve and pious in feeling, and if people did not lose the capacity for taking the same kind of intense pleasure in a birch leaf or a peacock's feather or the wing of a hooded crow that they may take in a great mountain range or a magnificent palace. What is small is not small in itself, just as that which is great is not – great. A great and eternal beauty passes through the whole world, and it is distributed justly over that which is small and that which is large; for in important and essential matters, there exists no injustice anywhere on earth. (*Letters on Life*, p. 67)

Rilke's markedly modernist sensibility dispenses with a higher, transcendent authority and recognises the hollowness of most redemptive ideologies by writing letters that seek to make sense of, and make tangible in his use of language, the phenomenal world. These letters functioned as Rilke's work-shop, laboratory and rehearsal space for some of his loftier ideas where he experimented with language and yet remain grounded in what he called 'life' or 'reality'.

From the letters we gain an understanding of how much emphasis Rilke placed on the actual observance of objects and occurrences. This stance of mindfulness, however, led Rilke to examine carefully every sensation, even if it seemed innocuous, positive, or altogether pleasing. For pleasure can obscure the world to us as effectively as pain: we tend not to see beyond strong emotional reactions. If something makes us happy, we should not simply stay with this happiness but examine to what new state of awareness of ourselves and the world we might be led. To Marguerite Masson-Ruffy, on 4 January 1923, Rilke writes:

> It is true that even happiness can sometimes serve as a pretext for initiating us into that which by its very nature surpasses us. But in such cases it is far easier to understand instantly that something good is happening to us, even if the difficulty *to make use of* this good that we receive through happiness is no smaller than that of divining what could be positive at the bottom of those absences imposed on us by pain. We must advance in this region with far greater determination.　　　　　　　　　　　　　　(*Letters on Life*, p. 96)

Although much is subjected to careful scrutiny in the letters, they are no less filled with joyful anecdotes and even apparently pointless passages with a kind of humour not normally associated with Rilke. The following letter was written when Rilke spent his first winter and spring in Switzerland.

> I am quite concerned about the frogs. They had reached already a quite considerable love temperature; they behaved quite like June-nights in the pond. They have this kind of heart around which the entire rubber body expands most wonderfully, and they were singing with this heart. Elastically. – But at night, before the weather changed, one of them suddenly stopped. In the middle of his rhapsodising he simply did not sing along any longer. Everyone stopped, perplexed; a pause, you could hear the fountain. He gathered himself, began again, responded to his cue at the wrong moment, corrected himself, recited half a stanza, got stuck, – said something incomprehensible, fell silent. All now with him, were silent, taken aback. Suddenly, right into this new pause, another one yelled at him, from the other side of the pond: '.........' (a curse in Froggy that cannot be translated) 'Out with Love!' He apologised, his voice sounded hoarse, – apparently another lead singer was named and a small group joined him, – a few beats, forced, without passion, – it did not work, he also broke off and stopped singing. Silence. Now the first, this spoilsport, this visionary who was responsible for everything, this one tried again, he did his utmost to save the overall mood. He put his hand over his heart, raised his head into the peculiarly indifferent April night and said: I will try again. – Oh no, how false it sounded, dry, dreary –, everyone discouraged him, enough, enough . . . Then, finally, silence. His beloved, however, whispered to him: 'My God, you're not going to get sick?!' – – I fear that's what he is, sick due to returned love and poetry, and she's probably also got a cold, is stuffed up, – looks quite unbecoming; he, feverish, stares at her blankly, at the one who just three days ago was still so dear, and thinks: her mouth is actually common, vulgar –, even to admire her eyes is an effort, something to think about, her golden eyes out of which stares the flu.　　　　　　　　(*Briefe*, I, 408)

On one level, the pond scene is an allegorical description of Rilke's own inability to write poetry during the war years and of his doubt whether he would ever regain his poet's voice after that painful period. But crucially, the passage reveals simply Rilke's joy at describing a mundane scene and his pleasure in casting in language beyond the constraints of syntax sensations, sights, sounds and experiences that are at the edge of expressiblity. It is also crucial to note that from everything Rilke said about his own letters, this passage was for him of equal importance to many other things he wrote. Rilke's entire project, in these letters, is to force himself to pay attention to the world without deciding in advance what is significant or useful. If we take these letters seriously, we will then also refrain from deciding in advance which letter serves us in understanding the poetry better, which letter reveals something about Rilke's life, and which one signals his political or other convictions. In short, Rilke tried to stop himself from slighting the world in front of him, and the letters offer a welcome occasion for his readers to do the same. Instead of instantly dismissing the letters as of secondary importance, it might prove useful to consider the correspondence as an achievement that equals Rilke's literary output.

Nonetheless, it is of course possible in some of the letters to see how Rilke arrived at some of his striking formulations and metaphors. Rilke begins with the detailed description of an artwork, an object, or an incident only to arrive finally, after many sentences, at a striking metaphor that we then encounter again in one of his poems. In his poetry, Rilke's deft intermingling of narrowly focused and expansive perspectives may take the form of one governing metaphor such as 'falling' that allows him to present as a continuous movement the falling of the autumn's leaves, our own inevitable falling and demise, and the directionless falling of our planet through the vastness of space (see, for example, 'Autumn'; KA I, 282). By linking the sight of leaves through a chain of metaphors to our existential situation of groundlessness, he interlocks the description of an everyday occurrence with a transcendent theme. By thus interlocking the everyday and the transcendent, Rilke suggests in his poetry, and minutely explains in his letters, that the key to the secrets of our existence might be found right in front of our eyes.

In the letters, Rilke insisted that we can be shaken in our certitudes, convictions and beliefs by losses *and* by gains, that we may be unsettled as much by negative encounters, adversity, difficulty, illness, loss and death as by the peculiar intensification of our being in the experiences of joy, rapture, friendship, creation or love. But Rilke also stresses that during those experiences, even when they bring us closer to others, we are fundamentally alone. In such moments, when our life is suddenly open to questioning, we are cast back on ourselves without support from any outside agency. Every rite of passage – birth, adolescence, love, commitment, illness, loss, death – marks an experience where we are faced with our solitude. But this is not a melancholic thought for Rilke. He revalorises solitude as the occasion to reconsider our decisions and experiences and to understand ourselves more accurately. Since this reconceptualisation of solitude takes place in letters, however, Rilke averts the risk of becoming hermetic, by opening up his language to his recipient as a concrete addressee.

Letters often allow writers to experiment with language and try out ideas before committing them to established genre or to publication. Rilke was no different, and we know much about his life and creative process from the correspondence. He admitted to placing his art above his personal relations: 'I know that I cannot cut my life out of the fates with which it has grown intertwined,' Rilke wrote in a letter of 11 August 1903 to Andreas-Salomé about his decision to leave his wife and young child, 'but I have to find the strength to lift life in its entirety and including everything into calmness, into solitude, into the quiet of profound days of labour' (B 1, 161). There are also passages in his novel *The Notebooks of Malte Laurids Brigge* that Rilke first wrote as letters and then included in their entirety in the book.

Rilke's commitment not to avoid but to become cognisant of the varying contours of difficulty we may encounter in the world finds its parallel in his views on art. His work does not constitute an aesthetic education where the appreciation of beauty leads one to recognise the truth. In the following excerpt from a letter, Rilke parts ways with the Romantic tradition defined by Schiller and Keats:

> What appears inexorable must be present [in poetry] for the sake of our greatest desires. Beauty will become paltry and insignificant when one looks for it only in what is pleasing; there it might be found occasionally but it dwells and is awake in each thing where it encloses itself, and it emerges only for the individual who assumes its presence everywhere and who will not budge until he has stubbornly coaxed it forth.[6]

Since beauty 'dwells and is awake in each thing', the focused search for beauty blocks our path to the true purpose of art, which is truth, or integrity and honesty, as he prefers to say. We must look *everywhere*, including in sites that strike us as unpleasant. In his life, similarly, he could not pretend to ignore the parts that did not make sense, hurt him or others badly, or that he would rather have denied, repressed, and forgotten, hence the large number of letters where Rilke strives to understand himself as both an artist and father. Rilke also ended the Romantic myth that the body must be given up in feverish and ecstatic surrender as a sacrifice to art. He did not forget his body's needs while he was living the life of the mind: 'You know that I am not one of those individuals who neglect their body in order to turn it into an offering for their soul; my soul would not at all have appreciated such an offering.'[7] He tried to listen to his body and translate its idiom into intelligible words. And he eschewed the seductions of ironic detachment and self-declared irrelevance indulged in by the modern masters. Without writing, Rilke's letters suggest, we might fail to grasp what exactly happens and become numb to reality itself; we might assume the obvious and latent hierarchies around us and unwittingly acquiesce to unjust conditions, not through cowardice, but through our failure to find meaningful expressions for them, and thus make them apparent to us. His search for the 'simple and quiet words', then, does not amount to quietism. Rilke's sense that one's mere presence on this planet deserves affirmation fuelled his commitment to search his experiences for a guide to life.

For this reason, Rilke attempted to cast himself in words: he had an urgent need to testify to his life in this world. 'How is it possible to live since the elements of this life remain completely ungraspable for us?', Rilke asks in a letter to Lotte Hepner on 8 November 1915 (B 1, 599). To the daunting nature of life and its difficulties, Rilke's correspondence is itself an answer.

In his letters, Rilke achieves what his aesthetic principles also mandate for true art: all things and experiences are allowed to speak to him from their proper place in the world, and not only as they are framed there and made sense of by him. Just as he invests his poetry with the power to intertwine everyday affairs and transcendent ideas, Rilke writes in a letter that the essence of true help, for instance, might consist in a modest piece of string offered at the right moment, when it is truly needed. This little piece of string could be 'no less helpful in saving our strength' than the most elaborate, long-term assistance, Rilke writes to Nanny Wunderly-Volkart on 20 May 1921 (*Briefe*, 1, 433–4). For Rilke, both his artistic credo and his most fundamental insight into how to live one's life call for a wholly inclusive view of the world.

There courses through Rilke's work the steady commitment to celebrate life in all its manifestations. This desire is announced already in the title of one of his first books of poetry, *To Celebrate Myself* (1899). Rilke's willingness to get to the bottom of life by any means differs fundamentally from that which characterised poets such as Baudelaire, Verlaine and Rimbaud against whom the young Rilke defined himself. The point became not to observe and comment on life, describing it as if from the outside, or to wrestle it to the ground and overwhelm it with the aid of intoxicants and provocation. Rather, Rilke considered the writer's task to consist in joining his voice to the sounds of agony, suffering, ecstasy and exhilaration, but also to the everyday exchanges between individuals and the interior monologues of all of us.

Rilke's descriptions of sites, people and objects achieve a simplicity and analytic precision which Rilke found nowhere in the learned European cultures of which he was a part. By honing his receptivity, attentiveness and mindfulness, he eschews the shortcuts of received opinion. Instead of tethering himself to a rigid work ethic, however, Rilke sought to bring all of his experiences, including unproductive periods of 'infertility' and 'idleness', into one uninterrupted state of mind. Like all major writers, he creates from an inchoate awareness of the inadequacy of all available explanations of the world, but does not allow this frustration to become the focus of his inquiry and thus drown out the world a second time. Nothing that Rilke read made sufficient sense of his life for him. As a consequence, he wrote a guide to life himself, as can be gleaned from the following excerpt of a letter to Jelena Woronina on 6 May 1899:

> So much has been written about things (both well and badly) that the things themselves no longer hold an opinion – but appear only as the imaginary point of intersection for certain inspired theories. When someone wishes to say something about a given object, he in fact speaks only about the views of his predecessors in the field and lapses into a semi-polemical spirit that is directly opposed to the naïve-productive spirit with which each object wants to be grasped and understood.                    (*Letters on Life*, p. 138)

In addition to serving as the workshop for his poetry, then, Rilke's letters claim a perspective on the world that breaks with traditions of knowledge handed down to him. Because in his correspondence Rilke hopes to reach individuals of varying perspective and backgrounds, he often invents several ways of expressing similar or even identical thoughts. In order to be heard by his correspondents, Rilke abandons established ways of saying things and in this process deepens and frequently expands his own insights. Some of the passages in Rilke's letters are so vibrant, creative and rhetorically animated precisely because Rilke surprised himself with a discovery that could not have been planned.

> Wherever an individual's philosophy develops into a system, I experience the almost depressing feeling of a limitation, of a deliberate effort. I try to encounter the human each time at *that* point where the wealth of his experiences still realises itself in many disparate and distinct ways without coherence, and without being curtailed by the limitations and concessions which systematic orders ultimately require.[8]

Rilke's willingness to recognise all facets of existence and experience without relying on any meta-theoretical framework, as provided by theology or the humanities, results in a double focus. On one level, there is Rilke's unceasing yet patient quest to determine what allows us to assume that life might have a meaning beyond our mere material existence. Then, as a contrapuntal theme, there is his equally diligent dedication to account for the irreducible uniqueness of existence, and thus also precisely for the physical and material aspects of our being in the world. Rilke was attuned to two different melodies (a metaphor for poetry of which he was fond): a cosmic bass line underscoring all creation, and the other melody that consists of the chatter and talk of everyday people in common situations. In his letters, he succeeds in achieving unusual harmonies composed of these two very different lines: he can be talkative and transcendent in the same phrase, at once full of deep wisdom and subtle irony in one paragraph.

The centre and heart of Rilke's letters are his reflections on love and death. (The heart, of course, is one of Rilke's essential metaphors and literal concerns: Rilke, possibly more than other poets, felt that rhymed language links us in fundamental ways to the bio-rhythms of lung and heart.) Love and death, of course, are also the great themes of Rilke's poetry. In his novel *The Notebooks of Malte Laurids Brigge*, completed after his first long stay in Paris in 1908 and intended to record the experience of survival in that disorienting, alienating and yet abundantly alive city, the narrator begins with the startling matter-of-fact observation that 'people come here to die' (*Notebooks*, p. 3). The book ends with a retelling of the biblical parable of the prodigal son who spurns conventional love for a kind of infinite striving of the heart that cannot know any aim, object or end. In Rilke's rendition, the prodigal son's project becomes one to love without an object – to love for love's sake. To transcend the ego does not mean, for Rilke, to enter into the spiral of radical self-doubt and philosophical scepticism, or to open the floodgates of unconscious desire and irrationality. It means, as he explains in his letters which are far more often addressed to women than to men, to be swept up by the movement of one's heart (or soul, if you like, or serotonin levels) without ever reaching a level where this movement will lose its purpose and desire by being fulfilled. In the *Duino Elegies*, this thought is expressed in a tone that mixes urgency with earthliness. Sometimes, however, life alone is urgent enough and we may not need any more intensity. Instead, what many of us want is what Rilke calls in a letter of 19 February 1922 to Margot Sizzo, 'space for the spirit to breathe'.[9] This is where the letters come in. They express Rilke's conviction that 'our heart always exceeds us' (second *Duino Elegy*; KA II, 205) in striking yet accessible images and by giving us precisely that 'space for the spirit to breathe' with a patience, mindfulness and near-serenity that befits a conversation between individuals who have trust and hope in each other but – like the poet and his readers – are not encumbered by too much intimacy.

## NOTES

1 Rainer Maria Rilke, *Briefe an Nanny Wunderly-Volkart*, ed. Rätus Luck and Niklaus Bigler, 2 vols. (Frankfurt am Main: Insel, 1977), vol. I, p. 341. References will be given in the text as *Briefe* with volume and page number.
2 Rainer Maria Rilke, *Letters to a Young Poet*, trans. M.D. Herter Norton (New York: Norton, 1993).
3 Rainer Maria Rilke, *Briefe I–VI*, ed. Ruth Sieber-Rilke and Carl Sieber (Leipzig: Insel, 1930–7).
4 Rainer Maria Rilke, *Letters on Life*, trans. and ed. Ulrich Baer (New York: Random House, 2005), pp. 108–9. Further quotations will be given in the text.
5 First *Duino Elegy*, in *Ahead of All Parting: The Selected Poetry and Prose of Rainer Maria Rilke*, ed. and trans. Stephen Mitchell (New York: Random House, 1995), p. 331.
6 Rainer Maria Rilke, *Briefe an Sidonie Nádherný von Borutin*, ed. Bernhard Blume (Frankfurt am Main: Insel, 1973), pp. 94–5.
7 Rainer Maria Rilke, *Briefe aus Muzot 1921 bis 1926*, ed. Ruth Sieber-Rilke and Carl Sieber (Leipzig: Insel, 1935), p. 14.
8 *Rilke und Russland*, ed. Konstantin Asadowski (Frankfurt am Main: Insel, 1986), p. 293.
9 Rainer Maria Rilke, *Die Briefe an Gräfin Sizzo, 1921–1926*, ed. Ingeborg Schnack (Frankfurt am Main: Insel, 1977), pp. 22–3.

## PART II
# Works

# 3

CHARLIE LOUTH

# Early poems

'I can imagine no knowledge more blessed than this: that one must become a beginner.'[1] The question of how to begin preoccupied Rilke throughout his writing life. A beginner was never something he just was, he had to become it: 'recover the initial innocence, come back to the place of naivety', he wrote in 1920.[2] It is probably true to say that Rilke began as a poet too easily, and that as he became a better poet he found it harder and harder to begin. At the same time he understood his work itself as a process of becoming and self-realisation. In Paris in 1902, confronted with the hostile diversity of the city and the immense focus of Rodin, he realised he would have to start all over again. He did, but could never have done it without the many beginnings he had already made, which even at that point, and much more so if we include everything written before the first volume of *New Poems* in 1907, make up a body of work that can only be bracketed off as 'early' because of the importance of what followed.

Rilke's earliest verse, from *Lives and Songs* (1894) to *To Celebrate Myself* (1899), is not much read, and has suffered not just from the great shadow thrown by the later works but simply from there being so much of it. Though many contemporaries had trouble freeing themselves from the *fin de siècle* inheritance, it is hard to find another poet who not only wrote but published so prolifically before producing major work. Still, Rilke himself, despite misgivings, repudiated very little of it: only *Lives and Songs*, his first book, was allowed to pass from view, the other collections of the Prague and Munich years – *Offerings to the Lares*, *Dream-Crowned* and *Advent* – being re-edited as *First Poems* in 1913. Even Rilke's contributions to the magazine he briefly edited in 1896, *Wild Chicory* (*Wegwarten*), only ever intended as ephemera, were reprinted in a collection which Rilke felt uncomfortable about but still allowed to go ahead as late as 1921. By contrast there are plenty of references in the letters which dismiss the early work pretty thoroughly: as 'dishonest', as not the beginning of his oeuvre but the 'extremely private end of the helplessness of my childhood and adolescence', and, apart from the *The Book of Hours*, as 'null and void'.[3]

It is easy to see why Rilke disliked but did not disown these early poems: they are of their time, and Rilke too in his early years was very much a product of his time. He was remarkably absorbent of the fashions and tendencies that shaped his surroundings, but since his surroundings were largely confined to the German-speaking enclave in Prague there was a limit to what he could receive in the way of contemporary signals, particularly as German poetry was at the end of the nineteenth century itself something of an enclave, still dominated by the Romantic idiom from the other end of the century and basically unaffected by the shifts in understanding of what poetry could do stemming from the French Symbolists in particular. *Lives and Songs* reads like a compendium of the available styles and forms, without even a trace of a personal voice. As soon as any theme is broached it gets dragged to its most obvious exemplar: 'It was in May' (SW III, 11) evokes Goethe's 'May Song' ('Mailied'), and the next poem, 'The Old Invalid' (SW III, 11–12), turns to Heine's 'The Grenadiers' ('Die Grenadiere'). Later we find an Eichendorff compilation ('Wish', SW III, 16–17) and in 'Can you tell me where the island is?' (SW III, 78–79) a remake of Goethe's 'Do you know the land where the lemon-trees blossom?' ('Kennst Du das Land . . . ?'). The collection was barely noticed, and Rilke later hoped that it had been pulped,[4] but whatever its shortcomings it already demonstrates surprising technical ease and virtuosity – the poems may have no value in themselves, but in terms of learning the craft they show that Rilke was well into his apprenticeship.

*Offerings to the Lares* came out a year later in 1895. It stands out from the early collections in its main subject-matter, the topography and history of Prague, which it covers almost in the manner of a guidebook. This turn might be read as an acknowledgement of the failings of *Lives and Songs*, since a greater discipline is implied by confronting the acquired facility in given forms with a real time and a real place. It is an attempt to correct the exclusively literary provenance of the first collection, though some of what might appear more actual in *Offerings to the Lares* has its literary source and style too, naturalism, which Rilke was also assaying in his writing for the stage (his first full-length play, *Hoar-Frost*, was written at about this time). The poems remain heavily indebted to Eichendorff, Heine and the Romantic folksong, but at times their derivativeness becomes expressive. As the title suggests, *Offerings to the Lares* would pay tribute to Rilke's home town and forge a connection to it through writing, but he wanders through it as a foreigner, apprehending its landmarks and historical moments in sepia tints and isolating them as vignettes. The collection has a dim awareness of this – the very first poem presents the town in twilight: 'The city blurs as if behind glass' (KA I, II). The inherited literary styles can only reveal so much, and if we read the poems generously that is their point since Rilke is really an outsider whose act of piety was soon belied as he turned his back on Prague. The inability to quite inhabit an acquired voice itself corresponds to the uncomfortable sense of exclusion which the desire to construct a 'Heimat' – a home country or native land – betokens.[5] At the same time, once we have accepted the perspective from which Prague is given us, Rilke's lyrical appropriations have considerable charm, and we can read the intricacies and preciosities of his style, which has become significantly more complex and recherché since *Lives and Songs*, as a playful equivalent to the ornate flourishes and abrupt juxtapositions of the city's architecture. In 'By St Vitus's' the characteristic heterogeneity of Prague, here in the shape of St Vitus's cathedral and an adjacent house, is rendered in the facetious rhyming of 'Rokoko-Erotik' with 'Gotik' (KA I, 13), which works because its self-conscious exuberance has been prepared in the previous verse that explicitly links architecture and language by saying that each part of the cathedral 'still speaks its own idiom'. Such mixing of styles is also a feature of the collection itself, so that the cityscape becomes an image of Rilke's lack of direction and poetic flightiness. He is still looking for an identity and a voice, and in the end is not that much further forward in finding it than in *Lives and Songs*. Accordingly, there are some fascinating glimpses of poets he might have been: 'Behind Smichov' (KA I, 43) seems to anticipate the expressionism of Ernst Stadler, and 'Landscape in Mid-Bohemia' (KA I, 62) sounds like Trakl. Nothing yet sounds like Rilke. There is though a half-serious attempt to connect with the Czech hinterland, and fragments of Czech and Slovak are scattered through the poems. Rilke seems to have dreamt for a while of a republic of letters in which German-Czech differences would be overcome,[6] a dream which implicitly extends to his next project, *Wild Chicory*, the short-lived periodical of 'songs for the people' which Rilke distributed himself in workers' clubs and hospitals (as well as bookshops).

With *Dream-Crowned* (1896) Rilke took a different course and turned inwards, away from the external world that *Offerings to the Lares* drew on. At the same time, the retreat into an inner realm, a dreamscape inhabited by the 'dark soul' (SW I, 85), is also a conjuring of potential; *Dream-Crowned* and, more programmatically, the following collection, *Advent* (1897), are oriented towards the future, led by 'longing, the pale woman' (SW I, 77) across inner landscapes of white, unoccupied space. Though the dominant tone is still neo-romantic (the second section of *Dream-Crowned*, 'Loves', conveys the growth and decline of a love affair in the manner of Heine), more contemporary modes also make themselves felt: the vague evocations of mood seem to hesitate now between romantic 'Stimmung' (mood) and the *état d'âme* (soulscape) of French Symbolism. Parks and gardens, as well as a chaster style, seem to point to the poetry of Stefan George, and the frequent organic imagery and pale stylisation to the influence of *Jugendstil* or art nouveau. Munich, where Rilke moved in autumn 1896 and where most of the poems in *Advent* were written, was the capital of *Jugendstil*, and Rilke immediately assimilated the new atmosphere. By contrast with *Dream-Crowned*, *Advent* attempts to reconnect with the contemporary world through a section entitled 'Gifts', poems which in the original edition carried dedications to people Rilke wanted to associate himself with, including Jens Peter Jacobsen, Maurice Maeterlinck and Hugo von Hofmannsthal. The opening poem was dedicated to himself and announces a process of ripening to be achieved by 'reaching deep into life'. But not immediately: for the moment he will 'roam through the days, dedicated to longing' (SW I, 103). The next poem, in a significant juxtaposition, was for Jacobsen, whom Rilke had just discovered and saw more as a poet of decadence ('a pale moon-poet' [SW III, 566], a poem written at the same time calls him) than as the poet of childhood who would shortly become so important to him. This poem is closer to the tone of the book as a whole, which is concerned not so much with life as with its deferral, a kind of saving up of the self in anticipation:

> You my sacred solitude,
> you are rich and pure and open
> as a garden awakening.
> My sacred solitude –
> hold the golden gates closed
> where desires wait.
>
> (SW I, 103)

The inner space of solitude is vast because it is potential, a spring garden that points to the many unfoldings to come. Its power is increased by being confined: whether desire is waiting to enter or to leave (whether the golden gates speak of the promise of what lies beyond them or the preciousness of what they enclose), it is maintained as desire by being denied passage. What almost all of Rilke's poetry has been lacking, considering that its implicit theme, in the absence of any other pressing reason to be written, is itself and the possibility of becoming something more, is reflection on its own workings, some thought as to *how* it might become. This is not quite a poetological poem, but there are hints of a consciousness of the form's complicity in what is evoked: the expansive movement of line two – 'you are rich and pure and open' – is held back by the imperative of line five, and the poem closes on itself like walls protecting the growth in a garden. In a very modest way, this poem discovers how form may express something it cannot grasp and, at the same time, intimates a proper relationship between poetry and life. But as the golden gates suggest, it is essentially a fairy-tale realm that the collection opens onto, and this seems a deliberate preliminary to going out into the world. Key words are 'lauschen' ('hushed listening'), 'leise' ('soft') and 'warten' ('waiting'). The third section, 'Finds', is a series of love poems, but the *du* (intimate addressee) is mostly distant and strange, her mouth 'cool' (SW I, 129). The real focus is the self's potentialisation of the self: 'I lay / in a silver sky between dream and day' (SW I, 131).

Rilke's next published collection was *To Celebrate Myself*, which though it appeared two years after *Advent* still has much in common with it, but two collections left unpublished are more significant and give us a better sense of his range and originality. *Christ. Eleven Visions* was begun at about the same time as *Advent*; and *To Celebrate You*, obviously enough, was conceived as a counterpart to *To Celebrate Myself*.

*Christ* reveals a whole dimension to Rilke's writing that leaves no trace in the contemporary published work. For the first time, Rilke has a subject that compels him not simply to conform with poetic convention but to break it and re-invent it. There could hardly be a greater contrast with the languid, small-scale variations on common *fin de siècle* currency that René Maria Rilke was serving up to his public. *Christ* does indeed have a kind of vision, making Christ traverse the world that is his legacy in various manifestations (fool, beggar, wandering Jew) and in various locations familiar to Rilke (the October Festival in Munich, Venice, the Jewish cemetery in Prague), bitter with remorse at the ravages his teachings have worked on life. In particular, he appears to regret not having fathered a child with Mary Magdalen ('The Fool') and seeks belated comfort in the arms of a prostitute who urges him to 'live life' ('Night', SW III, 150).

The main ideological impulse obviously comes from Nietzsche, and in that sense Rilke is still being carried by a current of his time, but the poems have nothing derivative about them, and the boldness of the conceit – the wrongs of Christianity demonstrated 'on the body' of its author, and historical time telescoped into poetic time – is matched by an energy and amplitude of language that anticipates *Malte* and the *New Poems*. There is a fiercely anti-lyrical, colloquial strain, and a satiric edge not found again before the tenth *Elegy*. The first poem, 'The Orphan', begins 'They pushed off. It was a bad business' (SW III, 129), and each setting is equally vivid, travestying biblical language ('You want to enter life: I am not that', SW III, 137), working in everyday detail ('patient chickens roasted themselves / a golden breastplate on the spit', SW III, 143), and allowing flarings of 'fine excess' (Keats): 'Star buds burst at the celestial poles' (SW III, 156). What sets the *Visions* apart from the contemporary verse and makes them reach forward into Rilke's maturity though is the handling of syntax, as exemplified by this extract from 'The Painter':

> The gentle light, that with its fine antennae
> probed the silent darkness from the fireplace,
> awakened here and there a thing to life
> that rising rich and strange into a secret
> took on form in the light's brief grace.

> Das leise Licht, das wie mit feinen Fühlern
> ins stumme Dunkel suchte vom Kamin,
> erweckte da und dort ein Ding zum Leben,
> das seltsam fremd in heimlichem Erheben
> sich formte in der kurzen Gunst des Lichts.
> (SW III, 139–40)

The shifting of firelight over the objects in the artist's studio is precisely enacted by the sentence as it unfolds. We can see how language and light both flicker in the words 'suchte vom Kamin', where one direction, outward, turns back to its source; and how the formation of a 'thing' in the final line grows out of the vagueness of sense in the fourth, so that meaning and object acquire definition together. Also the to-and-fro: the repetition of 'Licht', and the way the things come into view, fade, and reappear over the last three lines. In context, these lines evoke a stirring in the artist's mind as well. At moments like this, the *Christ* poems rival the movement of the long narrative lyrics of the *New Poems* like 'Orpheus. Eurydice. Hermes'. The anti-Christian thinking behind them reappears almost unaltered in the *Letter of the Young Worker*, which Rilke wrote more than twenty years later when completing the *Elegies* and *Sonnets*, and it remained his credo.

In a more modest way, *To Celebrate You* also represents a great advance. Technically, there may not be much to distinguish these poems from *Advent* or *To Celebrate Myself*, but where the published verse mostly sounds, up to *To Celebrate Myself*, as if it arose because Rilke *wanted* to write, it now sounds as if he *had* to. There is an ease and simplicity, a reciprocity between life and work, inside and outside. The shift can be simply ascribed to the meeting in May 1897 with Lou Andreas-Salomé, the addressee of the collection of almost a hundred love-poems which was left unpublished at her request.[7] This turning-point in Rilke's life, which changed his handwriting and his name from René to Rainer, was also a turning-point in his writing, though it is only the beginning of it we see in the poems he wrote to Andreas-Salomé. They present the relationship as an ushering of an 'I' into life by a 'you', and the life is both actual and poetic. This passage appears as a process of healing, as an exit from dream, and as a new childhood. The focus, again and again, is on Lou's hands – she is named in one poem ('The rain clutches with its cool fingers', SW III, 178) – 'white, your hands sleep in your lap' (SW III, 177), 'your hands shine in your lap' (SW III, 182):

> As you live your life towards me
> softly, and all at once, smiling barely
> lift your hand from your garments,
> your beautiful, lucent, slender hand . . . :
>
> into the proffered bowl of *mine*
> you lay it gracefully
> like a gift.                    (SW III, 191)

Pallor and gesture belong to *Jugendstil*, but are transformed by intimacy into something beyond stylisation. The initiation into life the poems recount has a religious quality, and the hands perform a ritual of 'never-desired tenderness' (SW III, 173). Lou's enable the speaker's to grasp life as never before: 'We'll take it in our grasp, / we have no fear of life' (SW III, 182). The languid, weary movements and tone that *Dream-Crowned*, *Advent* and *To Celebrate Myself* are full of is transmuted into attentive repose: 'your hands are not tired when they rest: their repose is only a hushed listening' (SW III, 183). The love-relationship played out by the hands is what gives the poems substance: whereas previously night and retreat were an escape from life, as the locus of sexual experience they now become its centre (see the poems 'And when I give you my hands in rest' and 'If you ask: What was in your dreams . . .', SW III, 189 and 193).[8] And this corresponds to a general and decisive shift at this time: Rilke is no longer writing for its own sake or to become a writer, but because writing has become his way of 'living life'. Later, *The Book of Hours* will be 'Laid in the hands of Lou' (SW I, 250).

But it was the counterpart to this volume that Rilke put before the public, the volume he several times called his 'first' book, one which 'my development has passed right through the middle of'.[9] *To Celebrate Myself* is marked by 'the longing for oneself' that Lou Andreas-Salomé had released in him.[10] Rilke began work on it in Berlin, where he followed her in autumn 1897, and it was a conscious attempt to make a new beginning. It is still greatly indebted to *Jugendstil* motifs and altogether more stylised than *To Celebrate You*, but the poems are richer than before and the available language is given a more individual inflection, as when the folded wings of an angel are compared to 'a white cypress' (SW III, 215). Transition is the great theme, and the poems are intended as a space of self-realisation, as a transit towards a (Nietzschean) affirmation of life, though it is the hesitant experience of the interim that holds most attraction: 'I am at home between day and dream' (SW III, 209) is the burden of one poem, still echoing *Advent*. And the favoured embodiment of this state is still 'jeunes filles en fleurs', girls on the verge of womanhood. Though on the whole the poetics formulated in the lecture 'On Modern Lyric Poetry', given in Prague in March 1898 about halfway through the composition of *To Celebrate Myself*, is ahead of his actual practice, we can better understand what Rilke is about by calling to mind the theory he develops there of 'pretext', according to which the apparent subject of a poem is only the means by which 'more subtle, totally personal confessions' (KA IV, 65) are articulated. Or, as he put it more radically and solipsistically in a letter, 'all things exist in order to become images for us in some sense'.[11] The girls' situation on the brink of themselves is thus (also) an index of Rilke's becoming and a means for him to explore it:

> *You girls are like gardens*
> *on April evenings:*
> *the many journeys of spring*
> *but no destination.*
> (SW III, 233)

Girls, gardens, evening, April, spring, journeys, the emblems of being 'ever more about to be' are amassed, and the point of arrival is negated, held off. This makes for a curious mixture of frustration and promise, as Ben Hutchinson has pointed out.[12] It is not yet the case that the space opened up by 'a passive attending upon the event' is filled by the poem itself, since the poems rarely offer enough. They are then poems which betoken poems, and Rilke's 'poetics of becoming' runs the risk of exhausting itself in intransitivity. Despite his resolve to take hold of life he has not yet found a way of doing so without undoing what is essential to it in the first place, its fugitive, ungraspable quality. Rilke re-issued *To Celebrate Myself* in 1909 as *The Early Poems*, reworking many details. One tendency of these revisions is to underline the theme of becoming in them, as if to accentuate the more complete forms of the *New Poems*.[13]

From this point on (the poems of *To Celebrate Myself* were finished by the end of 1898 and published a year later) it becomes much harder to trace Rilke's development by going from collection to collection. Though they are perfectly distinct in themselves, the two major works of this 'early' period, *The Book of Images* and *The Book of Hours*, are curiously imbricated in composition and publication: the three books of *The Book of Hours* were written at two-year intervals, beginning in 1899, but not put together and published until 1905. In the meantime the first edition of *The Book of Images* had appeared in 1902, and all its poems (with two possible exceptions) date from before the second part of *The Book of Hours*, whereas the new poems added to the second edition (1906) go back as far as 1899 (in the case of 'The Tsars' even to before the composition of part one of *The Book of Hours*) and range forward to the summer of 1906, by which time about a third of the first volume of *New Poems* had also been written. In addition, there is a host of uncollected verse from these years, some of which Rilke gathered unofficially, as in the manuscript he sent Heinrich Vogeler for his birthday on 12 December 1900 with the title *In and After Worpswede* (SW III, 844–86). In what follows I shall try to keep the implications of this complicated chronology in view without neglecting the discrete status of each collection. Three biographical moments are also worth bearing in mind: the journeys to Russia in 1899 and 1900, which were a premise for *The Book of Hours* (especially the first two books), Rilke's marriage to the sculptor Clara Westhoff in April 1901 – which has something to do with the greater concreteness and attention to form in *The Book of Images* – and the move to Paris in 1902, which provides the material for the third part of *The Book of Hours* and for most of the poems added to *The Book of Images* in 1906. Some of the intersections between life and work, for the years 1898 to 1900, can be traced in the early diaries.

Just before returning from his first trip to Russia, Rilke wrote a letter expressing his conviction that '*Russian* things will give me the names for those most fearful pieties of my being that since childhood have longed to enter my art'.[14] A few months later he wrote a long sequence of poems full of 'Russian things', unlike anything he had written before. They became the first part of *The Book of Hours*: 'The Book of Monastic Life'. For the first time, he had written a poetic cycle, a form that was to become important. Rilke's infatuation with Russia stemmed directly from Andreas-Salomé, in whose company the Russian journeys were made, but was also part of a widespread interest in Russia as a counter-image to the decadent West. Among other things, Russia represented for Rilke and many of his western contemporaries an unbroken tradition of spirituality still in touch with its beginnings, where 'the first day still goes on, the day of God, the day of creation'.[15] The form Rilke eventually chose for his new work, which was later supplemented by 'The Book of Pilgrimage' and 'The Book of Poverty and Death', was that of a book of hours, a devotional work intended to accompany the lay person through the canonical hours of the day. The famous medieval examples were lavishly illuminated and valuable works of art. The persona of (most of) the poems is an icon-painting monk, and icons are another example of the conjunction of art and devotional purpose towards which *The Book of Hours* seemingly tends.

The poems thus appear to be 'prayers', which is what Rilke initially called them. Genetically though, they can be seen to grow out of the invocations of the poems to Lou. The span of a world is created by putting an I into relation with a You (or Thou), but this difference is also an identity, the positions reversible: 'a call from your or my mouth' (KA 1, 159), 'The day when you began us was / the day of your own vast beginning' (KA 1, 170). God stands for an experience of totality, life felt as a whole, in which self and other are not distinct. The reciprocity the poems continually seek and develop is that of love poetry (again following an old technique). God 'comes and goes' (KA 1, 182) according to the wave-like rhythms of the poems which rise and fall in movements of outward extension and lapsing return – he is not referred to but created. And the self is equally changeful and voluble:

> I am, you fearful one. Can't you hear me
> breaking over you with all my senses?
> My feelings, which have found their wings,
> surround your countenance in a flurry of white.
> Can't you see my soul, standing close
> before you in a dress of silence?
> Doesn't my May-time prayer ripen
> in your gaze as on a tree?
>
> If you're the dreamer, I'm the dream you dream.
> But if you want to wake I am your will
> and take possession of all your splendour
> and arc myself like a star-filled silence
> over the wondrous city of time.      (KA 1, 166)

This poem begins with an inversion: God rather than the self is anxious, and the voice speaks God's words 'I am'. One could just as well read the words as spoken by God. The interdependence of the two poles is thus written into the structure of the poem, and this uncertainty of direction affects the other poems too: even when they are clearest about the identity of I and You, they show it to be reversible – 'What will you do, God, when I die?' (KA 1, 176). Whatever its nature, the I speaks in a multiplicity of aspects: the senses break like waves, the feelings circle like birds or moths, the soul stands like a woman or angel, the prayer is a fruit. The different metaphors offer no unity, in fact they work against the ready correlation of senses and feelings, soul and prayer. It is impossible to assign any character to this voice other than movement, a restlessness continually assaying its object. The notion of ripening, a central one in *The Book of Hours*, applying equally to I and You, captures this movement, but no maturity is ever reached: process is all. In the second stanza, the You assumes the active part, dreaming the subject, but the lines which then follow, though they seem to obey the same pattern ('if you want to wake I am your will'), actually run I and You together into a parity in which their movements coincide.

The main impression *The Book of Hours* makes is a rhythmic one. Both in scope and intensity Rilke's writing has moved into a different rhythmic dimension, one that can also be experienced in *The Lay of the Love and Death of the Cornet Christoph Rilke*, written in the same autumn as 'The Book of Monastic Life'. The powerful rhythms, which together with the rich texture of sound the poems create tend to dominate over the lexical sense (one poem sets 'act' against 'sense' in precisely this way: 'You are only grasped by an act' (KA I, 186)), are the heart of the poems' meaning, because they are the equivalent to or actually part of the experience of totality out of which the poems arise. In them, as we read, we can sense the spirit in which Rilke wrote them, as initiatory entrances into life. But these entrances are effected with astonishing ease: there is no tension, no real opposition, God is called into presence almost automatically, the intimacy is always there from the start. The poem reasserts it rather than discovering or restoring anything.

This changes, more or less, after the first part of *The Book of Hours*, as, perhaps affected by troubles with Lou Andreas-Salomé, Rilke's organic view of life becomes unsettled and 'God' ungraspable. The composition of 'The Book of Monastic Life' was a founding experience to which Rilke always returned even as he knew he had to work away from it. A much-quoted poem written in his 'Worpswede Diary' in September 1900 can be read as voicing dissatisfaction with the mode (though in modified form it was to continue serviceable for many years):

> All feeling, in figures and actions,
> becomes endlessly vast and light.
> I will not rest until I've achieved it,
> this: to find the images for my transformations.
> The rising fall of song is not enough.
> Once and for all I must make the attempt
> to utter into visibility
> what hardly happens when it's felt.
>
> (SW III, 699)

One might think that with *The Book of Hours* Rilke *had* found 'images for my transformations' (cf. KA I, 742), but these lines suggest that the poems were not images or pictures in the required sense of being 'visible', and that the kind of utterance he aspired to should enable transformations of the self which could hardly occur in the rise and fall of song. This is the beginning of a shift towards the poetics of the *New Poems*, and its first obvious though imperfect result is *The Book of Images* of 1902. It is hard not to see the title as an express turning against song, since it recalls Heine's *Book of Songs* (*Buch der Lieder*, 1827). The desire for a more distinct and resistant form is partly a response to George's hard-edged poetics, and the physical appearance of this first edition, which prints all the poems in capital letters, clearly also owes something to George's carefully designed books with their esoteric typeface and punctuation. It is really only the poems added to the second edition (which reverted to normal type), almost all of them written in Paris, that fulfil the demand for visual clarity in their actual substance, but there is nevertheless a distinctly new understanding of the poem operating in the first *Book of Images*. This can be seen in the opening poem, which in the second edition acquired the title 'Entrance' ('Eingang'):

> Whoever you may be: at evening step outside,
> leave the room where you know everything;
> beyond your house the distance begins:
> whoever you may be.
> With your eyes, which in their tiredness can hardly
> free themselves from the worn threshold,
> very slowly you raise a black tree
> and place it against the sky: slender, on its own.
> And have made the world. And the world is big
> and like a word still ripening in silence.
> And as your will grasps its meaning
> tenderly your eyes let it go . . .          (KA I, 257)

Whereas in 'The Book of Monastic Life' self and other were intimately connected and the poem could simply witness the connection, here coming into relation with the other requires an effort of dissociation from the familiar and an active process of perception. The poem works an encounter in which You and tree form a world. It is only a passing moment: the eyes let the world go again as they grasp it ('tender' now rather than 'tired'), the poem acknowledges that the correspondence is something one traverses and gains knowledge of but cannot hold onto. The poem has become a much more tentative, fragile thing, and consciously, almost programmatically so.

That is one side of the new understanding of poetry that begins to form in *The Book of Images*. Another is suggested by the penultimate poem in the collection, the long 'Requiem' written in Clara Westhoff's voice for her friend Gretel Kottmeyer. This, not for the first time but with particular deliberateness and ceremony, presents the poem as an artefact, as a thing assuming a place in the world. 'An hour now there's been one thing more / on earth. One thing more: a wreath' (KA 1, 341). Clara weaves her mourning into a wreath which is also the poem, and both replace the life of Clara's dead friend, adding something to the world that has just been diminished, almost as a counterweight. The wreath acquires a life of its own, it is massy and strange, almost appalling in its quiddity at the same time as being subject to time, a creation that will wither and go brittle or, in the parallel case of the poem, need to be reanimated with each rereading. 'Entrance' and 'Requiem' were both written in 1900 when *The Book of Hours* only existed in its first part, but they point forward to the poetry of things that is one significant aspect of the *New Poems*.

These shiftings make themselves felt more hesitantly within *The Book of Hours* itself. Several of the poems in 'The Book of Pilgrimage', written in a week in September 1901 in Westerwede, gratefully recover the mode of the first part. But the figure of life as pilgrimage, with its implications of a 'horribly long' (KA 1, 230) path from the self to God (no longer a 'neighbour', KA 1, 159), alters the tone distinctly. The poems themselves tend to be long, the relationship with God is difficult and one they have to work their way towards. The first poem remembers 'Entrance' in the lines:

> The summer was like your house
> where every thing has its place –
> now you must go out into your heart
> as out onto the plain.     (KA 1, 201)

The heart is estranged too, no longer at one with the world, and the self is exposed as in the later poem 'Exposed on the mountains of the heart' (KA 11, 115). Precisely because of this, there is more world in the poems, and more openness to the negative aspects of experience, true to the 'miracle' that *'alles Leben wird gelebt'* (KA 1, 211), meaning both that all life must be lived and that all the life we have is in the living. Living through a crisis by writing through it became an important pattern for Rilke from about this time, and 'The Book of Pilgrimage' shows its success: the poems begin to make of the transitional, pilgrim state an ideal mode of existence, a new exposed kind of ripening. But the third book, the product of a week's work in Viareggio in April 1903, follows a much greater unsettlement, and in confronting it the mode comes under more strain than it can really withstand. Rilke had fled to Italy after the best part of a year living in Paris. As *Malte* and many letters testify, he experienced the city as a place of suffering and overwhelming existential vulnerability, though that didn't stop it becoming the nearest thing he had to a geographical centre at least up until the beginning of the war. Though he went there to study Rodin, and had written his monograph on him within a few months, the close concentration on the 'immovably centred' sculptor and his art seemed to accentuate the sense of dispersion and perdition embodied in Paris, which Rilke saw as an Old Testament City of the Plain, ripe for destruction.[16] The images of oppression, terror and condemnation that open 'The Book of Poverty and Death' reflect and refract the time in Paris, but have clearly also been nourished by Baudelaire, through whose eyes Rilke saw Paris from the start. The poems are neurotically fraught with sexual imagery, especially with childbirth as a kind of affliction, and the negative view of female sexuality in particular probably comes from him ('Are we only the sex / and womb of women that grant their favours freely?', KA I, 237).

Poverty and death all but displace God from the focal point of *The Book of Hours*, and although elements of a prayer-book can still be discerned, especially in the poems about the poor which recall the suffrages of the saints, we have moved into much stranger territory now. Rilke begins to lay down some of the preoccupations which will accompany him for the rest of his life, such as the idea of dying one's own death and death as the crowning of a life. The second poem ends with a statement of abjection which is the book's premise: 'I am no longer master of my mouth / which keeps on closing up like a wound; [...] You force me, Lord, to an alien hour' (KA I, 234). It stands in exact contrast with the opening of the first part, where the inclining hour inspires the self, enabling him to grasp the day (KA I, 157). But by the end of this third book the 'I' is singing a hymn to St Francis: 'But then the pollen of his song dispersed / softly drifting free of his red mouth' (KA I, 251). It is possible then, that according to the revised poetics he was simultaneously working out and putting into practice Rilke now saw the undergoing of estrangement and loss as a condition of writing. Poetry proceeds less from favour than from its withdrawal.

The shape of overcoming a predicament is therefore still present in outline, but there are more remainders than before. The sequence is full of arresting images which the overall structure cannot absorb:

> For we are only husk and leaf.
> The great death all beings have in them,
> that is the fruit on which all turns.

> Denn wir sind nur die Schale und das Blatt.
> Der große Tod, den jeder in sich hat,
> das ist die Frucht, um die sich alles dreht.
>
> (KA I, 236)

What drives the poems is horror of an ill-lived, superficial life ('husk and leaf'), which is envisaged as a miscarriage of death, an idea which leads fairly naturally, if esoterically, to that of the 'Tod-Gebärer' – 'the one who gives birth to death' (KA 1, 239), a kind of Messianic figure who might provide relief from inauthentic life by saving it with a perfect death, a death which would make sense of life. The mythical figure itself is extreme and unconvincing, but the thought behind it is a firm rejection of other-worldliness and a pledge to 'serve the earth' (KA 1, 221).

The other mythologised figures are the poor, who people the poems and, in Baudelaire's manner, are examined for their affinities with the poet, though as has been noted it is not the poet who is reduced to their level, as when Baudelaire writes about rag-pickers, but rather the poor who are raised to his.[17] Indigence is precariously conflated with being 'poor in spirit' (Matthew 5:3) and poverty gradually unanchors itself from its primary meaning and original cause in the poems (the confrontation with urban destitution in Paris) and drifts towards an ideal, so that in the notorious single-line poem 'For poverty is a great shining from within...' (KA 1, 244) it seems that 'Armut' (poverty) is striving to become 'Anmut' (grace), as if words could be enough on their own. Whatever there is to say against Rilke here (and much has been said) it also needs saying that he has at least noticed and written about the social conditions of his time and place (as he would do much more effectively in *Malte*), even if his transfiguration of them runs the risk of suggesting that all is well. Poetically, the short poems on the poor, in which God's and our attention is directed towards them, are finely poised between lament and celebration, a duality of voice which Rilke has already called 'a fragrance and a cry' (KA 1, 240).

A poem written in the winter of 1902–3, so before the last sequence of *The Book of Hours*, considers crying out as an alternative to prayer:

> Cry out, cry out!
> Perhaps that would help and fetch
> the saviour here that prayer cannot reach.
> Rising cry out of the deep of nights,
> you'll be heard perhaps
> by a.... (SW III, 768)

This remained an imagined possibility right up to the *Duino Elegies*, but like there it is implied that no-one would listen to that kind of utterance. As the fragment breaks off and opens out it realises the improbability of what it desires. Since the mode of *The Book of Hours* ('prayer') also appears ineffectual, some other way needs to be found. Both cry and prayer are directed out towards the unknown, they are perhaps, as the seventh *Elegy* puts it, 'immer voll Hinweg' – 'always full of away' (KA II, 223). Rilke had of course already begun work on a poetry of focus, a poetry that cultivates knowledge of the 'earthly' (KA I, 222) and an intimacy with things. This was hugely encouraged by the example of Rodin: by the end of 1902 he had almost certainly written 'The Panther', the first of the poems that would go into the *New Poems*, and it provided a standard of concentrated utterance that all his poems for the next few years were measured against.[18]

Those poems added to the second edition of *The Book of Images* in 1906 may not have met that standard, but besides having a more personal tone which the *New Poems* hardly allow, they continue to develop the emphasis on the visible that we saw in the first edition. They also show an attention to diction and to the articulations of syntax that is much more sustained than before. Take 'The Saint':

> The people were thirsty; and so she went alone,
> the girl who had no thirst, to beg the stones
> for water on behalf of all the people.
> But the fork of willow gave no sign,
> and walking all that way exhausted her
> until her only thought was of the one
> who suffered pain (an ailing boy whose eyes
> met hers one evening with quiet surmise).
> Then like a thirsting animal the rod
> of tender willow stirred and dipped in her hand:
> and now she walked on flowering in her blood
> which roared inside her, a river underground.

> Das Volk war durstig; also ging das eine
> durstlose Mädchen, ging die Steine
> um Wasser flehen für ein ganzes Volk.
> Doch ohne Zeichen blieb der Zweig der Weide,
> und sie ermattete am langen Gehn
> und dachte endlich nur, daß einer leide,
> (ein kranker Knabe, und sie hatten beide
> sich einmal abends ahnend angesehn).
> Da neigte sich die junge Weidenrute
> in ihren Händen dürstend wie ein Tier:
> jetzt ging sie blühend über ihrem Blute,
> und rauschend ging ihr Blut tief unter ihr.
>
> (KA I, 267)

Much of this is reminiscent of the *New Poems*. The syntax extends sure-footedly over the iambic lines, and the use of language embodies the story it conveys – the rhyming couplet that opens the poem is followed by three initially unrhymed words mirroring the lack of response from the divining rod and the exhaustion of the girl, the inner event is in brackets, there is a clear turning-point signalled by 'da', and the last four lines, in which water is found, fall into regular rhyme (and chiasmic pattern) for the first time. We are given a situation without context, which might be based on a picture. And especially, the 'saint' announced in the title soon becomes a 'girl'; what brings her success is not self-sacrifice in a general cause but personal involvement, and in divining water (possibly even instead of divining water) she divines herself, including her sexual self. The originally Christian framework is radically secularised and Rilke completely reinvents what may be his source, the legend of St Geneviève of Paris, frescoes depicting which he had seen in the Panthéon (see KA I, 807). But though this poem anticipates much in the *New Poems*, *The Book of Images* also contains poems that operate quite differently.

One example is the opening verse of 'The Drinker's Song' from the sequence 'Voices' (KA I, 323–9), which were the last poems Rilke wrote before deciding that the second edition was complete:

> It was not in me. It went in and out.
> I wanted to hold it. The wine did that.
> (I don't know any more what it was.)
> Then the wine held this for me, then this
> until I was only held by it.
> Fool that I was.

> Es war nicht in mir. Es ging aus und ein.
> Da wollt ich es halten. Da hielt es der Wein.
> (Ich weiß nicht mehr was es war.)
> Dann hielt er mir jenes und hielt mir dies
> bis ich mich ganz auf ihn verließ.
> Ich Narr.       (KA I, 325)

With the greatest simplicity and surety of voice, the words convey the inability of the drinker to keep a purchase on himself despite a lucidity about his situation. This was not the direction Rilke's poetry pursued, but it shows how even when he was settling into the syntactic intricacies of his 'new' style he retained the ability to inaugurate a new one. This will to re-invent himself is part of the untiring search for the 'smallest basic element, the cell of my art'.[19] 'I will take every path leading back to this beginning until I get there, and everything I have done shall be nothing'.[20]

## NOTES

1 'Notes on the Melody of Things' (1898; KA IV, 103).
2 Rainer Maria Rilke and Merline, *Correspondance 1920–1926*, ed. Dieter Bassermann (Zurich: Max Niehans, 1954), p. 92 (letter to Baladine Klossowska, 18 November 1920).
3 B I, 709 and B II, 196 and 209 (letters to Fritz Adolf Hünich, 19 February 1919, Robert Heinz Heygrodt, 24 December 1921, and Erika Dieckerhoff-Suihotta, 4 January 1922).
4 See *Rilke-Chronik*, ed. Ingeborg Schnack, second edition, 2 vols. (Frankfurt am Main: Insel, 1996), vol. I, p. 28 (quoting a letter to Zdenek Broman Tichy, 7 January 1906).
5 See Judith Ryan's reading of the poem 'Auf der Kleinseite' as a 'deliberate rewriting' of Eichendorff's 'In Danzig' in her *Rilke, Modernism and Poetic Tradition* (Cambridge: Cambridge University Press, 1999), pp. 17–21.
6 See Rainer Maria Rilke, *Briefe zur Politik*, ed. Joachim W. Storck (Frankfurt am Main and Leipzig: Insel, 1992), p. 9 (letter to Jaroslav Vrchlický, 29 January 1896).
7 Only about half survived; see SW III, 791–2.
8 See Jutta Heinz, 'Die frühen Gedichtsammlungen', in *RHB*, pp. 182–210 (p. 202).
9 See *Rilke-Chronik*, ed. Schnack, vol. I, p. 82 (letter to Stefan George, 7 April 1899) and p. 314 (letter to Anton Kippenberg, 28 September 1908).
10 See Rainer Maria Rilke, *Tagebücher aus der Frühzeit*, ed. Ruth Sieber-Rilke and Carl Sieber (Frankfurt am Main: Insel, 1973), p. 37.
11 Letter to Frieda von Bülow, 7 June 1899 (B I, 41).
12 See Chapter VI of Ben Hutchinson, *Rilke's Poetics of Becoming* (Oxford: Legenda, 2006).
13 Compare the two versions of 'Senke dich . . .' ('Sink down . . .') (SW III, 258 and SW I, 195–6).
14 Letter to Frieda von Bülow, 7 June 1899 (B I, 41).
15 From the essay 'On Russian Art' (KA IV, 153).
16 *Auguste Rodin* carried as one of its epigraphs Emerson's words: 'The hero is he who is immovably centred' (KA IV, 404).
17 Andrea Pagni, *Rilke um 1900: Ästhetik und Selbstverständnis im lyrischen Werk* (Nuremberg: Hans Carl Verlag, 1984), pp. 99–100.
18 See the letter to Clara Rilke of 1 February 1906 (quoted at KA I, 790).
19 Letter to Lou Andreas-Salomé, 10 August 1903 (B I, 158).
20 Letter to Lou Andreas-Salomé, 8 August 1903 (B I, 153).

# 4

WILLIAM WATERS

# The *New Poems*

*New Poems*, published in 1907, and *New Poems: The Other Part*, published in 1908, together constitute the first of the four major works on which Rilke's reputation rests. We follow Rilke in using the shorthand *New Poems* to speak of both volumes as a unit, since, notwithstanding differences between the two volumes, they are parts of a single poetic project. Readers have generally agreed with Rilke that these 189 poems (under 172 titles, nine announcing sequences), written mostly in Paris between 1903 and 1908, are something 'new' in his work. Strongly influenced by the example of the sculptor Auguste Rodin, whose secretary Rilke was from September 1905 to May 1906 and on whose work he had written and lectured, Rilke turned in the *New Poems* to a sharp focus on the individual poem as a crafted and freestanding structure. The resulting poems have often been called 'made things', the more so because the most famous of them are also *about* individual objects, and although we shall have to emphasise other, sometimes countervailing, aspects of the poems as well, it is not hard to see the reasons for this description.

Taken as a collection of self-sufficient things, the *New Poems* have been characterised as a museum. All but a handful of the 172 titles could very easily be the names of paintings or sculptures. Some *are* the names of paintings or sculptures: 'Early Apollo', 'Cretan Artemis', the three Buddha poems, 'L'Ange du Méridien', 'Portrait of My Father as a Young Man', 'Self-Portrait 1906', 'Archaic Torso of Apollo', 'Lady Before the Mirror'. Other titles are architectural: 'The Cathedral', 'The Portal', 'The Rose Window', 'The Capital', 'Quai du Rosaire', 'The Steps of the Orangerie', 'The Square', 'The Tower', 'The Pavilion'. The array of museum-compatible titles also embraces many animals and plants; fountains, graves, landscapes, parks, morgues, and other sorts of places; events historical ('The Last Count of Brederode Avoids Capture by the Turks'), mythic ('The Birth of Venus', 'David Sings Before Saul', 'Alcestis') and mundane ('Night Ride', 'The Arrival',

'Corpse-Washing', 'Encounter in the Avenue of Chestnuts'); people ('The Blind Man', 'The Group', 'Family of Strangers', 'The Reader', 'The Bachelor'); and quotidian objects ('The Ball', 'The Bed', 'Lace'). If this is a museum, then, there is remarkable variety in it. The miscellany is itself one argument against the old practice of designating the *New Poems* as a whole as an assemblage of 'thing poems' ('Dinggedichte'); at the very least, invocations of this familiar term must allow the concept of 'thing' considerable elasticity, as Rilke himself did in his letters and essays of this time.[1] But we should also remain aware that many of these noun-titles actually head dramatic monologues, or poems that are in other ways – once we read beyond the title – anything but evocations of an object. The titles, in other words, give a much stronger impression of a museum or collection than do the poems themselves.

For the reader, moreover, many of the *New Poems* are as much prepared experiences of kinetic motion, or rides, as they are things in a static sense. In this characteristic Rilke both emulates the dynamism he admired in Rodin's sculpture and conveys his sense of language – when it is read – as a process undergone in time. Finally and most importantly, if the craftsman's attention to the delimited individual work before him is rightly one celebrated quality of the *New Poems* (in contrast, say, to the closely interlocking cycles of poems in the earlier *Book of Hours* or the later *Duino Elegies* and *The Sonnets to Orpheus*), the other side of that coin is that the *New Poems* are founded on a network of manifold interconnections. Though explicit sequences are few and the range of topics and approaches diverse, a reader familiar with more than a handful of the texts will constantly find this or that feature of each poem bringing to mind others in the volume.

Family resemblances among the poems are too subtly varied to catalogue in full. They begin with broad groupings of topic (objects; persons; legendary, historical or literary scenes) and go on into more specific, sometimes intersecting categorisations: there are numerous poems on classical, biblical and medieval motifs; scenes of the Paris streets; clusters of poems on cathedrals and on Belgian and Venetian sights; animal poems and flower poems; poems about buildings, public sites, or gardens; poems about interiors; poems about saints, prophets and other heroes; poems about statues or portraits; and many other categories of this sort, each of which can be further subdivided and cross-linked to others. A different sort of natural grouping is that according to poetic kind and form: there are the role-poems or dramatic monologues, the sonnets, the poems of address, poems in blank verse, densely rhymed verse and so on. Linguistic criteria (patterns in the use of person, tense, mood, and so on) may suggest fruitful interpretative clusters as well.

Formal and grammatical preoccupations generate some of the poems' trademark features: in the *New Poems* we see Rilke 'handling line and syntax as "materials" out of which to sculpt contours and build torques and tensions'.[2] Enjambment, the tension produced by breaking a line in an unexpected syntactical place, is pursued to bold extremes in search of particular effects. Poems may consist of a single intricate and drawn-out sentence, or play long clauses and short ones off each other. Negations or subjunctive clauses build up elaborate counterfactual alternatives to what is said to be the case. Participial forms may take the place of inflected verbs in order to portray the static dynamism of a portrait (life arrested, as in for example, 'Self-Portrait 1906') or a fountain (always in motion but always the same, as in 'Roman Fountain'). Adjectives become neuter nouns ('ein Grünes' – 'a green thing'; 'ein Schönverbundnes' – 'a lovely linked thing'), making familiar things opaque while their qualities become abstract and curiously independent of the object to which they belong. With command of rhythm comes an art of dramatic tempo; poems that start slowly can gather momentum and end with a flourish. Sound-patterning is dense and daring, even mannered, with a rich abundance of line-internal consonance and assonance (i.e. sound echoes of consonants and vowels respectively) and rhyme, and with prepositions and articles sometimes pushed into the spotlight as end-rhymes. The craftsman Rilke is a virtuoso, in the *New Poems* more than anywhere else in his work; and the signature of his technical *finesse* with language as a shaped material is unmistakable in this collection.

Questions of perception are often at the heart of these poems: the perspective from which something is perceived generates the contradictions whose depiction and resolution occupy the poem. In a related poetic structure, many poems pivot on a moment of sudden reversal (often perceptual, often near the end of the poem), which resolves in a transformation of one kind or another. These are then two more ways in which poems on widely differing subjects yet constantly bring one another to mind.

Certain recurring motifs and themes, too, work to tie poems to one another. Some are readily apparent, while others appear in such inventive variation that interconnections may not reveal themselves before repeated reading. Prominent motifs range from social class (urban poverty, faded gentility, vanishing aristocracy), to portent, danger and doom, or heroism. But there are also general themes such as vision, or pretence or imagination set against reality. Time, in many inflections, is a central preoccupation: many poems centre on ephemerality or memory. Gestures of negation and the counterfactual subjunctive, mentioned above as grammatical features, frequently join up with the theme of temporality to contribute to the motif that may be the most pervasive of all in the *New Poems*: absence and loss.

Finally, many of the *New Poems* are densely allusive, enigmatic, or of an intricate construction that impedes comprehension. In a surprising number of cases it would not be possible to identify the poem's subject at all if we did not have the title (one of several reasons for attaching special importance to the status of titles in this collection). Other poems, while not difficult to follow in themselves, present accounts of an experience of bafflement or unexplained portent (for example, 'In a Foreign Park' or 'In the Drawing-Room'). This attraction to riddles is yet another family resemblance drawing the collection together.[3]

The *New Poems*, then, for all their emphasis on specific and disparate objects of attention in the world, are also each deeply occupied with one another. Robert Musil, in his homage for Rilke's memorial in 1927, wrote that in this poet's work, 'things are interwoven as in a tapestry; when you look at them, they are separate, but if you attend to the background, they are linked by it. Then their appearance changes, and strange connections emerge among them.'[4]

Musil's image may allude to Stefan George's 1900 poem 'The Tapestry' ('Der Teppich'), a poem about a woven work of interlaced figures which, in a rare hour, comes to life in revelatory fashion, clarifying not just the confusion of the figures in the carpet but something in the mind of the viewer as well. If so, the comparison is apt for the *New Poems* in suggesting not just the interconnection of one poem with another but also the metaphoricity of each poem, the way that within each text, poetic comparisons draw us repeatedly away from the thing described as a way of showing it to us afresh. This is a second sense, then, in which interconnections, the relations among things, are at the heart of each poem's attention to its specific object. Again and again in the *New Poems*, objects or events are evoked in terms that, whether in the development of one image or in the accumulation of a succession of images, range far from the original thing ostensibly being evoked. The process is occasionally pushed to the extent that a reader may lose track of which is the object and which the thing to which it is compared.

A particularly clear case of such carefully prepared uncertainty is 'The Swan' (KA I, 473), unusual among the *New Poems* in that it is organised around a single explicit and extended simile (in two parts), a simile moreover that explicitly analogises the object seen to the concerns of the human world. Or is it the other way around? What is being compared to what? This is the point of special interest.

> This toil and struggle, passing on, heavy
> and as if bound, through things still undone,
> is like the makeshift walking of the swan.

And dying – this no longer grasping
of that ground on which we daily stand –
like his nervous settling himself –:

into the waters, which receive him gently,
and which, so happy in their passing,
draw back under him, wave after wave;
while he, infinitely still and sure,
ever more confidently and majestically
and serenely deigns to glide.[5]


Diese Mühsal, durch noch Ungetanes
schwer und wie gebunden hinzugehn,
gleicht dem ungeschaffnen Gang des Schwanes.

Und das Sterben, dieses Nichtmehrfassen
jenes Grunds, auf dem wir täglich stehn,
seinem ängstlichen Sich-Niederlassen –:

in die Wasser, die ihn sanft empfangen
und die sich, wie glücklich und vergangen,
unter ihm zurückziehen, Flut um Flut;
während er unendlich still und sicher
immer mündiger und königlicher
und gelassener zu ziehn geruht.

Some critics have taken this text as a poem about the experience of life and death, of which the swan's movements are an image. Others have argued the opposite, that this is a poem about swans – another thing-poem – and that the comparisons to living and dying are just particularly apt and original evocations of the object.

The debate cannot be helpfully resolved in its own terms, but it points us to a finer art of balance in the poem's structure and syntax. The explicit comparisons in the first two stanzas tell only part of the story. By the last six lines, the awkwardness of the poem's beginning – a 'front-loaded' simile, yoking this together with that, and this other thing together with that other thing, meanwhile relating each point of the second comparison back to its corresponding term in the first comparison – all of that has simply disappeared. An encumbrance has fallen away, and in that final stanza the swan has become all swan, nothing-but-swan.

And yet no part of the last stanza is grammatically complete. The *syntax* of the poem makes the last six lines continue to describe what dying is like, while that same extended, trailing grammar, getting further and further from the verb 'is like' ('gleicht' in the German) back in line 3, separated from the mention of 'dying' by the idiosyncratic dash-colon at the end of line 6 and by the white space of the stanza break – that drift works deliberately against the syntax to make the image in the second half of the poem independent and, as it were, self-sufficient. But also: the poem is called 'The Swan' (it is not called 'Dying').

What in this text is the foreground and what is the background? Some readers and critics have thought they knew the answer. But the poem is at work to press the question, to pit syntax *against* image so that the swan both is and is not there to serve the idea of what it is like when we die. (In lines 7–9 it is surprisingly not the swan that moves on the water but rather the water that moves under the swan, so that his 'going' is instead an increasingly tranquil 'ceasing to go'.) What the end of the poem shows is that the 'thing' must, so to speak, forget the comparison in order to complete it: the more serenely the swan becomes just a swan, the more adequately it represents the falling away of dividedness, difficulty and self-consciousness that the poem says dying is. What the poem says best is what it is hardly 'saying' at all any more: as dying ceases to be spoken about in the poem, as it recedes into the background, the foreground comes to express it more and more fully. The 'swanness' of the swan is felt in its gliding away from metaphoric duty, from meaning something; but really *in* the gliding away, such that if the tension of the comparison were not present to be departed from, neither the swan nor the experience of dying would be as fully conveyed as Rilke's poem conveys them both.

The interlocking of figure and ground in the *New Poems* was perceived in the earliest review of the volume, written by Stefan Zweig in 1908. Of Rilke's technique in this collection Zweig writes:

> Only as images does he grasp things, as a continual process of things reminding us of one another. In this way all of life becomes, around him, a tremendous association, an eternal mutual explanation, a meshing together. Nothing can be separate or insignificant to the poet who always sees it, even quite unconsciously, in relation to other things, who possesses a mysterious insight into the essential, so that he can peel away colour, tone, gesture and story from people and things like petals, can arrange them individually and layer them according to his will.[6]

Anthony Phelan rightly drew attention to this review of Zweig's as a still unsurpassed critical insight into 'a coherence in the collection which is sociable, as mutual interaction, but also interpretative as "ein ewiges Sicherläutern"' ('an eternal mutual explanation').[7]

The mutually interpretative powers Stefan Zweig recognised in the *New Poems* may be observed as well in the poems' recurrent preoccupation with questions of perspective. A single object seen from two or more angles is no longer a single object. Its faces or aspects, the different lights in which it is seen, are entities set into charged mutual relation. Critics' search for 'objectivity' or an 'essence of the thing' in this volume – like the putatively opposing, deconstructionist view that the poems are so many inevitable failures in the struggle to capture such an essence – has impaired the recognition that Rilke's things are instead artfully, almost cubistically, constituted out of these interacting views. In fact the poems strikingly refrain from suggesting that there *is* a locatable essence behind or apart from this interaction of facets and reflections; where the titles might seem to speak of entities, the poems show 'things' to be compositions of motion and abstraction. After Rodin – whose sculpture Rilke praised for its paradoxical ability to convey motion and for its art of interacting surfaces – Rilke's other great inspiration in the *New Poems* was the painter Paul Cézanne, often seen as a forerunner of cubism because of his experimental, 'planar' renderings of spatial depth and position. Rilke had already completed the first volume of the *New Poems* and half of the second volume before his intensive study of Cézanne began in October 1907, so the painter's influence as such can be sought only in a portion of the second volume; but Rilke himself felt, and critics have agreed, that in Cézanne he found a correlative and a confirmation of artistic processes that were already underway in his own work. The perspectivism in the *New Poems* is both widespread and variously enacted, and its far-reaching implications call for the examination of several instances of such perspectival construction.

Many of the poems about human beings are concerned to contrast two points of view, usually the 'inside' view of a person on him- or herself and an outside view by others. Poems like 'The King' and 'The Standard-Bearer' are explicitly organised around this contrast. 'The King', for example, first portrays the boy monarch – 'sixteen years old and already the State' – as his councillors see him: 'The death-sentence before him sits / unsigned a long time. / And they think: how he suffers'. But, the poem goes on, 'They would know, if they knew him better, / that he is merely counting to seventy slowly / before he signs it' (KA 1, 484). The appearance is of one kind of feeling (suffering), but on the inside, the boy king is instead inflating his actions to make them convey – he hopes – the gravity that is expected of him. The strategy is both childish and effective; the pathos of the figure is that he must cultivate that misperception and that loneliness in order to function as the king he is.

Another poem, 'The Standard-Bearer' (KA 1, 485–6), turns on a graver disjuncture between two radically different perceptions of a single set of events: the other soldiers, 'very alone and loveless', view the standard-bearer's protection of their flag under attack as 'courage and fame'. In their midst, though, the standard-bearer himself is at a dreamlike remove from their ordinary view. He sees ('when he closes his eyes'), and he feels, the flag as a woman. When he rips it from its pole to protect it from the hands of the enemy, what he experiences is violent sexual consummation. The hallucinatory disjuncture between these two perspectives conveys the standard-bearer's fervour for and existential absorption in his assignment: like saints, readers and other figures of heroic concentration in the *New Poems*, he inhabits an inner world whose difference from the outside – the pitting of one against the other, the irreducible doubleness of the supposedly single figure – is the poem's point. Where the title noun may have led us to expect an identity, we find instead the tension between two things, which is to say a relationship.

Differing views can occupy disproportionate shares of a given text. In a poem like 'The Bowl of Roses', the long poem that concludes the 1907 volume, the first stanza is jarringly at odds with the remaining seven. A street fight between two boys is evoked in a jostling succession of images: fire, stinging bees, overacting, crazed collapsing horses, faces peeling away from skulls. The images disturb but also disorient, not least because the first-time reader looks in vain for a connection between the poem's title, 'The Bowl of Roses', and this opening. The second stanza belatedly provides this missing orientation:

> But now you know how that is forgotten:
> for before you is the full bowl of roses,
> which is unforgettable and filled
> with that utmost of being and inclining,
> holding out, never being able to give, standing there,
> that can be ours: the utmost also for us.
>
> (KA I, 508–9)

This shift of attention – in this example 'perspective' is not quite the right word – propels the poem dramatically; the delicacy and depth of the roses, the unfolding of their meaningfulness, exists in pointed tension with the confused violence of the poem's first stanza. This shift goes one way only; the poem remains focused on the roses until the end of the poem, when, by virtue of the poem's own seemingly endless ability to compare the roses to other things – 'what can't they be?' Rilke asks – they come to include everything:

> the world out there
> and wind and rain and patience of the spring
> and guilt and restlessness and masked fate
> and darkness of the earth at evening
> out to the clouds' changing, flight and approach,
> out to the vague influence of distant stars.

All this the roses include, while transforming it into 'a hand full of inwardness' (KA I, 510). The tumult of the poem's opening, in other words, 'is forgotten', but it had to be there to be forgotten; and the opposition introduced by that beginning between inwardness and the outer world, the imagined and the real, drives the poem forward while it gradually reveals that these supposedly opposed categories are instead one and the same. Thus 'The Bowl of Roses', too, presents not a unitary object of attention but a series of views and differing terms whose identity is in, or is, their relation to one another.

In 'Woman Going Blind', 'The Blind Man', 'The Convalescent', 'The Courtesan', 'A Prophet', 'A Doge' and many other poems about human beings, perspectival contrast is less pointed than in 'The King' and 'The Standard-Bearer', but no less deeply informing. 'The Courtesan' (KA I, 487) is a role-poem, in form a freely rhymed sonnet but in tone a song-like self-characterisation rather than a Browningesque dramatic monologue. Its seductiveness comes from the courtesan's evocation of herself as she is seen or imagined by others, which is to say as mysterious and dangerous:

> My brows, which
> are like bridges, do you see them
>
> leading over the soundless peril
> of my eyes, which a secret intercourse
> joins to the canals, so that the sea
> rises and falls and changes in them.

> Meine Brauen, die
> den Brücken gleichen, siehst du sie
>
> hinführen ob der lautlosen Gefahr
> der Augen, die ein heimlicher Verkehr
> an die Kanäle schließt, so daß das Meer
> in ihnen steigt und fällt und wechselt.

The strangeness of this perspective – a person speaks about herself as if she were talking about an enigmatic other – also plays a part in its fascination. The inner self, if there is one, is dark. The courtesan's business is to reflect desire, to be what she is fantasised to be. The replacement of her interiority with a bewitched perspective that cannot, strictly speaking, be her own creates a hall of mirrors that itself becomes in turn her most compelling enticement.

In this respect 'The Courtesan' shows affinities with another characteristic of many of the *New Poems*, especially those whose titles name non-human things: the poems represent not objects as such but the *experience* of objects, making it wrongheaded to speak of these texts as either 'objective' or 'subjective'. A vivid example is 'The Tower' (KA 1, 492). The poem's subtitle – 'Tour St.-Nicolas, Furnes' – locates the tower on the map, and may conjure up a postcard view of it. But against those expectations the poem begins incomprehensibly, with the freestanding 'sentence' 'Earth-interior' ('Erd-Inneres'). This is followed by a single, winding sentence of twelve lines and a bewildering succession of six relative clauses, evoking not, as it turns out, the tower as seen from the town around it but the claustrophobic experience of climbing up its dark steps 'as if only in that place to which / you blindly climb / would you reach the earth's surface'. This tortuous trudge through subterranean fears – the poem suggests it is like being dead and undergoing resurrection – gives way, in the poem's second half, to the bright and sudden freedom of arrival at the tower's top:

> At last you feel the wind and see blue sky
> and you are plucked out into gusty day
> and all is light – it is as if you fly
> above a land which waits expectantly[.][8]

> Da aber nimmt dich aus der engen Endung
> windiges Licht. Fast fliegend siehst du hier
> die Himmel wieder, Blendung über Blendung,
> und dort die Tiefen, wach und voll Verwendung[.]

The arts of the poem are bent not at all on depicting or describing a tower 'in itself', but rather entirely on rendering the perspectival experience of the ascent. The observing self has literally entered into the thing, 'undergoing' it both physically and psychologically.

In other poems, the qualities of the observing mind appear as descriptors of the observed thing, or vice versa. In 'The Apple-Orchard' (KA 1, 582) for example, 'the evening green of the grass' looks

> as if we had long
> collected it and saved it up inside us
>
> in order now from feeling and remembrance,
> new hope, half-forgotten joy,
> to spread it lost in thought before us
> still mixed with darkness from within

> als hätten wir es lange
> angesammelt und erspart in uns,
>
> um es jetzt aus Fühlen und Erinnern,
> neuer Hoffnung, halbvergessnem Freun,
> noch vermischt mit Dunkel aus dem Innern,
> in Gedanken vor uns hinzustreun[.]

The exterior sense-object, in its depth of colour, has the 'look' of psychological interiority, world and mind interrelating so intimately that it becomes dubious whether they are distinct things at all. In other poems, conversely, the qualities imputed to an object may transfer to the observing subject. 'The Beetle-Stone' (KA 1, 585) is an example. The poem begins with negated rhetorical questions put to an addressee, which yet again seem at first mystifyingly unrelated to the poem's title: 'Are the stars not almost near to you / and what is there that you don't contain'. Only then does the sentence proceed to connect the mystery of this cosmic self to the titular object:

> Are the stars not almost near to you
> and what is there that you don't contain
> since it is impossible to grasp
> these hard scarabs' carnelian kernel
>
> without helping to bear on your whole blood
> that space that holds their carapaces down[.]

> Sind nicht Sterne fast in deiner Nähe
> und was giebt es, das du nicht umspannst,
> da du dieser harten Skarabäe
> Karneolkern gar nicht fassen kannst
>
> ohne jenen Raum, der ihre Schilder
> niederhält, auf deinem ganzen Blut
> mitzutragen[.]

The scarabs, rocked to sleep by millennia, are – like the Buddha in the poem that follows this one and concludes the book – the stone of the fruit that is the universe: all of space is centred on their ancient rest. What these lines describe is an interpenetration of object and subject, as the person who holds these scarabs himself intuits, even inhabits those same vast spaces, which emanate from the object even as they enclose and support it.

What the *New Poems* often portray, then, is not objects but interaction among perspectives; and these perspectives are not just views of an object but experiences of it, even reshapings of the subject under the object's power. It makes sense, then, that the many images of mirrors and mirroring in the collection betoken something other than a traditional conception of artistic representation. Such poems – like 'The Bachelor', 'Black Cat', 'Blue Hydrangea', 'The Coat of Arms', 'The Gazelle', 'Lady Before the Mirror', 'Last Evening', 'Quai du Rosaire', 'Roman Fountain', 'Venetian Morning' – show consciousness captivated by its own perceptual field,[9] but the fascination is always fascination by difference. When the flowers of the 'Blue

Hydrangea' (KA 1, 481) 'reflect' their own blue colour 'from far away', 'tear-stained and inexactly / as if they wanted to lose it again', this elusiveness of the object *is* at the same time the poem's attempt to say what the object is: the watery colour of blue hydrangea flowers is a blue that seems to be always really somewhere else – like the letter-writer of bygone time evoked in the next line's 'old blue letter-papers' – or something else, as the blue of the paper is composed of 'yellow, violet and grey'. Non-self-identity is this blue's identity.

In 'Lady Before the Mirror' the mirror appears as a vessel of liquid into which the woman releases her carefully composed appearance at the end of an evening. Having let it steep, and drinking it in like a sleeping potion, she finds, as the 'dregs' at the bottom of the mirror, the room around her and her waiting chambermaid. This inside-out structure, in which the deepest point of reverie is also the point of disillusionment, does not depend on a moment of reversal; the lady returns to reality in and through her absorption in the ensorcelled mirror world, rather than by being distracted from one to the other. At the same time, the apparent paradox corresponds closely to the fact that while you may look into the mirror to inspect yourself, the mirror gives an equally exact account of the prototypically not-attended-to: that which is behind you. This perspectival shift turns foreground into background and vice versa, an adjustment of attention in which the boundaries between the scene and the mirror-image of the scene turn out not to be boundaries at all. Discussions of this poem have sometimes supposed that it can be understood in terms of a traditional opposition between existence and the appearance of existence, reality and the mirror-world, but 'Lady Before the Mirror', like many of the *New Poems*, studies the inapplicability of this distinction.

The beginning of this essay emphasised the poems' formal qualities, their deliberate highlighting of language as a material with tensile and sensuous qualities that are to some degree independent of what the poem is 'saying'. This independence means that the pleasure of reading comes in part from following the intelligence with which subject matter and artistic means are balanced against one another.[10] This equilibrium, too, works to reduce the substantiality of the 'thing' or subject matter – it draws part of our attention to the language and so away from its supposed referent – even as by the same token the poem itself comes to seem more 'thing-like' than would be the case were the poems less rhetorically crafted. The second volume bears a dedication, in French, to Rodin; Rilke's publisher expressing doubts about the French, Rilke wrote back that the French would not really be a foreign language in this context, because (appearances to the contrary) the book is not written in German: 'the language proper to the book, having been completely absorbed into the artistic material, is not to be regarded in the first place as German, but altogether as poem'.[11] Whatever one thinks of this curious argument – the French dedication was in any case allowed to stand – Rilke's remark is telling. Material, language translated into 'poem', becomes a thing in its own right and comes in the place of what it seems to present. To some extent of course a similar claim could be made for all literary language, or in another sense even for all language. But what is special about the *New Poems* – in addition to their sheer virtuosity – is that here this effect connects with and contributes to the poems' motifs of hesitating and uncapturable identity.

More should be said about the *New Poems* as an elegiac volume. If the hidden theme of the *New Poems* is loss, or more radically the elusiveness of reality altogether, then this is a point with many interrelated aspects. There is an evident socio-cultural dimension: the early twentieth century was in many ways the end of an era in the European economic and social order, and Rilke felt that fact deeply. In this light, the book's many variations on the motif of transitoriness represent the poems' engagement with their cultural moment. The *New Poems*, with their Wilhelmine interiors, portraits and gardens, are 'monuments to the demise of a social class and its way of life'.[12] In a larger number of poems, the sense of the elegiac is abstracted away from this specific scenery to appear rather as a fascination with the material traces of the past. Throughout the volume, remnants – tokens of earlier times – haunt the present ('In the Drawing-Room', 'Tanagra', 'In a Foreign Park', 'The Parks', 'The Pavilion'). Sometimes the history of an object or place can be so intensely imagined as to become resurgent ('The Rose Window', 'Quai du Rosaire', 'Late Autumn in Venice'); sometimes the encounter with it can set the present moment ablaze ('Archaic Torso of Apollo'). The relation of present and past called up by an object surviving from an earlier time is never exactly the same from poem to poem – think of 'Early Apollo', 'The Portal', 'Roman Sarcophagi', 'Tombs of the Hetaerae', 'Lace', 'The Beetle-Stone', 'The Square', 'The Steps of the Orangerie', and so on – but in each case the pastness or diminishment of the object is essential to its effect, even where that effect seems, in the poem, to be one of revivification. The past cannot actually be restored; even if it could, to do so would be to abolish its fascination. But what the *New Poems* testify to is that the worn vestiges of earlier times, speaking obscurely of what is gone, may be the most intensely expressive features of the world of here and now.

Rilke's era was also awash in a certain philosophical psychology, influential in literary circles, that can be related to the theme of the instability of identity in the *New Poems*. The late-nineteenth-century 'elementarist empiricist' psychology of Ernst Mach and others accorded with the *fin de siècle* literary disposition by analysing experience as a transient flux of impressions. Undermining the sense that we live in a world of stable subjects and objects, the theory seemed to transfer into the philosophical realm the fluidity of living in a time of rapid social change. In this decentred world-view, the properties of objects are not separable from the mind that perceives them, while that mind in turn is nothing but the continuous river of these perceptions.[13] In such an intellectual climate, it should not be surprising that many of the New Poems address the insubstantial and elusive quality of the world explicitly through themes of mutability and disappearance. But more radically if less overtly, as our discussion of perspectivism began to indicate, even poems that lack these themes tend to reveal the 'thingness' of the things they evoke as an active effect of interacting forces or as a presence shot through with or overlaid upon absence. The effect is potent – the celebrated feeling that these poems capture the quiddity of their things is right, in a way – because it is a fact of our experience that things, like people, are often most strongly felt to be themselves when they are departing from what they recently were, or when they are irrevocably gone.

This conspectus of the New Poems should serve only to point the reader back to the poems themselves, in all their variety and individuality; summary must be faint and very partial compared to the specific life of these works. Their diversity is not the least of their surprises. The New Poems have not exactly been neglected by Rilke scholars, but they are still too often reduced to a handful of familiar 'representative' poems – the present survey too has had to omit much more than it could include – and still too seldom recognised as an achievement ranking with any other work of Rilke's and indeed with the richest works of European modernism.

## NOTES

1  The term is not Rilke's; it originated with the critic Kurt Oppert in a 1926 critical essay. Rilke's prose writings most closely connected to the New Poems are the letters to Lou Andreas-Salomé of 3, 8, and 10 August 1903, which do express his yearning to make 'things' in language that would be analogous to Rodin's sculptures (although a 'thing'-poem in this sense need not be a poem about an object). Other pertinent prose writings are the Rodin essays and the Letters on Cézanne, as well as certain sections of Malte.

2  Edward Snow, 'Introduction', Rainer Maria Rilke, New Poems: The Other Part [1908], trans. Edward Snow (San Francisco: North Point, 1987), xi.

3  See Paul Claes, Raadsels van Rilke: een nieuwe lezing van de Neue Gedichte (Amsterdam: De Bezige Bij, 1996).

4  Robert Musil, Essays, Reden, Kritik, ed. Adolf Frisé (Reinbek: Rowohlt, 1983), second edition, pp. 1238–9.

5 Rainer Maria Rilke, *New Poems [1907]*, trans. Edward Snow (San Francisco: North Point Press, 1984), p. 87, modified. Unless specified all other translations are my own.
6 Donald Prater (ed.), *Rainer Maria Rilke und Stefan Zweig in Briefen und Dokumenten* (Frankfurt am Main: Insel, 1987), p. 46.
7 Anthony Phelan, *Rilke: Neue Gedichte*, Critical Guides to German Texts (London: Grant & Cutler, 1992), p. 34.
8 Rainer Maria Rilke, *New Poems*, trans. Stephen Cohn (Manchester: Carcanet, 1992), p. 105.
9 Ray Ockenden, 'Rilkes *Neue Gedichte*: Perspektive und Finalität', in Adrian Stevens and Fred Wagner (eds.), *Rilke und die Moderne* (Munich: iudicium, 2000), pp. 89–108.
10 I borrow this phrasing from Helen Bridge, who, in 'Rilke and the Modern Portrait', *Modern Language Review*, 99.3 (2004), 681–95, uses it to describe the quality of Cézanne's painting to which Rilke was drawn (p. 684).
11 Rainer Maria Rilke, *Briefe an seinen Verleger 1906–1926*, 2 vols. (Wiesbaden: Insel, 1949), vol. I, p. 49 (letter of 26 September 1908).
12 Phelan, *Rilke: Neue Gedichte*, p. 89.
13 See Judith Ryan, *The Vanishing Subject: Early Psychology and Literary Modernism* (University of Chicago Press, 1991).

# 5

ANDREAS HUYSSEN

# The Notebooks of Malte
# Laurids Brigge

*The Notebooks of Malte Laurids Brigge* occupies a singular position in the
history of modernist prose. Rilke's only 'novel', written in the Paris years
during a pivotal crisis of the poet's creative imagination and finished with
some difficulty far from Paris, is fundamentally concerned with issues of
poetic language, vision and imagination. It tells the story of Malte, a twenty-
eight-year-old aristocratic Dane whose artistic aspirations bring him to Paris,
where he begins to record his life crisis, experiences and memories in a
series of diary-like notations. However, Rilke soon abandons the fictional
convention of telling the story of an individual bound by a defined space and
by chronological time. Especially in the second part, fictional plot gives way
to a series of literary and historical reflections that push the work toward
allegory and essayism rather than providing narrative and plot. Read in
light of this second part, even the first, more directly narrative section of the
text, which is focused on Malte's traumatic reactions to city life, appears
less like a novel and more like a concatenation of narrative fragments and
miniatures not primarily controlled by a storyline, but by a consciousness
and subjectivity in crisis.

Thus it makes sense that Rilke should draw on the convention of the
diary form. But here, too, the suggestion of a sequential diary is abandoned
as soon as it is introduced. There is only one conventional diary heading, the
one on the first page: 'September 11, rue Toullier'. After that, the reader's
expectation of a stable progression in time and space is again undermined.
The informed reader soon begins to wonder to what extent the figure of
Malte serves as a screen for the writer himself – Rilke in Paris, his own life
crisis as a poet, his sense of alienation and estranged perception, of ego loss
or ego dispersal – all displaced and rewritten as the life crisis of an other,
a fictional figure. And, indeed, key passages of the text are lifted almost
verbatim from the poet's correspondence, not even rewritten, but simply
copied into the text.

Yet *Malte* is not simply a veiled autobiography either. The German title *Aufzeichnungen* gives a hint. 'Notebooks' is an imprecise rendering. It weakens the tentative sense of 'Aufzeichnung' as written notation, disjointed jottings; it loses its visual connotation as drawing ('Zeichnung') or sketch; and it loses its documentary sense as recording. Subjective and objective dimensions are merged in this very word, just as the usual separation of the written from the visual is suggestively overcome. Dispersal and fragmentation of text and subject alike are assumed. The micro-organisation of the text into seventy-one distinct sections of varying length and weight corresponds to this sense of 'Aufzeichnungen' at the level of form, just as Malte's key project in Paris, learning how to see, confirms it in the register of subjective consciousness and sensuous perception.

The literary result is a text that remains elusive both in content and in form. But as soon as one focuses on the dispersed nature of these 'Aufzeichnungen', rather than searching for some unifying principle of composition such as the novel of sentimental education, the *Bildungsroman* or the artist novel, the *Künstlerroman*, a key inspiration for Rilke's extraordinary prose text emerges. It is Baudelaire's *Little Prose Poems* (*Petits poèmes en prose*, 1869), also known by their earlier title *The Spleen of Paris* (*Le Spleen de Paris*). Baudelaire's seminal attempt, after the completion of *The Flowers of Evil* (*Les Fleurs du mal*), to write a form of poetic prose that would capture the movements of the psyche is creatively continued in Rilke's *Malte*. At a key point in his reflections on writing, Malte copies down a passage of Baudelaire's 'At one in the morning' ('A une heure du matin'), which articulates the writer's despair at not being able to produce poetic verse (*Notebooks*, p. 53). Indeed, Rilke's text as a whole can be read through the Baudelairean veil as an attempt to write the city in a new way, to create a poetic prose adequate to the confusing and disorienting experience of the modern metropolis, an experience which required another, not yet known mode of poetic expression beyond verse, metre and rhyme, but also beyond fictional plot.

But the comparison with Baudelaire does pose a problem. In contrast to Baudelaire, Rilke is rarely seen as a poet of the city, and rightly so. We picture Rilke in the isolated North German artist colony of Worpswede; we remember the recluse on the Adriatic in Duino or at Muzot, the castle in the Alps, places that gave rise to the high ambition of his late works of poetry, the *Duino Elegies* and *The Sonnets to Orpheus*. Even in the poems of his earlier Paris period, it is never the street, the bustle of people, the energy of urban movement that provides the material for the 'Dinggedichte' of the *New Poems*.

Paradoxically, it was Rilke's fundamentally anti-urban sensibility that gave rise to the figure of Malte, who may represent one of the most persuasive poetic embodiments of Georg Simmel's metropolitan type of individuality, a figure that captures Simmel's intensification of nervous stimulation in the extreme. But while subjective and objective culture does fall apart in Malte's experiences and perceptions, he is Simmel's metropolitan individual, only with a significant traumatic twist. For in Simmel, as in Walter Benjamin's work on Baudelaire, the metropolitan type develops a protective organ that shields him from the onslaught of images and impressions. Malte, however, completely lacks this Freudian protection against stimuli ('Reizschutz') that would either neutralise the shock experiences of modern urban life or strike poetic sparks out of the urban experience as in Baudelaire.

The main problem Malte faces in his encounters with Paris as a city of poverty, misery and death is his inability to protect himself against the onrush of stimuli and shocks. He is totally permeable to the outside world. Everything he sees and hears seems to go right through him, even to annihilate him. This inability to fend off the aggressions of the outside world is narratively linked to Malte's childhood experiences on his family's estate, experiences which Malte remembers with great intensity and an overwhelming sense of loss and disorientation during his stay in Paris.

Here Rilke draws on a theme typical of the nineteenth-century novel, the move of the protagonist from country to city. But the paradigm is significantly rewritten. It is not some innocence and naïveté of pre-urban life that give way to a sense of alienation and disillusionment in the city. Memories of childhood past and urban present are rather uncannily intertwined in Malte's psyche, with one exacerbating the other. The text thus suggests a fundamental affinity between the haunting psychic aspects of Malte's early childhood experience and the disrupting fragmenting perceptions of the modern city. Rilke probes a dimension of perception and experience not found in the reflections of either Simmel or Benjamin. Malte, the solitary foreigner in Paris, never becomes a man of the crowd. He is neither flâneur nor dandy, both of which would require some identification with metropolitan life which Malte lacks. Issues of exchange, commodification and consumerism, so prominent in Simmel and Benjamin, are all but absent from Rilke's urban world. And Benjamin's concern with the impact of modern media and information culture on the structure of experience appears in Rilke at best as part of a vague and fairly unoriginal critique of the superficiality of modern civilisation against which he posits his project of modernist writing.

At the same time, the novel can be read in its very form as a paradigmatic example of how the city can affect and radicalise basic structures of perceptual experience in a way not imagined by Simmel, Benjamin or Freud. Malte's inability to gird himself with an armour against the onslaught of urban shocks and stimuli, it turns out, is grounded in early childhood perceptions. Rather than parrying the shocks of metropolitan modernity and transforming them into verse – an image Benjamin took from Baudelaire's 'The Sun' ('Le Soleil') – Malte remains defenceless. The shocks of urban perceptions penetrate him down to the deepest layers of unconscious memory traces, hurling themselves, as it were, into the quarry of childhood memories, breaking loose large chunks that then float up to the surface and merge grotesquely with his vision of city life.

In the first half of the text, Malte thus reproduces fragment upon fragment of his past, fragments that lack the explanatory intervention of the analyst or the interpretative framing of a narrative voice. The modernist narrative with its tortured subjectivity, its experimental ruptures and discontinuities, emerges out of the constellation of a childhood trauma of the fragmented body and the shattering and unavoidably fragmentary experience of the metropolis. The absence of an adequate 'Reizschutz', resulting from a deficiently developed ego structure, characterises Malte and determines the course and structure of the narrative. It is particularly the haunting imagery of the body that couples childhood trauma with the threatening encounters with figures and events in the city. The text is littered with descriptions of body fragments which take on a life of their own, thus disrupting the imaginary unity of the body surface. Clearly these are not Oedipal anxieties of loss in the sense of the Freudian account of castration anxiety. They are rather anxieties of excess, of flowing over, of unstable boundaries between inside and outside, and they make the threat of invasion of the self ubiquitous. At the same time, these experiences of excess are not to be misread as exuberant expansions of self, nor do they represent the pleasurable symbiotic merger of self and other as in Freud's 'oceanic feeling'. Rilke's persistent use of the imagery of disease and filth aggression and death points in a different direction. The paradox is that these visions of bodily excess carry with them a phantasmagoria of loss and death, a voiding of any sense of self. Malte describes himself as a nothing that begins to think, a blank piece of paper that is waiting to be written on. The voiding of self appears as precondition for the new mode of writing the text itself aspires to. But this condition for writing is indissolubly linked to the visual, to Malte's project of learning how to see in a novel way. This new vision takes shape in the famous passage in which Malte describes the horrifying, almost hallucinatory recognition of the residual inside wall of a demolished house as now outside wall of the adjacent building. With the rust-spotted open channels of former toilet pipes, the residues of mouldy paints, and pieces of wallpaper still sticking to the walls of bedrooms at various heights, it is a sight of nauseating traces of a decayed, ghostly inside. This inside has now become the outside, a visual and spatial urban void that is captured with images of a decaying body, of digestion, filth and disease. Terror overcomes Malte and he runs (*Notebooks*, pp. 45–8).

Here the dissolution of boundaries destroys any differentiation between the animate and the inanimate, between body and things, the perceiving subject and built urban space in both its real and phantasmagorical appearance. But then the experience of terror cannot be attributed to the city alone which, as it were, would overwhelm an overly sensitive, but deep down authentic, subject. No, the terror, as Malte writes, is already at home inside him.

Thus even if initially Malte hopes to find some relief from the city by remembering his non-urban childhood, it soon turns out that his childhood itself is packed with very similar experiences of the horrifying and the uncanny. If Malte's loneliness in Paris makes him want to escape into the past, the past provides no relief. His childhood traumas resurface with a vengeance, but the reader never quite knows whether the city triggers childhood memories or whether these memories structure and shape Malte's city experience in the first place.

Malte's uncanny experiences have been variously explained with a variety of psychoanalytic approaches (Freudian, Kleinian, Lacanian and Winnicottian), but the text has remained elusive to such approaches which, by focusing on Malte/Rilke's familial relations, usually ignore the dynamic links between childhood anxieties and city experience. They also pay scant attention to Malte's fearful identification with shattering fragile objects, his fear of going to pieces which not only marks key experiences of the child and of the young adult, but which energises and shapes his writing project. In a key passage that weaves the imagery of shattering objects back into that of the fragmented body Malte conjures up an image of apocalypse in writing and language that might bring all his pains to an end:

> For the time being, I can still write all this down, can still say it. But the day will come when my hand will be distant, and if I tell it to write, it will write words that are not mine. The time of that other interpretation will dawn, when there shall not be left one word upon another, and every meaning will dissolve like a cloud and fall down like rain. [ . . . ] But this time, I will be written. I am the impression that will transform itself. It would take so little for me to understand all this and assent to it. Just one step, and my misery would turn into bliss. But I can't take that step; I have fallen and I can't pick myself up (pp. 52–3).

Clearly, this is aesthetic theology. Put in more secular terms, it would be the moment of the modernist epiphany, the transcendence into a pure realm of writing that would leave all contingency behind and overcome all splits and fissures of subjective perception and articulation. What Malte expresses here is the intense modernist longing for another kind of pure language and vision that would, in psychoanalytic and ontogenetic terms, correspond to a phase preceding the development of language and sight, both of which are constituted quintessentially as differentiation in relation to others. But the desire for such a 'glorious language' (*Notebooks*, p. 257) before differentiation is accompanied by Malte's equally strong acknowledgement that such a language cannot be attained, that the desire for it is an impossible, even dangerous desire.

Rilke's novel remains one of the most powerful and haunting articulations of a crisis of subjectivity under the pressures of urban modernisation, but in its theological coding of the desire for that other language, that other vision uncontaminated by the spatial and temporal contingencies of modern life, it is also a powerful and symptomatic evasion of the problem. What remains with the reader is rather the urban imaginary and its disturbing affiliation with childhood memories that refuse to produce comfort or reclaim the past. In the narrative fragments of the first part, Rilke's writing joins a post-Baudelairean archive of short prose writings by authors as diverse as Hugo von Hofmannsthal, Franz Kafka and Robert Musil, Siegfried Kracauer and Gottfried Benn, Ernst Jünger and Walter Benjamin, whose importance for the trajectory of modernist short prose and its symptomatic mix of the narrative and the aphoristic, the existential and the essayistic, the visual and the writerly still remains to be assessed.

# 6

KATHLEEN L. KOMAR

# The *Duino Elegies*

One of the most famous cycles of poems written in German in the twentieth century, and arguably one of the best known from any era, Rainer Maria Rilke's *Duino Elegies* (published in 1923) have remained remarkably influential into the twenty-first century. Translations into many languages are still being actively produced, with at least seven new translations into English alone since the turn of the millennium. Rilke's work has inspired not only major English-speaking writers such as American novelists Thomas Pynchon, British poet W. H. Auden, and American poet James Merrill but also writers from Iran (Sadegh Hedayat), the former Czechoslovakia (Milan Kundera), and India (Amitav Ghosh) – among many others. Composers such as Britain's Oliver Knussen, Russia's Dimitri Shostakovich, Denmark's Per Nørgård, Norway's Arne Nordheim and America's Morten Lauridsen have all set Rilke to music. Popular culture continues to absorb Rilke's writing and reproduces it in surprising venues ranging from self-help manuals to films to contemporary Indie rock groups. What is it about Rilke's work, and in particular the *Duino Elegies*, that fascinates so many readers?

One answer might be that Rilke draws from a diverse cultural background. As a world traveller and lover of other traditions, Rilke is influenced by many cultures in addition to those of German-speaking countries: including, among others, Russia, where he travelled with Lou Andreas-Salomé, Scandinavia, where he stayed with Ellen Key, and France, whose poets, Baudelaire, Mallarmé and Valéry, he admired. He even mentions in his letters that he reads the *Qur'an*, and in his famous letter to his Polish translator Witold Hulewicz of 13 November 1925 he compares the angels in his *Elegies* to those of Islam (B II, 377). Readers from many lands, therefore, might feel a connection to Rilke's work.

Equally important, however, are several themes and issues that continue to make Rilke's work resonate throughout the world, including the problem of time and, by extrapolation, that of death, the uncertainty of a world after Einstein and the search for a new non-scientific wholeness to offset it, the nature of the relationship of individual consciousness to physical objects and, perhaps most importantly, the ontological status of our limited, physical, human existence. Can human beings transcend their limits to reach a more perfect state? Or is this limited human world enough? The Romantic poets explored many of these issues a century earlier but failed to establish a new transcendent unity. Living in a world of intensified disorientation for the individual human consciousness, Rilke must re-examine the problem of transcendence and rethink immanence. Can human consciousness find metaphysical wholeness without denying the limited human world? These questions lead Rilke to investigate the power of poetry to transform the external world through consciousness. These themes and questions make Rilke the artist par excellence; his *Duino Elegies* form a meta-text that explores the apprenticeship of the poet. But they also connect him to the spiritual realm in which angels become objects of poetic investigation and the search for a reunification of isolated consciousness with something larger and more unified is an urgent poetic quest. This dual role of artist and spiritual seeker broadens Rilke's readership and helps to keep his *Duino Elegies* alive.

## Contexts

At first glance, Rilke's *Elegies* can appear hopelessly idiosyncratic with images ranging from gnats to angels and a cast of characters from acrobats to heroes. And indeed, the *Duino Elegies* took shape in the midst of a chaotic world in which science yielded not a new system of order as the Enlightenment and the nineteenth century had hoped, but instead radical relativity (with Einstein's theory of special relativity, for example, published in 1905) and uncertainty (Heisenberg's uncertainty principle formulated in 1927). In addition, Sigmund Freud was making human beings aware that an even more mysterious subconscious level underlay the world of apparently logical control. Artists responded to these new developments with an explosion of aesthetic experimentation ranging from Cubism to Surrealism and from the narratives of Franz Kafka and James Joyce to the poetry of T. S. Eliot. Rilke's *Duino Elegies* participate in this exploration as they seek to understand how human consciousness can relate to such a disorienting world.

In the social and cultural realm, Europe faced the devastation of the First World War and the end of an older tradition that had defined western civilisation. In his 1923 volume *The Modern Theme* (*El Tema de Nuestro Tiempo*) Spanish cultural historian and philosopher José Ortega y Gasset suggests that European man after World War I is confronted with the loss of old values without any new ones on the horizon to replace them; this results in a radical disorientation of the individual. Rilke's *Elegies* attempt to deal with this disorientation. He explores how the individual human consciousness can respond when confronted with the loss of ordering principles and of access to any unified transcendent realm.

Written between 1912 and 1922 in two bursts of creative activity separated by the trauma of the First World War, Rilke's *Duino Elegies* simultaneously record his creation of a poetics and exemplify that poetics. In these poems Rilke wrestles with the problem of isolated self-conscious humans in search of a new unity with existence. The *Elegies'* beginning was dramatic. Standing atop the tower of the castle of Duino that belonged to his supporter, Princess Marie von Thurn und Taxis-Hohenlohe, Rilke describes hearing a voice during a driving storm giving him the first lines of the *Elegies*, 'Who, if I cried out, would hear me among the angelic / orders?' ('Wer, wenn ich schriee, hörte mich denn aus der Engel / Ordnungen?'; I, 1–2; KA II, 201). Rilke's ten elegies form a response not so much to this question as to the impulse to ask it. They record the isolation of individual human consciousness seeking some escape from the trauma Ortega y Gasset describes, which was so strongly felt by writers and artists between the two world wars. Like the acrobats he depicts in the fifth *Elegy*, Rilke is caught at the moment between the 'no longer' and the 'not yet' (KA II, 216–17), between a disappearing past order and an uncertain future one. Rilke's *Elegies* explore the role of the poet in this increasingly chaotic world and the possible strategies of the individual human consciousness faced with radical alienation and still longing for transcendence.

Given such a context, it is unsurprising that Rilke's cycle of poems is elegiac in tone, often lamenting lost unities. But the poems also emulate the traditional form of the elegy, the elegiac distich that consists of a line of dactylic hexameter followed by a line of essentially dactylic pentameter (that is a line of six dactylic feet, each one consisting of a stressed syllable followed by two unstressed ones, followed by a line with five dactylic feet). While not consistent throughout the cycle, Rilke's meter is predominantly dactylic, and he sometimes produces perfect elegiac distichs. These echoes of earlier poetic forms link Rilke to an older poetic tradition even as he laments the loss of that past. Thematically, Rilke examines possible interactions between the angelic and human realms. He will begin by looking to the divine realm and man's separation from it. His poems then trace a path that examines man's status in relation to the transcendent realm. Rilke is not, however, a linear thinker. He meanders through a series of reflections and reconsiderations as the cycle progresses. Finally, however, he arrives back in the realm of the humanly possible. Rilke's *Duino Elegies* dramatise the construction of a poetics as well as an ontology. He is concerned with the task of the poet, but also with an understanding of the human world in broader terms.

## The cycle of consciousness

All of this makes it difficult to decipher the meaning of the *Elegies*. There are, however, coherent models that underpin the cycle. Rilke points to his most crucial model already in *The Notebooks of Malte Laurids Brigge* in a striking passage depicting the possible interaction of the physical and transcendent worlds, the worlds of objects and of angels (KA III, 509–10). Malte describes an old man, whom he compares to an old rain-battered doll, feeding birds. He is sure that if this old doll stood long enough, angels would come and feed from his hand. Only the intrusive presence of the self-conscious spectators prevents the interaction between doll and angel. This passage from *Malte* (which in many ways could be seen as a prequel to the *Elegies*) points to very similar imagery in the fourth *Elegy* and suggests the model that helps shape the *Duino Elegies* in general.

Around 1911, shortly after publishing *Malte* and shortly before beginning the *Duino Elegies*, Rilke studied Hölderlin and Kleist. Friedrich Hölderlin spurred his interest in classical poetic forms, but Rilke was also attracted to Hölderlin's development of a model of consciousness that moves from the non-conscious state of objects through man's troubled and isolated self-conscious position to the all-conscious state of the angels. Heinrich von Kleist developed a similar theory of consciousness in his essay 'On the Puppet Theatre' ('Über das Marionettentheater', 1810), which provides a working model and some of the imagery for Rilke's *Elegies*.

Kleist's essay describes a discussion between the narrator and a famous dancer whom he is surprised to meet at a puppet theatre. The dancer explains that the puppets are perfect models of grace because they are not self-conscious; they are perfectly at one with the forces of their environment. The inanimate, non-conscious puppet's grace is only reproduced when self-consciousness is overcome and extended into infinity, into the super-consciousness of a god. The puppet and the god can therefore interact whereas self-conscious man is excluded from this unity. Kleist thus articulates a system of levels of consciousness and a movement from the unconscious object totally at one with its environment to the self-conscious human adult alienated from himself and his world to the super-conscious god who achieves a total unity with all of existence by subsuming it in his all-encompassing consciousness. This model also echoes the Christian tradition of man beginning in innocence in Eden, experiencing self-consciousness and alienation, and moving toward a transcendent reunification with the divine after death.

These models of a cycle of consciousness help to structure the *Duino Elegies* and offer a way to understand their imagery. If we think of Rilke's images in the *Elegies* as arrayed around a circle that begins with the non-conscious (objects) and meets at the other end with the super-conscious (angels), the images begin to make poetic sense. Puppets, gnats, animals, children, heroes, lovers, poets and angels, taken as a progression, move the cycle of consciousness forward from inanimate puppet towards all-conscious angels. The fourth *Elegy*, which encompasses a profound philosophical consideration of the limits of human consciousness, presents the most direct embodiment of this model of consciousness. The self-conscious adult is distracted by knowledge of future decline and death and troubled by the contrast between himself and that unselfconscious world inhabited by the animal and the child. Rilke invokes Kleist's essay for his central images depicting the reunification of the cycle of consciousness, the union of the unconscious and the super-conscious realms in the interaction of the puppet and the angel. 'Angel and Puppet: now – at last – a *play*! / Now all can fuse together, all that we / Divide by merely being here' (*Elegy* IV, 57–9).

In this cycle of consciousness, self-conscious adult human beings are always excluded from that moment of completion in which non-conscious puppet and super-conscious angel meet. Self-conscious man – and the poet at this point – are like the spectators in the passage from *Malte*, whose very presence keeps the moment of transcendent unity of existence from happening. Self-conscious human beings operate by drawing distinctions (*Elegy* I, 80–1) and are thus relentlessly aware of time and physical boundaries and, as a consequence, of parting, separation, expectation and finally death. This knowledge traumatises human consciousness and generates anxiety and distraction unknown to either the puppet or the angel. The speaker of the *Duino Elegies* seeks to find a way to escape this state.

### *Elegies* I–VI: possible models to access the transcendent realm

The *Duino Elegies* open with the speaker in crisis. He is painfully aware of the limits of his self-consciousness. In the first *Elegy*, Rilke ponders how self-conscious man (who speaks, as he must, in the first person) could gain access to the transcendent realm represented by the angels. The poet first considers a direct assault. What if he called directly to the angels? Unlike the mythical Semele, who demanded to see Zeus in his divinity and was destroyed by the experience, the poet quickly realises that his limited consciousness is not yet conditioned to survive a direct apprehension of the transcendent. He withholds his call. Incapable of directly approaching the transcendent realm, Rilke maps out other possible models that might teach him how to overcome self-conscious isolation and move toward the angels. He suggests that some human beings occupy a privileged position in the cycle of consciousness, and might, therefore, serve as models: first, children and those who die young, who are not yet trapped in self-consciousness; second, the hero, who bypasses paralysing self-consciousness to move directly into action; and finally, lovers, particularly unrequited lovers, who have moved beyond isolated consciousness toward a larger unity with another consciousness (the beloved) or with consciousness at large if the love is unrequited.

Each of these models escapes adult human self-consciousness. Children are still close to the innocence of pre-consciousness. They are not yet aware of the separation of self from world; they can live the present moment and eliminate boundaries between themselves and the exterior world as they do in the imaginary world of play, which occupies 'the in-between space between world and toy' (*Elegy* IV, 73). To die young, without suffering the full trauma of self-consciousness, preserves this privileged state.

Like the man of action (versus the man of thought) discussed in *Notes from Underground* (1864) by Fyodor Dostoevsky, the hero bypasses self-conscious reflection by acting directly in the world and thus escaping the paralysis of self-consciousness. Rilke explores the hero in the sixth *Elegy*, where he compares him to the fig tree which seems to thrust directly into full fruit rather than tarrying at intermediate stages just as the hero acts rather than reflects. And like those who die young, the hero preserves this privileged state by dying. For Rilke (as for his predecessors, the German Romantics), dying presents a direct means of transcendence since it allows one to lose the insular self-consciousness and physical limits that separate the self from unified existence. This access to the transcendent realm, however, is not useful to human beings remaining in the world or to the poet seeking to fulfil his mission.

Lovers are Rilke's third possible model of access to the transcendent realm. Lovers surpass the isolated, self-conscious individual in their capacity to interact intensely with at least one other consciousness. If the love object is removed and the love is unrequited, that intense participation in consciousness becomes unbounded and available to gain access to existence at large. The unrequited lover thus gains a privileged status that moves self-conscious man forward in the cycle of consciousness (unlike either the child or hero who carry us back toward the non-conscious). Unrequited lovers such as the Italian Renaissance poet Gaspara Stampa therefore figure prominently in the *Duino Elegies*.

Rilke mentions Stampa along with Renaissance French poet Louise Labé and the Portuguese nun Mariana Alcoforado, each of whom turned their unrequited love into poetry. Their examples point Rilke toward the poetic realm and create a viable model of poetic transformation as a means of perpetuating the personal moment of transcendence. Through the examples of these women, the poet comprehends that an unrequited love relationship can thrust the lover beyond the single beloved (as the tension of the bowstring propels the arrow out into space in the first *Elegy*) in order to become more than the isolated self. The speaker now believes that lover and poet must make this outward leap, 'For remaining is nowhere' ('Denn Bleiben ist nirgends'; *Elegy* I, 53).

This phrase, 'Denn Bleiben ist nirgends', is a remarkable linguistic construction that presents the second major factor (along with Kleist's cycle of consciousness) necessary to understand Rilke's *Elegies*. Rilke uses language itself to transgress the boundaries of logic and categorisation that hold human beings captive within self-consciousness. In order to do this, he must force language to violate its own categories and allow the reader to catch glimpses of a unified realm that does not draw such distinctions. The phrase 'Denn Bleiben ist nirgends' participates in this linguistic alchemy and allows Rilke to confront one of the major sources of self-conscious human anxiety – namely time.

Linear time creates a past and future. Memory generates an elegiac lament for unities lost, and the anticipation of the future makes new loss and eventually death a constant distraction. To escape the anxiety of time, Rilke must find a way to short-circuit time by turning it into space – in which all exists simultaneously (as it does in the realm of the angels). Phrases such as 'Denn Bleiben ist nirgends' accomplish just this task. 'Bleiben', to remain or stay, is a temporally defined category; it implies persistence through time. 'Nirgends', nowhere, is a spatial category. By linking these two concepts with 'is', Rilke creates a definition of time that turns it into a spatial category. Time is space. Rilke, however, defines time not just by any spatial category, but by one which negates itself. 'Nowhere' is a spatial term that denies division or specific location or limit in space. Time is defined by space, which is in turn defined as boundless. Rilke thus recreates in his poetic language the unboundedness that characterises the transcendent realm of the angels. This kind of linguistic alchemy provides in the *Duino Elegies* that transformation that Rilke will come to accept as the poet's task later in the cycle.

The first *Elegy*, then, accomplishes a great deal. It announces the problems of transcendence versus immanence, posits models of access to the transcendent realm, and creates a linguistic construction that forms the seed of Rilke's ultimate discovery that language has the power to transform existence.

In the second *Elegy* the poet confronts further the problem of the transcendent realm. But how does one describe an angel, how does one delineate a being that is beyond the rational, beyond all distinction and division, literally beyond words? Rilke does this by linguistic innovation. He creates language that violates its own semantic boundaries – as did the phrase 'Denn Bleiben ist nirgends'. The angels are defined as 'pollen of blooming divinity' ('Pollen der blühenden Gottheit'), 'spaces of being' ('Räume aus Wesen'), 'shields of rapture' ('Schilde aus Wonne'; *Elegy* II, 12–14). Each of these phrases fuses a natural or physical category (pollen, spaces, shields) with one belonging to the transcendent realm (divinity, being, rapture). Rilke joins the concrete and abstract, natural and transcendent, in order to undermine such categorisation entirely. Distinctions necessary to the rational human mind are transgressed to allow the poet to describe something beyond language, namely the angels. Rilke cannot describe angels directly; he can only give the reader a sense of their wholeness by forcing the reader to imagine beyond normal linguistic limits, to reunify that which rational man puts into separate categories.

Through his linguistic innovation in the second *Elegy*, the poet begins to understand that his true work will be changing human consciousness through language itself. The poet must create a new, timeless space, like the 'in-between-spaces of time' ('Zwischenräume der Zeit'; *Elegy* II, 3) of the mirrors in Part II of his *Sonnets to Orpheus*. But this space cannot be found among the angels; Rilke does not seek that final mystical union. The poet's domain must be found in that pure, restrained, narrow human realm that can create a harvest of language somewhere between 'river and rock' ('Strom und Gestein'; *Elegy* II, 76) – between the moving, flowing completeness of the angels (whose self-projection and re-absorption represents a constant stream of being in pure consciousness) and the stasis and stability of being in the pure physicality of the inanimate world of objects. Not unlike the acrobat who must balance between rising and falling in the fifth *Elegy*, man and the poet must balance between pure consciousness or flow and the non-conscious or stasis, between energy and matter. As the acrobats of this *Elegy* demonstrate, however, such a moment of balance is precariously difficult to maintain. Like the tumbler who cannot remain at the apogee of his somersault, man constantly misses the moment of perfect fulfilment, 'where the pure too little / incomprehensibly transforms itself – , springs around / into the empty too much' ('wo sich das reine Zuwenig / unbegreiflich verwandelt – , umspringt / in jenes leere Zuviel'; *Elegy* V, 82–4). Man's position is the conscious recognition of his participating in both the realm of pure physicality and that of pure consciousness, but belonging to neither. The poet's job is to stake a claim in the fertile human space that exists between two extremes.

Continuing to explore the models of consciousness he proposed in the First *Elegy*, the poet realises that none offers a true strategy for accessing the transcendent realm. Children grow up. Heroes (whom Rilke ponders in the sixth *Elegy*) are too unique to represent a general strategy for those who are already burdened with self-consciousness. Lovers often have the misfortune of being loved in return or the distraction of (male) sexual urgency (examined in the third *Elegy*) or future expectation. This realisation leads to a contemplation of man's fate in the fifth *Elegy*.

This *Elegy*, the last of the *Elegies* to be written and positioned in the cycle, presents the image of the acrobat as a metaphor for both the human condition in general and art more particularly. This *Elegy* was inspired by a combination of a painting by Pablo Picasso, *The Acrobats* (*Les Saltimbanques*, 1905), in which a group of acrobats is arranged roughly in the shape of a capital letter 'D' (to form the beginning of the word 'Dastehn' or 'existence' in line fourteen of the poem – often translated as 'destiny' to preserve the 'D' in the English version) and a troupe of street entertainers Rilke saw while living in Paris. The poem investigates the sham existence made up of the fleeting and empty action that the acrobats are forced to repeat while moving from inability to jadedness without ever being able to settle at the moment of wholeness. The acrobats and their audience form an artificial rose that encompasses both in a world of performance without feeling or meaning. The acrobats, hurled about by fate and necessity, produce an art of slick façade without genuine accomplishment. At the end of the *Elegy*, the poet imagines a world in which lovers might love so intensely that they actually performed a unified act so complete that even the dead, who already exist in a transcendent realm, would pay them homage. But he imagines this perfect act in the form of a question to the angels, a query directed to the transcendent realm. Rilke is still looking to the angels for answers. Within a few *Elegies* he will redirect his attention.

Rilke turns in the seventh *Elegy* to an entirely different perception, which he had anticipated in the first *Elegy*. The poet wonders in the first *Elegy* 'of whom then can / we make use' (*Elegy* I, 9–10) to help us to gain access to the transcendent. The angels are still unapproachable and take no note of us; self-conscious man is of no service, and even animals are suspicious of our need to interpret our world, our 'gedeutete Welt' (*Elegy* I, 13), to 'make sense' of our environment by imposing our organising logic on it. Finally, the poet suggests self-consciousness might be ameliorated by the small, familiar interaction of our isolated consciousness with objects in the world (*Elegy* I, 13–17). The contact between consciousness and object, the stability created for the physical world by means of consciousness is what human beings can use to draw the attention of the angels. This epiphany causes Rilke to change his poetic direction in the seventh *Elegy*.

### *Elegies* VII–IX: reversing course

The seventh *Elegy* presents a total reversal of the speaker's actions. What had been an attempt to call the angels in the opening lines becomes by the end of the seventh *Elegy* a celebration of the human condition with all its limitations, in fact because of all its limitations. Joy becomes a possibility for the unity-seeking poet when he stops yearning for transcendence and turns instead to the process of transforming the physical world within his consciousness and thereby also escaping solipsism. In this shift of direction, the poet finds his true task. Rilke discovers that 'the most visible joy / can only be discerned when we transform it within' (*Elegy* VII, 48–9).

Once the poet recognises that he can rescue objects from time by transforming them within, his task becomes one of praise and transformation. In a striking reversal, the poet can now proudly show the world to the angels for their appreciation (*Elegy* VII, 70–2), thus totally changing the direction and purpose of his poetic activity. Because the angels' all-encompassing consciousness does not recognise boundaries, they can only appreciate the limited human world through the intercession of the transforming poet. The poet ceases his attempt to access the transcendent realm and accomplishes, because of his own human limits, something the angels could not. He can now present human spaces and arts (architecture, Chartres, music, and even simply a woman in love) to the angels as worthy of their contemplation.

The poet finds in the seventh *Elegy* that his proper task is one of transformation not transcendence. He discovers that he can praise the physical and limited world, that 'Being here [in this physical world] is magnificent' ('Hiersein ist herrlich'; *Elegy* VII, 39). Human culture, architecture, religion, music and art, the transformation of the physical world by human consciousness has always had the power to create a kind of 'human transcendence'. Transforming the finite world becomes the task of the poet and his gift to the angels. Now the angel is asked to praise human beings rather than the other way around (*Elegy* VII, 76–7).

The poet now understands that what he thought was his poetic task as the *Duino Elegies* began – reaching the transcendent realm – is a misguided activity. He acknowledges that the isolated self-consciousness can never attain transcendence. In this *Elegy* the poet also discovers how to proceed beyond the isolated self not toward the transcendent realm but within the physical world; he discovers the ability to transform consciousness *and* world by having them interact in the poetic image. The poetic image, like the cry of the bird uttered in the opening lines of this poem, is taken up by larger forces of existence and thus expands far beyond the isolated self.

In the seventh *Elegy*, Rilke thus substitutes a realisable and fruitful poetic project for a futile one. Rather than completing the movement of the mystic in which individual consciousness achieves unmediated unity with the transcendent, Rilke turns back into the limited human world to enact poetic transformation through individual consciousness and thus create duration in the fleeting physical world. The poet here experiences an epiphany; he realises that a genuine poetic voice will grow beyond the personal and will outgrow the impulse to woo the angel. He realises that interaction with the world of objects and physicality, and not flight or pleading, will lead him away from solipsism and toward a new kind of unity. As an intense experience of being in the here and now ('Hiersein') becomes his focus, Rilke decisively changes his poetic aim from transcendence to transformation of and within the physical world. This moves Rilke toward a geocentric and anthropocentric poetics based on immanence rather than transcendence.

One might assume that this would complete Rilke's record of poetic apprenticeship and the cycle of poems, but Rilke is a non-linear thinker. His ruminations eddy and backtrack. The eighth *Elegy* is such an eddy that recalls earlier moments of anxiety. The troubled condition of being a self-conscious spectator in existence (so intensely felt in the fourth *Elegy* and more negatively depicted in the fifth) recurs in the eighth *Elegy*, 'we, spectators, always, everywhere turned towards everything and never outward!' (*Elegy* VIII, 66–7). Because he is conscious of himself as discrete, man looks out at existence and perceives boundaries that separate him – unlike the unselfconscious animals that can look into 'the open' ('das Offene'; *Elegy* VIII, 8). Man attempts to overcome this separation by controlling the world, by ordering it with his mind (*Elegy* VIII, 68–9). Like the acrobats in the fifth *Elegy* who order themselves into complex physical arrangements only to fall asunder, human consciousness cannot order the world for very long. Eventually the world escapes our imposed system of order, and time reimposes disorder and decay.

The fate of man is always and only to remain alien and opposite ('Dieses heißt Schicksal: gegenüber sein und nichts als das und immer gegenüber'; *Elegy* VIII, 33–4). From the moment of his expulsion from the womb, man is conscious of being alien in the world and separate from it. The speaker observes that children can almost remember a broader unity, and that one can regain it by dying (in which state all boundaries literally decay), and that lovers might catch a glimpse of unity if the beloved were not always spoiling the view. But as they did in the first six Elegies, all these living categories fall short of reunification with existence.

This inability to eliminate the boundaries between self and object to produce an indiscriminate unity torments human beings. To counter his anguish, Rilke creates another moment of linguistic alchemy. In the eighth *Elegy*, the poet complains that for self-conscious man 'It is always world / and never Nowhere without No' ('Immer ist es Welt / und niemals Nirgends ohne Nicht'; *Elegy* VIII, 16–17). The quadruple negative, 'never Nowhere without No', is, ironically, one of the most positive statements in the *Elegies*. Recalling his linguistic innovation in describing the Angels, Rilke must find a way to violate semantic categories and linguistic structures in order to describe a state that is beyond logical explication or discursive language. Rilke yearns to be able to eliminate boundaries of time ('niemals') and of space ('Nirgends') without any sense of negation ('ohne Nicht'). Human consciousness would need to nullify its own distinctions and imposed order, i.e., to get beyond itself, in order to experience existence as a unified whole rather than as 'Welt' or as that which is not the self. Rilke's quadruple negative does just that by violating grammatical boundaries and producing an affirmation from an intensely negative formulation composed of apparently impossible states. The poet thus transmutes the highly negative and limited into infinite affirmation through his linguistic alchemy.

The ninth *Elegy* re-emphasises the poet's acceptance of this task of transformation. The speaker of the *Elegies* realises that the physical world and its temporal limits are not purely negative but rather they are indispensable to man. The singular, ephemeral nature of the world gives it greater value. Along with this new appreciation of the physical, limited world comes the realisation that language enables man and the poet to escape time and create duration. As Rilke puts it, '*Here* is the time of the *Sayable, here* is its home. / Speak and acknowledge' ('*Hier* ist des *Säglichen* Zeit, *hier* seine Heimat. / Sprich und bekenn'; *Elegy* IX, 43–4). Language takes in the external world and transforms it within human consciousness in order to create a new and more durable state that can be shared with others. 'Hier' in the above quotation is both our earthly realm and the poem itself. Again, Rilke fuses time and space in an endless simultaneity, to create an aesthetic realm impregnable to linear time. 'Here is the time' unites spatial and temporal concepts so that 'Hiersein' is not just being here spatially, but also being so intensely in each present moment that linear time disappears into a constant present in the poem. The 'sayable', ultimately, provides the means of surviving in a fragmented world. Transforming the world through language is an act fit to present even to the angels.

Rilke's *Duino Elegies* begin as an attempt to storm the transcendent realm and escape the limits of the physical world. After testing a number of strategies for transcendence, Rilke comes in the seventh and more conclusively in the ninth *Elegy* to realise that the idea of transcendence itself is a distracting trap. The poet turns finally back to the world and to the consciousness he sought to escape. By making the two interact, he creates a form more permanent than either, the aesthetic form. The end of the ninth *Elegy* becomes a joyous acceptance by the poet of the task of transformation, 'Verwandlung'. Earth replaces the angels as the poet's interlocutor:

> Earth, isn't this what you want: *invisible*
> re-existence in us? [ ... ]
> What, if not transformation, is your urgent commission?
> Earth, you dear one, I want to.

> Erde, ist es nicht dies, was du willst: *unsichtbar*
> in uns erstehn? [ ... ]
> Was, wenn Verwandlung nicht, ist dein drängender Auftrag?
> Erde, du liebe, ich will. (*Elegy* IX, 67–70)

In recognising and accepting his task of transformation, the poet rescues the physical world of objects and his own consciousness from the distraction of time and death. Rilke arrives firmly at the point of 'Hiersein', of being in this world: 'Look, I live. Out of what? Neither childhood nor future are becoming less.... Supernumerous existence springs up in my heart' (*Elegy* IX, 77–79). The problem of linear time, of disturbance by memory and hope experienced in the first *Elegy*, resolves into a unity in the totally experienced present moment. Life thrives without using up past or future; it flourishes in a unified simultaneity. Immanence replaces transcendence as a unifying principle by the end of the ninth *Elegy*.

### *Elegy* x: falling happily back to earth

Rilke's final poem in this cycle recapitulates the journey of the speaker of the *Elegies* and of the poet. The poem reprises the apprenticeship in consciousness and in poetics. This repetition is not surprising since Rilke's poetics of transformation forces a constant renewal of the poetic act. The tenth *Elegy* re-enacts this process of transformation, which Rilke has already accomplished in the alchemy of his poetic language (in phrases such as 'Bleiben ist Nirgends' or 'niemals Nirgends ohne nicht', for example). Unlike the earlier poems of the cycle, however, this *Elegy* presents an allegory in which human emotion is turned into geography and becomes a landscape through which man moves in search of an ultimate joy.

This geography begins in a modern degraded city in which the restless acrobats of the fifth *Elegy* are echoed by more degraded carnival hawkers who display the breeding of money and other dehumanising distractions. The poet hurries past this sham landscape into one of more profound experience including death itself. He does so by following first a youth who is fascinated by a personified lament ('Klage') and then a newly dead youth who can follow mature lament to its source in joy. This combination of the youthfully dead and lament recalls the beginning of the speaker's journey in the first *Elegy* that closes on the lament for Linus, whose death creates earthly music and poetry since those who were stunned at his death were rejuvenated by the song of Orpheus.

Lament and early death, then, lead us to poetry and music, which transforms the sorrow and pain of living human existence into an experience of enlightenment that can transport us beyond isolated self-consciousness. In the tenth *Elegy*, the poet follows the recently dead youth who discovers the source of joy and enlightenment precisely by following an allegorical lament. Art becomes a means to experience whatever we can of transcendence without actually leaving the physical world. The poet surpasses the child, the hero and the lover in his movement through the cycle of consciousness since he can both experience this progression and perpetuate it for others in his art.

Here the poet employs an image which brings full circle the cycle of consciousness he has been exploring – the Sphinx. The Sphinx embodies all the levels of consciousness; it is stone, animal, man and god in one, and it wears the pschent, the pharaoh's double crown, that symbolises the unity of the upper and lower worlds of life and death. Beyond this figure of ultimate unity lies the source of both sorrow and joy; the Sphinx embodies the transformative power of the poet who can unite in language and image realms that cannot be fused in any other way.

The *Duino Elegies* close by affirming the lessons imparted in the course of the ten poems. The poems end on a movement back toward limited, earthly existence. But it is a productive earth that the poet has learned to transform through his consciousness and preserve in poetic language. Man's perception of distinction and singularity now becomes positive and the very fleetingness of the world itself is something to be cherished. Poet and reader have learned to celebrate the physical world and the human condition as fertile ground. The closing gesture of the *Duino Elegies* indicates to man that in order to move into a more expansive level of consciousness he must be like the seed pod and the rain which must fall to earth in order for the seed to grow.

This allegory of falling is carried over from the catkins and the rain to happiness itself in the last four lines of the *Elegies*; to find joy and to move forward in the cycle of consciousness, man must let himself fall into earthly existence rather than attempting to scale the transcendent heights. This final realisation reverses the *Elegies'* opening gesture, the desire to call up to the angelic realms. The poet instead must immerse himself in the physical and the earthly in order to create fruitful transformation. The reader too comes to understand that this limited human world is indeed enough; human consciousness and larger existence are reunified; self-conscious man finds a way to expand his consciousness without abandoning the human realm by death. Intensely experienced immanence replaces the desire for transcendence.

By the end of the *Elegies*, Rilke has transformed our human realm of limits and logical distinctions into an advantage rather than a prison to be escaped. He creates a more modern geocentric and anthropocentric poetics that overcomes the frustration of a focus on the transcendent realm. The *Duino Elegies* celebrate the intense experience of 'Hiersein', and in so doing convert human anxiety about time and death into joyous poetic transformation. In the course of his poems, Rilke learns that the poet's true calling is not up to the divine realm, but rather back to the humanly possible world transformed by human consciousness and given duration in poetic language. The *Duino Elegies* open with a call to the angelic realm, but they close with a gesture that returns poet and reader to the fertile earth. The poems begin by aspiring upward; they end by falling, happily, back to the earth to engender new poetic understanding. In this cycle, Rilke makes immanence not just tolerable, but a triumph of human consciousness in which the poet can create unity within our fragmented modern existence by transforming the physical world into language.

# 7

## THOMAS MARTINEC

# *The Sonnets to Orpheus*

When Rilke moved to the Château de Muzot in the Canton of Wallis, Switzerland, in 1921, he was hoping he had found the place where he might complete his *Duino Elegies*. And indeed, having worked on this cycle, with several long interruptions, for a whole decade, Rilke did finally manage to bring this project to a conclusion in February 1922. This is, however, only one half of the success story that took place in Muzot. The other half concerns yet another major work that came into being there: *The Sonnets to Orpheus*, Rilke's last poetic cycle in German. Even before Rilke completed the *Duino Elegies* he had composed almost the entire first part of the sonnets, twenty-six poems altogether, in only four days (from 2 to 5 February 1922), and immediately after the *Elegies* had been finished, the second part consisting of another twenty-nine poems, was written in little more than a week (15–23 February). While the sonnets of the second part were rearranged after their composition, the first part predominantly reflects the chronological order in which the sonnets were written. The whole cycle was first published in 1923 by Insel in Leipzig.[1]

In part because of the closely connected genesis of *The Sonnets to Orpheus* and the *Duino Elegies*, Rilke always viewed the former in relation to the latter. At first, the sonnets appeared to him to be a by-product of the *Elegies* because of the spectacular speed of their composition, in which, as he wrote to Katharina Kippenberg, 'my pen found it difficult to keep up with their arrival' (B II, 225; 23 February 1922). He wrote to Marie von Thurn und Taxis, 'Just as before, when it was possible for the *Life of The Virgin Mary* to emerge alongside the first of the great Elegies (in Duino), in hours before and after working on them when my mind was receptive, this time a series of (something over fifty) sonnets has arisen.'[2] Gradually, however, Rilke came to realise that *The Sonnets to Orpheus* manifested their own poetic value and as a consequence he no longer regarded them as by-products but placed them 'alongside their older, noble sibling, the *Elegies*'.[3] To his Polish translator, Witold Hulewicz, he wrote: 'The *Elegies* and *The Sonnets* are permanently supportive of one another –, and I regard it as an infinite boon that I was able to fill both these sails with the same breath: the little rust-coloured sail of *The Sonnets* and the *Elegies*' huge white sail-canvas' (B II, 378).

Even though Rilke scholarship has rightly noted that the *Duino Elegies* and *The Sonnets to Orpheus* represent two different stages in Rilke's oeuvre (nowadays commonly referred to as the 'late' and the 'very late' Rilke), it is still essential to consider some of the ideas that helped to shape the *Elegies* in order to establish the framework in which the *Sonnets* are to be seen as well. Taking Rilke's image of the two sails filled by one breath, one might say that it is necessary to investigate this breath in order to identify the direction in which 'the little rust-coloured sail of the *Sonnets*' is moving. The ultimate source of this breath is an ostensibly simple, yet essentially complex question: 'How shall we live?' For Rilke, as for many of his contemporaries, this question posed a great challenge, all the more so as the key responses that poetic tradition had so far brought forth appeared outdated in modern(ist) times. The most fundamental answer, that one should live according to God's will, had become definitively unreliable ever since German philosophy of the nineteenth century had declared God to be dead. Furthermore, around the turn of the century, belief in humankind's capacity for love had been thoroughly shaken by psychoanalysis, which had identified more mundane forces, such as the drives of sexuality and power, at the core of human relationships. In Rilke's particular case, a whole series of failed love-relationships with various women had helped to increase his doubts about love as a means of orientation or guide for life. A belief in progress seemed a promising option in the search for the meaning of life: a huge wave of scientific and technological progress in the nineteenth century gave rise to the assumption that, one day, mankind would be able to solve its problems for itself. As far as the modernists were concerned, however, the drawbacks of industrialisation and ultimately the horrors of mass destruction in the First World War ruled out this promise of meaning as well. Rilke was well aware of this void. Summarising his novel *The Notebooks of Malte Laurids Brigge* (1910) in a letter to Lotte Hepner he wonders, 'how is it possible to live if the elements of this life are wholly beyond comprehension? If we are constantly insufficient in loving, uncertain in our resolutions, and impotent in the face of death, how is it possible to exist?' (B I, 599–600).

The 'breath' with which Rilke filled the 'sails' of both the *Duino Elegies* and *The Sonnets to Orpheus* can be understood as the attempt to find a valid answer to this existential question. Rilke identified the origin of the modernist crisis in the fact that essential elements of life had been locked out of life because they were felt to be unpleasant; above all these are death, the ugly, and an attitude to life that does not satisfy the criteria of rationality. The result, Rilke argued, was an impoverished version of life that is unable to proffer deeper meaning to humankind. In an important letter to Countess Sizzo of 12 April 1923, Rilke explains that the purpose of both the *Duino Elegies* and *The Sonnets to Orpheus* is to reintegrate aspects of life that had been excluded by modern civilisation, in order to point those who search for meaning in a new direction:

> More than once now I have suggested to you how in my life and in my work I am more and more driven only by the endeavour to correct wherever possible our old repressions which have taken from us our secrets and increasingly made them alien when in them we might live infinitely from fullness. Formidableness has shocked and horrified mankind: but where is there anything sweet and marvellous that on occasion does not wear *this* mask, that of the formidable? Life itself [ . . . ] is it not formidable? [ . . . ] Anyone who has not acknowledged the fearsomeness of life on occasion, even acclaimed it, will never fully take possession of the ineffable authorities of our existence, he will pass by on the verges, and when judgement is made one day will be neither alive nor dead. To demonstrate how formidableness and blessedness are identical [ . . . ]: that is the core meaning and conception of my two books. (B II, 296)

Seeking to prove the identity of 'formidableness and blessedness' and thus to cure modern life from its fatal 'repressions', in Sonnet I: 9 Rilke addresses the point that humankind had repressed most rigorously, death:

> Only to him who dares take up the lyre
> even in the realms of the Shades
> shall it be granted in awe to aspire
> to unendingly praise.
>
> Only one who has dwelt with the Dead
> and eaten the juice of their flower
> earns and retains every sound that is heard
> now and forever.[4]

Just like the *Duino Elegies*, so too are *The Sonnets to Orpheus* to be read as an attempt 'to keep life open in the face of death'.[5] It is characteristic of Rilke's attitude towards death that, unlike in Christian belief, the realm of death does not set in *after* life, but it is already a component of life: 'if one makes the mistake of applying *catholic* concepts of death, the hereafter and eternity to the *Elegies* or the *Sonnets*, one will be led completely astray from their starting point and will pave the way for an ever more fundamental misunderstanding' (B II, 377). It is a key feature of Rilke's poetic search for the meaning of life that death is reintegrated into life by being transformed into a *dimension* of life. Life and death together form the 'double-realm'

('Doppelbereich') in which human existence is rooted: 'Death is the *face of life* that is turned away from us, not illuminated by us' (B II, 374), Rilke explains in the same letter to Hulewicz, and Sonnet I: 9, which praises communication with the dead, ends with the lines 'Not till the reign of the Double- / Kingdom can every voice sound / everlastingly kind'.

Rilke's attempt to reintegrate death into life is part of a more comprehensive endeavour to free human existence from the limits of the visible world. The prime target of this endeavour is not so much to enhance death by supporting our recollection of those passed away, but rather to enhance life by extending its boundaries far beyond the area of what is commonly regarded as life. Rilke believed that the world perceived with our senses (henceforth for simplicity referred to as 'the visible world') was only one dimension of our existence: 'All the worlds in the universe are hurtling into the invisible and as such into their next-deepest reality' (B II, 378). But do we appreciate this deeper level of existence? After all, reasonable investigation is limited to the visible world, and tends to deny what it cannot detect. Modern science, for instance, operates on the assumption that there is no God, but only nature (which then is investigated with great success). Rilke felt that this one-sided approach to existence leads to a constriction of reality since it locks out the entire invisible world. As a consequence he tried to reopen the door to the realm of the invisible. The key requirement to gain access to this realm was metamorphosis: 'The world has no other refuge than to become invisible: *in* us [ . . . ] only *in* us can we complete this intimate and durable metamorphosis of the visible into the invisible, a world no longer dependent on being visible and tangible' (B II, 377).

Like the *Duino Elegies*, *The Sonnets to Orpheus* seek to achieve metamorphosis by means of poetry and as a result the concept of metamorphosis is a core principle of poetic composition. Having described humankind as 'transformers of the earth', Rilke points out that 'the *Sonnets* manifest individual details of this activity' (B II, 378), and he identifies the purpose of his sonnets in the 'inclination to establish just that connection to the greatest and most powerful elements of our origins'.[6] The ancient myth of Orpheus, son of the Thracian king Oeagrus and the muse Calliope, appealed to Rilke as it presents a whole series of metamorphoses. Rilke probably knew this myth through his reading of Ovid, who tells the story of Orpheus in the tenth and eleventh books of his *Metamorphoses*. The fact that Rilke was given a parallel-text, Latin-and-French edition of this book by Baladine Klossowska at Christmas 1920 might have helped to trigger a turn to this particular myth. The same can be said of a postcard Baladine pinned opposite Rilke's desk in 1921: it features the reproduction of a line drawing by the

Italian Renaissance artist Giovanni Battista Cima da Conegliano, which shows Orpheus playing his lyre, surrounded by animals listening raptly.

Three moments of metamorphosis are identifiable in the Orphic myth. First, after his wife Eurydice dies of a snake-bite, Orpheus travels into the underworld in order to bring her back. He manages to touch Hades and Persephone, the guardians of the underworld, with his singing, so Eurydice is set free on condition that Orpheus does not look back at her while leading her out into the world of the living. When Orpheus fails to fulfil this condition, his wife has to return to the dead; Rilke had already adapted this part of the myth in 'Orpheus. Eurydice. Hermes', one of the *New Poems*. Second, when Orpheus sings, animals, trees and plants gather around him to listen to his songs; the postcard left by Baladine features this part of the myth, which in *The Sonnets to Orpheus* is presented in the very first poem of the cycle. Finally, after the Maenads kill Orpheus by pulling him to pieces and throwing him into the sea, his severed head continues to sing and his lyre continues to play: 'Mobbed by destroyers, you raised the sweet order of song!' ('aus den Zerstörenden stieg dein erbauendes Spiel'; I: 26). In all three of these instances, Orpheus transcends the boundaries of human existence by means of his singing: he enters the realm of death (for Eurydice) and overcomes his own death (at the hands of the Maenads); he also crosses the boundary between nature (animals and plants) and culture (music): 'His hands slip through the lyric fence, transgress. / His whole obedience rests in his excess' ('Der Leier Gitter zwängt ihm nicht die Hände. / Und er gehorcht, indem er überschreitet'; I: 5). Thus Orpheus serves as an ideal figure of metamorphosis who keeps the 'double-realm' of life and death, and of nature and culture connected: 'Steadfast among the messengers / far through the Gates of the Dead he bears / chalices heaped with fruits for praise' ('Er ist einer der bleibenden Boten, / der noch weit in die Türen der Toten /Schalen mit rühmlichen Früchten hält'; I: 7).

The opening sonnet on the metamorphic power of Orphic song sets the tone for the entire cycle:

> A tree rose up – O apogee of rising!
> Now Orpheus sings, all hearing's tallest tree.
> And nothing speaks but signals in the silence,
> new births and transformations, come to be.
>
> (I: 1)

Orpheus's singing transforms animals into cultural beings and thus helps them to overcome the boundaries of their natural existence. This process is indicated by a new kind of listening: in nature, animals are quiet in order to detect either prey or enemies, but when Orpheus starts singing, they are quiet in order to listen to him:

> From nests and earths deep in the melting wood
> the silence and its creatures hastening here
> stay hushed not out of cunning, not from fear
> but eagerly to hear what must be heard.
>
> No impulse now to bellow, howl or roar.

The results of this cultural, rather than instinctive, listening are 'Tempel im Gehör' – 'Temples of the Ear', places of divine adoration in which natural beings search for a higher dimension of life:

> Where nothing but the merest refuge was,
>
> answering only to the blackest need,
> a tunnel entrance propped by trembling spars –
> you built them their own Temple of the Ear!

It is important to note that this metamorphosis takes place *in* rather than *after* life: the animals emerge from their natural habitat, the forest, and Orpheus whose singing brings about metamorphosis is as fully part of the natural world as he is a figure of transcendence.

This double-existence, which makes Orpheus a 'counter-myth to Christ',[7] is a key feature of metamorphosis in *The Sonnets to Orpheus*. Rilke felt that with regard to the invisible world, humankind was confronted with a twofold challenge: on the one hand we are asked to achieve the spiritual act of metamorphosis on which the universe relies in order to reach a deeper level of reality; on the other hand we have to appreciate our present nature, because it, too, is a crucial dimension of our existence:

> Be, among Shades here in the Realm of Declining,
> a ringing glass until, ringing, you shatter.
>
> Be! yet at the same time remember the code of not-being,
> endless dimension for every inmost vibration;
> see you fulfil it this once and once-only time.     (II: 13)

Rilke's call for a metamorphosis not only implies that we ought to open the visible and terminated world to an invisible and timeless dimension, but by the same token it is aimed at celebrating the visible and finite world as one of the elements of life in general: 'So it is important not only not to denigrate and disparage the here-and-now, but precisely because of the temporariness that it shares with us, these phenomena and things should be comprehended and transformed' (B II, 376). According to Rilke's concept of a dual reality which he calls 'the whole', we are not meant to live up to a timeless being, like God, or an eternal reality, like heaven, or the promises of any ideology, but rather we are to bear the timeless dimension of life in mind while celebrating the moment. Sonnet I: 22 states this quite clearly in the opening line: 'Wir sind die Treibenden' – 'We are the strivers'. As we are finite beings in a visible world, to neglect this feature would cause us to miss the keynote of our existence. Thus Rilke's idea of metamorphosis counteracts the religious concept of martyrdom, according to which eternal life is to be attained via a neglect of human nature. The sonnets point in the opposite direction; they appreciate human nature on the way to eternity:

> For what we are, we the strivers
> are valued still by the Powers:
> part of the life the Gods live.
>
> (II: 27)

The sonnets refer to another figure of metamorphosis besides Orpheus. According to the subtitle, *The Sonnets to Orpheus* are 'written as a memorial for Wera Ouckama Knoop' (KA II, 237). On 1 January 1922, only a few weeks prior to the composition of the sonnets, Rilke received a letter in which Gertrud Ouckama Knoop gave an account of her young daughter's illness and death. Born in 1900, Wera died at the age of nineteen, and although Rilke met Wera only occasionally when she was still a child, he took great interest in her destiny. In a letter to Countess Sizzo he recalls:

> This pretty child, who only began to dance and was admired by all who saw her then because of the art of movement and metamorphosis innate to her body and to her temperament, explained unexpectedly to her mother that she could no longer dance and did not wish to any more ... ; [ ... ] In the time that was left to her Wera made music; finally she only kept up her drawing, as if the dance that was failing her was issuing forth from her ever more quietly, ever more discreetly. (B II, 298)

Like Orpheus, Wera also features as a metamorphic character in Rilke's view: not only is her dancing described as an 'art of movement and metamorphosis', but it also experiences a transformation into music and finally into drawing where it expresses itself more discretely. Moreover, it is the fact that Wera dies young that makes her truly a figure of metamorphosis for Rilke: she appears as the girl 'whose incompletion and innocence hold open the door of the grave so that, departed, she belongs to the powers that keep the half of life fresh and open to the other, wound-open half' (B II, 378).

Two of *The Sonnets to Orpheus* take up Wera's life explicitly; they are the last but one in each part of the cycle. Sonnet I: 25 discusses Wera's aesthetic metamorphosis:

> First as a dancer until her hesitant figure
> was halted – like youth itself cast into bronze; alert,
> motionless, grieving. Sent by those highest achievers,
> Music descended and entered her transient heart.

Corresponding to Rilke's understanding of death as yet another dimension of life, Wera's dancing is finally presented as a departure rather than the end of her existence: 'Then after terrible beating / entered the gate irremediably open'. The second Wera sonnet (II: 28) takes up the idea of metamorphosis through art and combines the girl's dancing with Orphic singing:

> Drift here, drift there, young woman still half-child,
> achieve the pattern of your dance; surpass
> the mere arithmetic dull Nature wields
> and for one fleeting instant touch the stars.
>
> For Nature's ears knew little till they heard
> the voice of Orpheus – which moved you so.

Even though only the two sonnets mentioned here refer to Wera's destiny explicitly, Rilke dedicated the entire cycle to her, as many of the poems echo the idea of metamorphosis in death and art which Rilke sensed in Wera's life. Thus he explicates in a letter to Anton Kippenberg of 23 February 1922: 'even though only two sonnets [ . . . ] touch on this connection literally, many hover around it, and the sub-title should be permitted and might often be helpful for the desire to understand of those not so intimate'.[8]

Both Rilke's interpretation of the Orphic myth and his reference to Wera mark the fundamental difference between *The Sonnets to Orpheus* and the *Duino Elegies*; they need to be considered if one is to understand why the *Sonnets* are commonly regarded to have inaugurated the final (i.e. post-*Elegies*) phase of Rilke's oeuvre. It is true that both cycles present metamorphosis of the visible world with all its constraints into the realm of the invisible as the key response in the modernist search for a fulfilled life. But the *Sonnets* present and treat metamorphosis quite differently from the *Elegies*. It is characteristic of their genre for the *Elegies* to lament the *absence* of metamorphosis in human existence; metamorphosis only comes into play through the figure of the angel, and thus via a non-human being who is able to achieve what human beings are not. At home in 'the great unity' – as Rilke expressed it to Hulewicz – angels are 'the beings that surpass us' (B II, 375). Humankind, on the contrary, is caught in an existence that lies somewhere between animal nature and the angelic sphere, doomed to suffer from the inability to transcend the boundaries of the visible world.

This is not the case in *The Sonnets to Orpheus*. Here the *Elegies*' lament is regarded as only the preliminary stage to the praise of life:

> Triumph *knows*. Yearning soon surrenders. Only
> Grief is still a novice. All night long she
> learns her lessons, numbering old sorrows.
>
> All at once – inaccurate and artless –
> she lifts a constellation of our voices
> to the high heavens undimmed by her own breath.
>
> (i: 8)

Unlike the angels, Orpheus and Wera are presented as beings who are rooted in *both* realms. Orpheus is a visible being who manages to transcend the world with his music thus 'replacing' the angel of the *Elegies* as a 'figure of transcendence':[9] 'Is he, then, mortal? No: formed by both / living and dead realms those qualities grew!' (i: 6). The dedication of the cycle to Wera emphasises the duality of the Orphic being. Certainly Rilke viewed Wera as a figure who entered the realm of the invisible, but the starting point of this process is a real human being. Rilke emphasises this earthly dimension by mentioning Wera's name instead of hiding it as he did with Paula Becker's name in 'Requiem for a Friend'.

Within the cycle itself human beings are shown to have metamorphic potential, too: 'Though ignorant of our true places / yet our acts are relevant and real' (i: 12). The speaker frequently addresses this potential with appeals such as 'Seek transformation. O take delight in the flame / in which boastful manifestations of change must be burned' that opens Sonnet ii: 12, followed in the next sonnet by 'Share in her death with Eurydice. Ascend in your song / and in praise ever-ascending combine with the pure' (ii: 13). Another way of addressing the human capacity of metamorphosis is to present it in the subjunctive:

> Imagine one who brought Things into the innermost heart
> of his sleep: from the depths he had shared in the night
> would he not differently wake to a different day? (ii: 14)

Sonnet i: 3 poses Orphic metamorphosis as questions:

> A God can do it. Mankind cannot press
> boldly through the narrow lyre and follow:
> [ . . . ]
> Singing is being. Easy for the God.
> When might *we* be? When will he turn around
> the earth and stars to face our mortal being?

Finally, the last poem of the entire cycle presents the redemptive answer to the question of proper living in a conditional phrase:

> And if earthly powers should forget you,
> to the constant Earth say this: I flow!
> Tell the rushing waters: I abide.
>
> (II: 29)

Thematising human metamorphosis in this manner leaves it in limbo: on the one hand it has an actual place in human existence, on the other hand it is a potential, a mission that still needs to be accomplished. That is why a group of sonnets warns of the obstacles on our way to metamorphosis. Above all these obstacles are a technology that has become independent – 'The machine will forever imperil all human creation / while it presumes to direct us instead of to serve' (II: 10) – and a mentality that focuses on continuity rather than change: 'Things that are pining to fly we burden with ballast, / adding ourselves to their load and exulting in weight' (II: 14).

Rilke's ideas on metamorphosis are also reflected on a more formal level in the way in which he handles the sonnet as a poetic genre. Prior to *The Sonnets to Orpheus* Rilke had used the sonnet form on many occasions. Many of the *New Poems* (1907) and *New Poems: The Other Part* (1908) are sonnets (the opening poems of each part, for example, 'Early Apollo' and 'Archaic Torso of Apollo'). However, while most of his poetic collections embrace a range of different lyrical forms, *The Sonnets to Orpheus* are Rilke's first and only cycle devoted to this single genre. With the sonnet, Rilke chose a poetic form that is above all characterised by two features: a long-standing tradition reaching back to medieval times and a fairly strict formal pattern. Both aspects appealed to Rilke. In a letter to Irmela Linberg of 24 March 1919 he explained:

> Because I have been working over the last few weeks on the translation of several old Italian sonnets, this form has been strongly revivified for me by virtue of my constant preoccupation with it. How pleasing it still is even to us, this form that permits an almost intensified sense of freedom within the most restrictive of bonds.[10]

The translation of several old Italian sonnets not only got Rilke 'in the mood' of sonnet writing (a moment not to be underestimated) but it also helped him to fulfil a crucial requirement of his aesthetics. By dealing with a traditional poetic genre he re-established a connection to the past, whose neglect he regarded as one of the main reasons for the impoverishment of modern existence:

The more tradition is kept fenced off from us on the outside and stifled, the more decisive it becomes for us whether we remain capable of staying open to the most varied and most secret traditions of mankind and of passing them on. *The Sonnets to Orpheus* are [...] an effort in this direction made in a last act of obedience. (B II, 307)

Admittedly, when Rilke is speaking of the 'traditions of humankind', he is primarily referring to ideas, concepts, beliefs, and myths, rather than to poetic forms. And yet, the latter are part of the tradition he seeks to revitalise, all the more as Rilke speaks, of course, as a poet.

The history of the German sonnet is primarily based upon the form employed by the Italian fourteenth-century poet Petrarch, whose famous collection *Canzoniere* contains over 300 sonnets: each with fourteen lines subdivided into two strophes of four lines (quatrains) and two strophes of three lines (tercets) (as opposed to the Shakespearian sonnet consisting of two strophes of six lines (sestets) followed by a couplet). Despite permitting a certain degree of variation, the rhyme pattern is part of the sonnet's formal strictness in so far as it serves to emphasise and thus stabilise the strophic structure. Very often, the two quatrains share the same rhyme pattern (sometimes even the same rhymes) as do the two tercets, thus highlighting the difference between both parts of the sonnet. Yet another element of formal strictness is to be found in the metre: ever since the early seventeenth century, when Martin Opitz claimed that alternating feet (i.e. iambs [stressed like 'behave'] and trochees [like 'beehive']) suit the German language best,[11] most German sonnets have been written in iambic metre. The typical verse of baroque sonnets is the alexandrine, consisting of six iambs, or the 'vers commun', consisting of five iambs. It is important to note that throughout the history of German literature the form of the sonnet has always been discussed in connection with its content: the structure, particularly the quatrain/tercet divide, was seen to support a particular way of presenting one's feelings and thoughts. Composing a sonnet did not therefore simply mean to express some ideas in four and others in only three lines, but it meant to present a problem in two quatrains in order to draw a conclusion in the tercets – to give just one example.

In *The Sonnets to Orpheus*, Rilke preserves some of the sonnet's traditional formal features while changing others. All the sonnets have fourteen lines, divided into two quatrains and two tercets; they are rhymed and they have identifiable metrical patterns, but Rilke treats these formal elements with a considerable degree of freedom. The rhyme pattern not only changes between different sonnets (which had already been common in the German tradition), but also between corresponding parts *within* a sonnet: the first quatrain of the opening poem, for instance, features an alternating rhyme (abab), while the second quatrain employs an 'embracing' rhyme (cddc). In several cases the metre changes within the poem as well. Some sonnets contain stanzas whose lines are of different length, such as 'Mag auch die Spieglung im Teich / oft uns verschwimmen: / *Wisse das Bild*' ('Though what reflects in the pool / grows indistinct as it flows: / *Know what it shows*'; I: 9); others combine different feet, such as dactyls (a stressed syllable followed by two unstressed ones) and trochees (a stressed syllable followed by an unstressed one), like 'Sieh, die Maschine: / wie sie sich wälzt und rächt / und uns entstellt und schwächt' (I: 18; see also II: 18) – which a translation can hardly hope to replicate. Several sonnets employ exclusively dactyls, which traditionally was a feature of the elegy rather than the sonnet:

> Rühmen, das ists! Ein zum Rühmen Bestellter,
> ging er hervor wie das Erz aus des Steins
> Schweigen. Sein Herz, o vergängliche Kelter
> eines den Menschen unendlichen Weins.

> To give praise! For praising, his high vocation,
> He was wrought: bell-metal from mineral stillness!
> His heart, O it is the ephemeral winepress
> Pressing the grape for Man's lastingest wine.
>
> (I: 7; see also I: 9 and II: 20)

Last but not least, Rilke frequently overrules the structure of the sonnet with the presentation of his thoughts; this is most evident whenever the divide between the quatrain and tercet is overrun by an enjambment, thus linking both parts of the sonnet:

> What we have given the scaffold over the years
> it will surely give back to us: just as a child may
> offer as gifts the toys of its previous birthday.
> It is not like this that a God truly merciful enters
>
> into the welcoming heart like a wide-open door.
> He would come as a God, all in light and in power enduring,
> so much more than a wind for the sails of the great and secure.

> Was es durch Zeiten bekam, das schenkt das Schafott
> wieder zurück, wie Kinder ihr Spielzeug vom vorig
> alten Geburtstag. Ins reine, ins hohe, ins thorig
> offene Herz träte er anders, der Gott
>
> wirklicher Milde. Er käme gewaltig und griffe
> strahlender um sich, wie Göttliche sind.
> Mehr als ein Wind für die großen gesicherten Schiffe.
>
> (II: 9; see also I: 3)

Just like the reference to the myth of Orpheus and to Wera's destiny, Rilke's free use of a traditionally strict form is ultimately rooted in his concept of metamorphosis. Thus, bridging the gap between past and present does not simply mean conserving traditions, but rather integrating them into present existence by means of application. Accordingly, Rilke employs a genre with a traditional pedigree in the twentieth century, seeking to achieve a metamorphosis of poetic form:

> I keep saying sonnets. Even if this entails the freest or, so to speak, most changed-about things that can be conceived of in the name of this usually so calm and stable form. But precisely this, transforming the sonnet, lifting it, in a sense carrying it whilst 'on the run' without breaking it – this was a peculiar trial or task for me here. (B II, 225)

In *The Sonnets to Orpheus*, the concept of poetry as a place of metamorphosis goes far beyond a particular treatment of the poetic genre. It also encompasses the idea that poetry in general plays a key role in the attempt to lead a fulfilled life. In antiquity the pre-eminent questions of mankind had been answered by mythology, which took up existential phenomena, such as love and hatred, birth and death, peace and war, in order to give meaning to them in a world of human beings, heroes and gods. In modern times, these myths were still known through their literary presentation by classical authors, Homer, Virgil, Ovid and many others, but they had lost their original power to give meaning to life, as the Enlightenment had replaced the mythological approach with rational investigation. As a result, war, for instance, was no longer seen as a battle of divine forces, but as a conflict in which various groupings pursue their political, economic, religious, ideological interests; these interests can be identified and explained by rational investigation. Likewise death was no longer seen as transition into another realm, such as the underworld or heaven, but as the outcome of certain biological processes that can be analysed (and even delayed) by scientific investigation.

Rilke was well aware of this shift in perception which had come into effect long before he started writing; it had been prepared since the Renaissance, then became a main feature of the Enlightenment, and it has shown its consequences ever since. By the same token Rilke felt the loss this shift had caused with regard to the search for life's meaning: there were no reliable sources to solve this problem anymore. Modern civilisation had managed to gather knowledge about the world, to solve many a mystery and to provide humankind with the technology that helped to improve daily life; simultaneously, however, modern civilisation had dismissed all (mythical) answers to the central questions of human existence. Under these circumstances *The Sonnets to Orpheus* can be seen as an attempt to step in and to fill the gap left open by modern thinking. In a situation where humankind shows the (endangered) potential to live such a life by means of metamorphosis, it is poetry's task to turn potential into action: poetry itself becomes the place of metamorphosis. The second part of the cycle opens with the line 'Breath, you unseeable poem', and in the subsequent lines the act of breathing is presented as an act of metamorphosis: absorbing the world (breathing in) and returning one's inner life (breathing out) represent an intimate exchange between the subject and the world: 'ceaselessly, freely exchanging / a measure of World for our being! / Counterpoint, of whose rhythm I *am*' (II: 1). We can read the poem as 'visualised breathing', thus identifying the poetic text as the place of this intimate exchange between subject and world.[12] This is at the core of Rilke's Orphic concept: it is poetry that accomplishes metamorphosis, thus transcending human existence to a higher sphere: 'True singing / is whispering; a breath within the God; a wind' (I: 3).

Rilke's ambition to contribute to the fulfilment of human existence also explains why he composed a whole cycle of sonnets rather than individual poems that were later assembled into a collection.[13] In a letter to Katharina Kippenberg, Rilke notes that he has 'eventually emerged from a merely accumulative process with Orpheus and the great Elegies'.[14] While collections gather a certain number of individual poems which are basically independent of each other, poetic cycles are characterised by a higher degree of coherence. In *The Sonnets to Orpheus* this coherence stems from the genre (all poems are sonnets), the mythological grounds (Orpheus) and a thematic centre (metamorphosis as exemplified by Wera Ouckama Knoop); it is supported by the fact that all the sonnets were written in the course of a few days, which is more unusual (as the *Duino Elegies* demonstrate). Furthermore a certain degree of coherence is to be found in the arrangement of some of the poems: the first part is framed in two layers by two sonnets presenting scenes of the Orphic myth (I: 1 and I: 26), and by two referring to Wera (I: 2 and I: 25); in addition, the last but one poem of both parts (I: 25 and II: 28) is about Wera. Of course, poetic cycles are by no means an invention of the modernists: Goethe's *Roman Elegies* (*Römische Elegien*, 1790) and Heine's *Germany: A Winter's Tale* (*Deutschland: Ein Wintermärchen*, 1844) are only two of the most famous examples of pre-modernist cycles. It is fair to say, however, that poetic cycles became strikingly popular towards the beginning of the twentieth century. The driving force behind the cyclic composition of *The Sonnets to Orpheus* is to be seen in the ambition to create a whole system of meaning rather than collecting meaningful pieces;

as Ulrich Fülleborn has pointed out, poetic inspiration is no longer limited to the individual poem, but ultimately leads to a rather complex response to eminent questions and challenges of life, similar to the one that in the past used to be given by myths.[15] As a result *The Sonnets to Orpheus* not only refer to ancient mythology, but they also seek to take on the *function* once fulfilled by mythology.

However strong the link to ancient mythology might be, Rilke's last poetic cycle should not be read as an attempt to continue a pre-modern way of contemplating life. It is not Rilke's intention to turn back the clock by simply ignoring the history of modern civilisation. He rather addresses the problems that have been caused by the development of civilisation in order to cure them with his poetry. The result is a poetry that Beda Allemann, referring to Herder, described as 'paramythic': the myth it presents features a tension that derives from Rilke's awareness that there is no way back to a mythological era.[16] The 'paramythic' quality of *The Sonnets to Orpheus* is reflected by the sophisticated presentation of modern (i.e. post-mythic) technology. Even though Rilke points to the hazards technology poses to human existence, he never condemns it as such, but urges a proper use of it. Sonnet I: 18, which is about a machine, ends with the lines

> Drawn from our own, its power
> owes but one favour:
> humbly to serve and impartially labour.

Next to the presentation of several modern phenomena, it is the way in which Rilke proposes meaning that makes the entire cycle an explicitly modern offering rather than the repetition of an ancient myth. Alongside the reliability of meaning offered by ancient mythology came the necessity to believe in the given answers without (enlightened!) doubts. Myths represented self-contained systems of meaning that did not tolerate changes made by rational thinking: either one shared the system wholeheartedly or one did not. This is not the case in *The Sonnets to Orpheus*, because they really *offer* their images to the reader without demanding dogmatic obedience. Having described the image of horse and rider, for instance, Rilke concludes: 'But if for a little while it pleases us / to trust the pattern would not that suffice?' (I: 11). Rilke employs mythical elements without turning them into a new system that forces those seeking for the meaning of their lives into a corset of belief. Instead he offers his latest poetry in order to stimulate the readers' imagination and to free their minds from the constraints of modern thinking – thus tuning them into the Orphic melody of life.

## NOTES

1 For a more detailed account of the process of composition see Ulrich Fülleborn 'Deutungsaspekte u. Stellenkommentar' (KA II, 712–64, here p. 706).

2 Rainer Maria Rilke, Marie von Thurn und Taxis, *Briefwechsel*, ed. Ernst Zinn, 2 vols. (Zurich: Niehans & Rokitansky, 1954), vol. II, p. 700 (25 February 1922).

3 Rilke, Thurn und Taxis, *Briefwechsel*, vol. II, p. 716 (14 June 1922).

4 Rainer Maria Rilke, *'Sonnets to Orpheus' with 'Letters to a Young Poet'*, trans. Stephen Cohn (Manchester: Carcanet, 2000), p. 31. All English translations of *The Sonnets to Orpheus* in this essay are from this volume; translations of Rilke's letters are by Robert Vilain.

5 Rilke, *Briefe*, ed. Ernst Zinn, 2 vols. (Zurich: Niehans & Rokitansky, 1954), vol. II, p. 852 (to Nanny von Escher, 22 December 1923).

6 Rilke, *Briefe*, ed. Zinn, vol. II, p. 838 (to Leopold von Schlözer, 30 May 1923).

7 Manfred Engel, 'Die Sonette an Orpheus', in *RHB*, pp. 405–24, here p. 411.

8 Rainer Maria Rilke, *Briefe an seinen Verleger, 1906 bis 1926*, second edition, 2 vols. (Wiesbaden: Insel, 1949), vol. II, p. 415.

9 Fülleborn, 'Deutungsaspekte', p. 722.

10 Quoted from *Rilke-Chronik*, ed. Ingeborg Schnack, second edition, 2 vols. (Frankfurt am Main: Insel, 1996), vol. II, p. 1380.

11 In his *Buch von der deutschen Poeterey* (1624).

12 See Fülleborn, 'Deutungsaspekte', p. 724.

13 On the matter of the cycle and its structure see Fülleborn, 'Deutungsaspekte', pp. 718–20 and *RHB*, pp. 420–1.

14 Rilke, Kippenberg, *Briefwechsel*, p. 599 (30 June 1926).

15 Fülleborn, 'Deutungsaspekte', p. 718.

16 Beda Allemann, 'Rilke und der Mythos', in Ingeborg H. Solbrig and Joachim Storck (eds.), *Rilke heute: Beziehungen und Wirkungen*, vol. II (Frankfurt am Main: Suhrkamp, 1976), pp. 7–27, here pp. 10 and 14.

## PART III

# Cultural contexts, influences, reception

# 8

ANDREAS KRAMER

# Rilke and modernism

This chapter places Rilke's writings and aesthetics within the broader context of modernism. Although there is little debate today about whether or
not Rilke can be regarded as a modernist writer, the question as to how
exactly he fits into the history and landscape of European modernism is
less straightforward to answer. Never a card-carrying member of any of the
numerous modernist movements that emerged during the modernist period,
nor a signatory to any of the manifestos issued by these groups, he was
given to styling himself as a solitary writer beyond movements. Rilke's relationship to modernism as a whole, and to individual movements within
it, thus represents an individual inflection of the modes and structures of
modernism to his own particular poetics.

First, though, because the term 'modernism' is much-debated and con-
tested, it will be necessary briefly to set out the way in which I will use
it. I have then divided my discussion into three sections, each of which is
broadly correlated to the widely accepted stages of development of Rilke's
work. 'Holistic modernism' charts the early Rilke's concerns to fuse art and
life, aestheticism and vitalism. 'Metropolitan modernism' discusses the middle phase of Rilke's work, the impact of Paris and the contemporary visual
arts in the *New Poems* (1907/8) and *The Notebooks of Malte Laurids Brigge*
(1910), while Rilke's late work, represented by the *Duino Elegies* (1912–22),
is configured as 'mythic modernism'. The division into sections is slightly
artificial as Rilke continually reworks concerns from an earlier period in a
later mode – an attitude which in itself echoes modernism's restless desire
for change and innovation.

Modernism, however, covers many things. It is sometimes constructed as
a distinctive movement, opposed to Realism or Romanticism. Other critics
see it as an umbrella term for a series of artistic and literary movements,
from Symbolism to Expressionism, which emerged between about 1880 and
1930. Modernism is sometimes characterised by its deliberate challenge to
traditional forms of art and thought, in particular the modes of Realism,

by its opposition to reason and scientific thought, and by its development of new, experimental styles. But modernism's forms, though often directly competitive, encompass both conventional and innovative modes, as can be seen in Rilke's life-long reworking of poetic tradition. Other attempts to define modernism have focused on the cultural response and the ideological position of their representatives. Modernism is thus often characterised by the experience of profound and pervasive crisis – a crisis of the self, a crisis of language, a crisis of perception and experience, as for example in Walter Benjamin's account of modernism.[1] All of these parameters become critical because, once assumed to be fixed and stable, they have been displaced by doubt and uncertainty. These crises are seen as symptoms of a wider sense of discontinuity of tradition, and a feeling of alienation from the modern world. But some modernists embraced technological modernity and attendant ideas about social or political revolution, while others opted to look to past or exotic cultures as sources of authenticity and inspiration against the modern world. Many modernists shared an anti-bourgeois outlook, but this could mean either an adherence to a valuation of art as a sacred realm, its redefinition as a vehicle for political revolution, or the complex dialectics between the two that we find in Adorno's theory of art.

Within modernist studies, it became increasingly clear that homogenising modernism to a more or less unified aesthetic or cultural response to the modern world was unable to account for the diverse, often complex and contradictory range of modernist texts. Critical theory, especially the new approaches emerging around post-structuralism, gender studies and New Historicism, have extended the way in which modernism is configured and investigated. The broad consensus today is that within modernism there is 'a wide variety of texts that articulate experiences of modernity in different aesthetic codes, from different subject positions, and with different political affiliations and national contingencies'.[2] As well as accounting for such kinds of divisions and difference, recent modernist studies have investigated the ways in which modernist texts relate to the discourses and institutions of modernity, in which a sociological theory of modernity as an ever-accelerating process of industrialisation and the rationalisation and bureaucratisation of all aspects of individual and social life, is legitimised by the idea of progress. Modernist works are not just transcriptions of individual symptoms of upheaval or crisis; at the same time they are active responses to the condition of social modernity. Modernist texts, rather than simply reflecting modernity (which would be a falling back into the ideology of Realism) or belonging to a separate realm (which would be the aestheticist view), are seen as dialectically related to modernity. In Fredric Jameson's words, there is a dialectic between 'the practice of language in the literary work, and the experience of *anomie*, standardisation, rationalising desacral-isation in the [ . . . ] world of daily life – such that the latter can be grasped as that determinate situation, dilemma, contradiction, or subtext, to which the former comes as a symbolic resolution or solution.'[3] This opens the way towards seeing literary modernism as a deeply fissured phenomenon, as a range of responses to modernity that involve profound inner contradictions and conflicts at every level, from author to text to work to movement. This is an approach that would also require us to look for precisely the shifts in emphasis and strategy we seem to have in the case of a non-affiliated modernist like Rilke.

## Holistic modernism: art and life

Like his contemporaries Stefan George or Hugo von Hofmannsthal, the early Rilke is situated in the aestheticism of the *fin de siècle*. Responding to the dominant mode of literary Realism, particularly in its heightened form of a scientific Naturalism, aestheticism turned away from objective reality by invoking art as an alternative and autonomous reality to which social or political concerns were subordinate. Apart from being firmly rooted in European aestheticism, Rilke was also one of the many *fin de siècle* writers who adopted a Nietzschean and essentially vitalist philosophy of life. In Rilke's case, this was a strategy which helped him overcome the aestheticist impasse by which art is rigidly separated from life and social reality.

In literary terms, it was French Symbolism that provided the most lasting impetus for aestheticism. Originating in France in the 1880s and 1890s, and championed by poets, Symbolism stressed the primary importance of suggestion and evocation, and heightened those aspects of literary language which emerge when the stress is no longer on reference to external objects; instead, internal relations and affinities, especially between sound, sense and colour, come to the fore which in turn enact a subtle play between presence and absence. As the poet Mallarmé, who was a decisive influence on Rilke, put it:

> To create is to conceive an object in its fleeting moment, in its absence [ . . . ].
> We conjure up a scene of lovely, evanescent, intersecting forms. We recognize the entire and binding arabesque thus formed as it leaps dizzily in terror or plays disquieting chords; or, through a sudden digression (by no means disconcerting), we are warned of its likeness unto itself even as it hides.[4]

Rilke's encounter with Symbolism confirmed his view that art was auto-nomous, independent from external reality; and that it was fundamentally non-mimetic, emphasising instead form and internal relations. At the same time, he showed an abiding interest in the issues that the above quotation only alludes to: the interplay between presence and absence, the autonomous act of creation and its implications for the creative subject.

Although clearly shaped by the Symbolist aesthetic, Rilke sought to overcome its strict separation of art from life, spirit from matter. In order to embrace 'life' without falling back into the modes of a shallow mimetic Realism, he looked to the post-Symbolist *Ecole naturiste* which applied the Symbolist aesthetic to phenomena of 'life' and 'nature'.[5] Rilke's attitude towards Symbolism and the post-Symbolist developments is part of his attempt to develop a holistic kind of modernism.

The Symbolist aesthetic and its impasse are fully present in *The Book of Hours* (1903), which is modelled on the medieval Book of Prayers, but in which Art has taken the place of religion. The first two books, 'The Book of Monastic Life' and 'The Book of Pilgrimage', develop the notion that 'God' is a human work of art rather than a transcendent being. The speaker of this cycle of poems is a Russian monk, who is also a painter of icons, suggesting a close link between visual art and the divine. Rilke's privileging of visual art, and of visuality, as a condition for producing modernist art will become more pronounced later.[6] Other poems display a longing for deserted parks and ruined castles, and the kind of nostalgia for the aristocratic, pre-industrial eighteenth century that we also find in the work of George, and which can be read as a strong response to the modernising present.

The final book, however, 'The Book of Poverty and Death', which was written in Viareggio in April 1903 following Rilke's first stay in Paris, introduces the world of urban modernity and considers its implications for the optimistic project of creative unity with 'God'. The poems imagine modernity invariably as causing distance between self and nature/God, and fragmentation within each of these. In a number of poems, the big city, with its systems of rapid transport and new communications, is criticised for being in thrall to the idea of progress; for thriving on illusion and dissimulation; for producing a mass of isolated individuals instead of organic communities; and for causing existential fear, 'the deep fear of over-large cities' (KA I, 233).

Faced with modernity in which human beings have lost their sense of self as well as their sense of place, the book's speaker develops a different strategy to overcome this kind of fear. Some poems seek to expose the idea of inevitable progress as illusory. The big cities are also portrayed as inimical to true social change and presented as if they were ruins (KA II, 235–6), a rare dialectical insight by Rilke into modernity's close link with the concept of linear progress and an idea that Walter Benjamin would develop in his reading of modernism. But Rilke is an aestheticist poet, not a materialist critic.

A similar kind of aestheticism informs the high-minded concept of 'Besitz-losigkeit', the condition in which nothing is possessed or owned, which he develops when addressing the plight of the urban poor. While not providing an insight into the workings of the capitalist economy, this notion serves at least to counter one of its more powerful myths. A similar move is associated with the idea of 'Tod', literally 'death': it refers to the death of the individual in mass society, the loss of organic community and the anonymous and abstract forces of modernisation. But loss of individuality is attractive for Rilke because it approximates his ideal of subject-free creativity – a modernist creativity in which the aestheticist position is curiously inflected. This idea finds its most paradoxical expression in the composite figure of a redeemer who gives birth to death. The possibility of social change seems slim for Rilke, but it might happen outside the bourgeois-capitalist categories of linear time and historical progress, as the 'Letter from the Young Worker' suggests.

Urban modernity becomes the Jamesonian subtext to Rilke's modernist poetry, albeit in an aestheticised form. Up to a point, Rilke's critique of social modernity resembles anti-modernist discourse that covered a wide spectrum from conservative to 'völkisch'-nationalist positions. Modern civilisation is criticised for being rationalised, commercialised and degenerate, a far cry from authentic (and authentically German) culture. Against deracination and degeneration, this discourse located authentic experience elsewhere, in pre-modern rural life, spatially and temporally removed from urban modernity and unaffected by rampant modernisation. Rilke had already encountered a pre-modern world during his Russian travels, which helped him articulate a view of the modern artist who could, from a distance, be at one with the world. Rilke's affinity with the conservative 'Heimatkunst' (local or regional art) movement around 1900 is a German example of this idea. It is no coincidence that it was in Worpswede, a small artists' colony on the North Sea coast, that he developed what may be called a provincial modernism, a kind of internal primitivism. This is a variant of holistic modernism which configures nature and landscape, alongside art, as modernity's other. In an enthusiastic review of a regional novel, *Jörn Uhl* by Gustav Frenssen (1901), Rilke praises the aesthetic values associated with 'Heimat', regionalism and chthonic modernism, completely ignoring the novel's sinister politics, in which a veteran of the Franco-Prussian war of 1870–1 returns home to the Northern German border with Denmark to cultivate his family's farmland and help defend his community against Danish invaders (KA IV, 269–72). In writing about the Worpswede artists and their portrayals of rural life, Rilke suggests that this kind of 'Heimat' art registers a fundamental loss of connection with nature, due to urbanisation, industrialisation and instrumental rationality. The true artist's proximity to, and affinity with nature is presented as a better way of communing with truth and spiritual meaning. Sometimes, Rilke's discourse reads like an ecological parable, as when nature is imagined ultimately to revolt against humankind's attempt to dominate and exploit, and as a result destroy human civilisation (KA IV, 307–9). But Rilke is less interested in ecology than he is in aesthetics. Nature is a realm of dormant powers and sacred knowledge which defy human reason, and an art based on rural nature could potentially resist the totalising logic of modernity. Rilke's chthonic modernism would later be reworked in the geocentric turn of the *Duino Elegies*.

In turning towards 'life' as a mode of resistance to devitalising modernity, Rilke was profoundly affected by Friedrich Nietzsche, whose writings became a pervasive and powerful influence on so many German-speaking modernists. For Rilke, Nietzsche's famous dictum that 'the world is justified only as an aesthetic phenomenon' proved a cornerstone of his aestheticist outlook. But perhaps more importantly for Rilke, Nietzsche's call involves a revaluation of the concepts of 'life' and 'form'. Some of Rilke's early fiction, such as 'The Apostle', features male protagonists who have renounced rationality to embrace earthy, chthonic life, rather like a Nietzschean 'superman', though Rilke does offer some irony to distance himself from his protagonists. His main concern was how chthonic 'life' could be shaped in and by aesthetic 'form'. Hence, *The Book of Hours* modifies a key idea from Nietzsche's *Thus Spake Zarathustra* so that the possibility of a God is dependent on the poetic subject, for example in the poem 'See, God, another comes to build on you' (KA I, 169). Moreover, the poem echoes Nietzsche's critique of historicism and his call for a radical break with the overly rationalised culture of modernity to embrace the powers of the 'unhistorical'. Overall, though, the emphasis of *The Book of Hours* on asceticism and solitude seems to hold such powers in check.

An interesting instance of how Rilke's aestheticism is modulated by a Nietzschean vitalism can be found in his notes on Nietzsche's *The Birth of Tragedy*, which were probably written in March 1900 (KA IV, 161–72). Discussing the well-known concepts of the Apollonian and the Dionysiac, Rilke accepts Nietzsche's view that the two principles needed to operate in tandem:

Because we are not in a position to bear force not directly applied (i.e. God himself), we make relations between it and individual images, destinies and figures and continually put in its path new things to form comparisons with it.                                                    (KA IV, 161)

In other words, for Rilke, in order to represent 'life', the artist must channel the overpowering force of Dionysiac earthiness (which he equates with God) into the beauty and clarity of 'Apollonian' form. In paraphrasing Nietzsche, however, Rilke uses a phrase from the Symbolist aesthetic when he suggests an art of 'relations' ('Beziehungen') and an idea of 'form' which is fluid, rather than static, organic rather than artificial.

Another influential figure who helped Rilke arrive at such a view was the sociologist and cultural critic Georg Simmel (1858–1918), whose lectures Rilke attended whilst he was living in Berlin. Simmel offered an account of modernity in which the concept of 'life' becomes central. 'Life' serves to unite perceptions of reality polarised between abstract reification and indifferent *anomie* with metaphysical and aesthetic values. Simmel regarded the modernist art movements from Naturalism to Expressionism as manifestations of an energising *élan vital*, whose spontaneous articulations could help break up the increasingly static and constricting forms of modern social life. Two poems from the *Book of Images* conjoin aestheticism and vitalism to imagine a unity of self and other, poetic form and formless life. The first stanza of 'At the Edge of the Night' (KA 1, 283) reads:

My room and this expanse
wakeful over the night-time land –
is one thing. I am a string,
stretched taut over broad
whirring resonances.

And the poem 'Progress' (KA 1, 284) begins

And once more my deep life rushes louder,
as if now it were channelled between broader banks.
Things are becoming ever more closely related to me
and every image is more looked at.

Using the standard vitalist imagery of music and water, the poems imagine a liquid self as part of an abundant *élan vital*, and a liquefying, yet form-conscious art which inherently resists the devitalising effects of social modernity.

## Metropolitan modernism

The aesthetic and existential shock of living in Paris, which Rilke experienced during several extended stays there 1902 and 1910, is routinely cited as the reason for Rilke's breakthrough to modernism, as properly defined by its

origin in and relation to the metropolis. But although the work in this middle
period represents a radical departure in aesthetic terms, it can also be read
as a reconfiguration of Rilke's earlier holistic ambitions. His work confronts
urban modernity, but is still driven by the desire to give the 'Dinge', or
things, of that modernity a new aesthetic form. His confrontation with the
visual arts of Rodin and later Cézanne fuels this desire.

The metropolis is the most important topos in modernist writing and also
one which embodies social modernity. But in modernism in general, and in
Rilke's in particular, the relationship between literature and modernity is
rarely straightforward. The augmented new edition of his *Book of Images*
(1906) includes 'Voices', a cycle of poems which gives voice to people living
on the margins of society. Although the themes of 'poverty' and 'blindness'
appear to be continuous with *The Book of Hours*, these poems largely
refrain from poeticising life on the social margins. They suggest instead an
affinity between the poet and those who have been deformed and deranged
by the demands of urban life. Such an affinity is particularly prominent in
those poems that deal with madness, some of which are dialogic. In rejecting
individuality as defined by bourgeois society, Rilke suggests an overcoming
of aestheticist self-absorption and arriving at some form of intersubjectivity.
Rilke's interest in social outsiders at this stage anticipates a key concern in
Expressionist poetry.

The *New Poems* radicalise this aesthetic. There is a renewed emphasis on
'Dinge', and their internal life or living form. Being non-mimetic, the poem
brings the silent object to life (in the vitalist sense). The poems collected here
are often characterised as 'Dinggedichte' – literally 'thing poems' or 'object
poems' – but the term can be misleading in its emphasis on the object.
Rilke's concern is not to remove the object from an anthropomorphic gaze
and subjective interpretation altogether. Instead, the *New Poems* present a
range of encounters between subject and object, interior and exterior, man
and animal, beholder and work of art, during which the boundaries of either
party are being called into question. Highly self-reflexive, many of the poems
refer to artistic perception and creation.

But again, Rilke's aesthetic concern is linked to the modern condition of
alienation, as this passage from a letter to his wife Clara Westhoff-Rilke
written on 8 March 1907 suggests:

> Gazing is such a wonderful thing, and one we know so little about. In gazing
> we are completely turned outwards, but at the very moment when we are
> most outward-turned things appear to happen within us that have waited
> longingly until they are unobserved, and whilst these things happen within
> us, without us, perfectly and strangely anonymously – their significance grows

in the object outside, a convincing, strong name, their only possible name, in which we blissfully and reverently recognise what is happening within us without ourselves reaching out for it, comprehending it only very gently, from some distance, under the sign of a thing that just now was alien to us and in the next moment will be alienated again. (B 1, 247)

Crucial to an understanding of Rilke's aesthetics at this period, the passage suggests that poetry is an impersonal, quasi-mystical process by which the conventional relationship between subject and object is inverted. At the same time, however, the statement reflects a typically modernist malaise, when it describes the distance between a rational subject and a world of the object alienated from it. Rilke uses the term 'entfremdet', alienated, not in a Marxian but in a vitalist sense. He gestures towards a dialectics of seeing, but privileges the aesthetic dimension over the material and historical ones. The spatial dialectic between closeness and distance, as in Walter Benjamin, has much to do with the problematic status of art's autonomy in modernity.

'The Panther', written in 1902/3, suggests the withering of an original, exotic vitality under the conditions of Western modernity. Caught and put on display as the object of a zoological gaze, the panther is split between the Dionysiac force still visible in its legs, and the tired gaze which it casts at those outside the cage. But the animal's gaze disrupts the logic of the objectifying human gaze, in a way that is similar to the blind and marginalised people Rilke depicts elsewhere. It is such deficiencies of human 'Anschauen', or gazing, that the New Poems bring up time and again, most famously in 'Archaic Torso of Apollo', which ends 'for there is no place there / that cannot see you. You must change your life' (KA 1, 513). Other poems, such as 'The Carousel' and 'The Ball', allude to the role of the unconscious and memory which help transform the moving object in question, and suggest a destabilising of the self which constitutes itself vis-à-vis the object only to become temporally and spatially displaced by it. Such a notion of displaced subjectivity is even more pronounced in the second part of the New Poems, where we also find poems which subvert the classical ideal of beauty and harmony, and again are concerned with the urban underclass, with depravity and morbidity, and – particularly significant in the context of classical aesthetics – the ugliness of a city like Rome seen from the countryside. Although urban modernity is not consistently represented in the New Poems, it has been identified as the subtext that Rilke works through, as their repressed Other. The poems' formal perfection conceals their disturbing deconstruction of subjectivity, and this concealment may be an indication of just how violent Rilke's response to urban modernity must have been.

In stark contrast, *The Notebooks of Malte Laurids Brigge* conceal much less of their confrontation with urban modernity. Rilke's only extended work of fiction, it is routinely described as the first modernist novel in German and ranks among Rilke's lasting contributions to modernism. Written between 1904 and 1910, the *Notebooks* consist of jottings by a first-person narrator, who lives an isolated life as a young Danish poet in modern Paris. Instead of the kind of chronological or linear narrative one would expect in a realist novel, the text eschews plot and development and the very fact that we have notes suggests disunity and fragmentation of form.

The *Notebooks* are modernist in three main ways. First, embedded in Malte's notes is a severe critique of urban modernity, as represented by its poverty, ugliness and depravation. Second, in response to his shock experiences, Malte resolves to 'learn to see' and describe his surroundings in a new way; and third, this new way of seeing leads to a radical deconstruction of the notion of the subject. The three ways indicate also how a response to modernity becomes an attempt to resolve the artistic problems associated with that response.[7]

Much of Rilke's Parisian detail focuses on the downside of modern life, suggesting a modernity which has begun to turn against itself. Malte's notes register modernity in terms of industrialisation and technology, but only in ironic reversals, such as when the Salpêtrière – a psychiatric hospital – is described as a place where dying is figured as a dehumanised industrial process, prompting Malte's ironic tribute to the factory-type output thus achieved (KA III, 496), or when the logic of monetary capitalism is applied to the deluded scheme of a Russian emigré to set up a 'timebank' in order to escape death (KA III, 575). The living and organic world becomes associated with dying; order becomes disorder; reason, madness; noise, silence; and individuality becomes translated into a faceless, anonymous mass. Ironically, it is a pair of masks which seem to hold the possibility of an alternative, more authentic existence within modernity. On passing the 'mouleur' (modeller) every day, Malte glimpses two masks: one is of a young woman who drowned (or drowned herself), and whose face, in death, is described as beautiful because of its smile; and the other is the mask of a male artist, whose face displays the knowledge of an art independent of visuality. That artist is easily identifiable as Beethoven. Such reversals – a key strategy that Malte uses to cope with the city – suggest how profoundly disturbed conventional views of reality have become.

Although deeply shocked by what he encounters, Malte learns to see, and the new kind of seeing involves uncovering the hidden structures within the visible world. The novel gestures towards an aesthetic vision of reality, in which the classical ideal of beauty has been reversed to become an 'aesthetic of ugliness'.[8] This kind of negative aesthetic is necessarily partial, since it registers modernity only to the extent that it pervades and meshes with Malte's gaze and his other senses. There are numerous analogies between the modes of perception in the *Notebooks* and Simmel's account in his seminal essay 'The Metropolis and Modern Mental Life' (1903), which charts the atomisation of urban experience, whereby rapid and incongruous visual impressions overwhelm the individual gaze. But whereas Simmel diagnosed the blasé, intellectual attitude adopted by so many city-dwellers as a defence mechanism to protect them from becoming wholly disintegrated, Rilke's *Malte* explores those kinds of disintegration and continually experiments with concepts of the 'self'.

*Malte* is one of the most radical deconstructions of the notion of self we find in modernist writing. Exiled in Paris, affected by the irrationality of modern Paris and unable to articulate a stable sense of self there, Malte uncovers the fragmentary nature of, and indeed psychic splits within, his own personality.[9] In a proto-Kafkaesque image, Malte likens himself to a beetle that is being trampled on so that its hardened shell – also Simmel's metaphor for having adapted to urban life – becomes useless. In the middle and final parts of the novel, Malte explores memory and imagination in order to immunise himself against the dispersal and fragmentation of his self in the city. A long series of notes is concerned with flashbacks to his aristocratic Danish childhood and what was formerly a seemingly stable identity. However, Malte's memory is increasingly fused with imagination and desire, and the references to people and events, whether experienced at the family home or gleaned from books, serve to undermine any sense of continuity of self. Malte finally draws on biblical myths, inverts the story of the prodigal son, and develops a curious idea of intransitive love as embodied by his younger sister Abelone. Sometimes read as private allegories of Rilke's artistic ideals, these myths also point to the profound disturbance in Malte's own sexual and family history.

Like much modernist narrative, the *Notebooks* gravitate into subjective consciousness, in which the conventional modalities of time and space are suspended. For Walter Benjamin, who attempted to locate the origins of modernism in nineteenth-century Paris, the experience of shock has become the norm in the metropolis, and Malte is no exception. The shock impacts on the very form of the notebooks, and Malte's attempts to deploy the inherited genres of memoir and parable only serve to emphasise the impossibility of coherent narrative. Some critics have suggested an affinity between the notes and the prose poem; and it was Baudelaire who identified that indeterminate genre as 'a child of the great cities, of the intersecting of their myriad relations'.[10] It is indeed Baudelaire who serves as a reference point in Rilke's novel. At one point, Malte quotes Baudelaire's poem 'A Carcass' ('Une Charogne'), which depicts the decaying cadaver of an animal and exhorts the poet to remember the rotting body. For Baudelaire, poetry's function was ultimately to sublimate what is repugnant by portraying it as part of kaleidoscopic modernity. Malte, however, remembering Baudelaire's poem, is unable to conjure any idea of beauty or art.

This failure points to an important difference between Baudelaire's and Rilke's modernism and between their views of the relationship between art and modernity. Baudelaire argued that modernity had fissured the aesthetic idea of 'beauty' into an eternal, timeless and a relative, time-bound element, which directly tracks the fleeting nature of modernity. By contrast, Rilke embraces the horrific and repugnant underbelly of the metropolis to construct this embrace as an appropriately new modernist aesthetic. In a letter to his wife Clara Westhoff-Rilke of 19 October 1907, he offers the following genealogy of modernist aesthetics:

> I was compelled to think about how, without this poem ['A Carcass'], the entire development towards objective 'telling' that we now think we can discern in Cézanne would not have been able to get off the ground. [ . . . ] For that to happen, artistic 'gazing' had to surmount itself to such an extent that it could perceive the core of existence even in what is horrible and apparently repulsive, things that are just as *valid* as everything else that exists. Just as no selection is valid, neither is it permitted to turn away from any form of existence.
>
> (B I, 279–80)[11]

According to Dorothea Lauterbach, Rilke's ideal of 'objective telling' involves more than a neutral statement about a concrete visual perception; it purifies seeing from all traces of subjectivity and thus enables the object to develop the most appropriate 'form' in which it may be depicted.[12] Rilke emphasises art's ability to confront the whole range of 'existences' of modern life – demonstrating the continued significance of the vitalist emphasis on the *élan vital*, 'Leben' itself. But in Malte's notebooks we plainly have a 'selection' that speaks loudly of the deformation of life – such are the fissures between aesthetic agenda and the text in Rilke's metropolitan modernism.

The letter's reference to Cézanne points to the role played by the visual arts in this phase. Rilke's interest in Rodin, van Gogh and then Cézanne, on whom he wrote extensively during 1902 and 1907, is primarily aesthetic. These artists interest him because they emphasise that the artistic process involves patience, contemplation and simplicity; that it requires the artist to ignore his or her subjectivity; and that it foregrounds the formal autonomy of the work of art. Rilke's discourse on these artists, however, grapples with modernity. Like their Worpswede counterparts, the French artists register loss of and alienation from nature, but in their attempt to confront 'life' in all its manifestations, they articulate universal artistic laws. The shift from representation (in the holistic phase) to underlying patterns of representation is akin to Rilke's new view of urban reality in *Malte*. But it seems that for Rilke, such underlying patterns, such a kind of 'objective telling' were meant to ensure the viability of a modernist tradition with which to confront modernity. As far as the visual arts are concerned, Rilke was ambivalent about abstraction and the violent rejection of tradition that accompanies it. The artists of Picasso's *The Acrobats* (*Les Saltimbanques*, 1905) figure in the fifth *Duino Elegy* as allegories of artistic and metaphysical homelessness. But the step towards abstraction that Picasso took shortly after in *The Young Ladies of Avignon* (*Les Demoiselles d'Avignon*, 1906), with its assault on classical mono-perspectivism and its representational violence, and subsequent developments in non-representational art indicated for Rilke the demise of the 'Dinge' and society's trend towards abstract functionalism. It was in his last phase that he reshaped his work to respond to those issues.

## Mythic modernism

In the *Duino Elegies*, *The Sonnets to Orpheus* and the uncollected late poems, Rilke's modernism takes a mythic turn. Once again, as mythical themes and figures have been a feature in the earlier work too, this phase can be seen as a reshaping of his earlier concerns. Written during a period of severe doubts about the legitimacy of poetry, and the adequacy of language, his poetry is still charged with the task to give form to a formless and disintegrating world. Rilke's mythic modernism remains preoccupied with the subtext of social and political modernity, which was then taking a catastrophic turn in the guise of mechanised industrial-scale warfare. In August 1914, Rilke wrote the ill-judged 'Five Songs', in which he, like so many writers and intellectuals in Europe, welcomed the war as a Dionysiac release of vitality and hailed the advent of the mythical war-god. Having been drafted into brief military service, he then witnessed the violent political upheavals in Central and Eastern Europe in 1917–19.

Within the context of literary modernism, Rilke's mythical turn is not unique. Especially after World War I, many modernists returned to some sense of order and their view intensified that the ultimate values of art, its intensity, its difference, needed to be vigorously defended against civilisation. Mythic modernism imagines a time-space that is both within and outside modernity. The mythic time-space responds to the time-space compression effected by modernity, and imagines an alternative time-space in which authentic experience and/or knowledge is located. To this end, Rilke's poetry literally performs a turn; as the poem 'Turning-Point' (KA II, 100–2) has it, a turn inwards – a transformation of the exterior into an interior landscape. 'Space' and 'inner space' become important tropes. As a result, the gazing and observing that were so crucial to *Malte* and the *New Poems* are newly configured. In a letter to Ellen Delp Rilke describes the Spanish landscape near Toledo: 'Appearance and vision everywhere come together in the object, in each one a whole interior world had emerged, as if an angel that was embracing the space were blind and looking inward.'[13] This is a curious, almost paradoxical version of the former dialectic of inner and outer, subject and object. On the one hand, seeing has been expanded to include an angelic perspective; on the other, it is inverted and blinded; and both moves seem for Rilke still to guarantee an experience of wholeness. The most famous of the mythic creatures is the angel of the *Duino Elegies*, who becomes a trope for viewing the human world from an extra-human perspective.

Another element of Rilke's mythic modernism also reworks earlier concerns. Creaturely life becomes an important trope for Rilke's confrontation with modernity.[14] Unlike in the *New Poems*, Rilke's creatures now inhabit a seemingly pastoral world, which allows the poet to comment indirectly on the deficiencies of the human world. The third poem of 'Spanish Trilogy' describes the internal split between frenetic urban modernity on the one hand, and the memory of a pastoral landscape (KA II, 44). Metaphysical homelessness is the norm, and as in *Malte*, it is through memory that the urbanised self imagines the city's other as a pastoral landscape with reassuring reference to home. In the first *Duino Elegy*, 'the resourceful animals have already noticed / that we are not reliably at home / in the interpreted world' (KA II, 201). Because human interpretation involves categorising and ordering the world, its primary effect is one of 'entzwein', 'dividing' or 'separating', the imposing of differences between self and other, man and nature. Another *Elegy* charts what may be considered an allegorical history of human consciousness, which is blinded by instrumental rationality, incomplete and ill-equipped to experience other time-spaces.

The mythic poems then suggest a world in which human beings, with all their reason and knowledge, are no longer in control. 'Exposed on the mountains of the heart' (KA II, 115–16) begins a famous poem, written in September 1914, which depicts humanity as exposed into a bleak landscape beyond the familiar parameters of reason, knowledge and language. The poem maps a critical situation in which a fragile and doubtful self is allowed a glimpse of the 'last locality of words' ('letzte Ortschaft der Worte') below and the 'final farmstead of feeling' ('letztes Gehöft von Gefühl') way above, in the unprotected realm of the unsayable. Alerting us to other forms of consciousness and knowledge, Rilke's mythic modernism becomes another way of speaking about modernity.

Many poems, although frequently moving beyond an easily definable reality, are still preoccupied with our knowledge of 'things'. The ninth of the *Duino Elegies* registers a withering of 'Dinge':

> More than ever
> things are slipping away, the things we can experience, since
> what is supplanting and replacing them is action without image.
>
> (KA II, 228)

Full and immediate experience is prevented by the reproducibility of things, and life has become formless activism. This is a process that Rilke suggests is akin to the psychoanalytic process of repression. The final elegy expands on these ideas in its portrayal of a global 'Leid-Stadt' or 'city of suffering', in which Rilke uses sexual metaphors to describe the capitalist circulation of goods and accumulation of money.

The lasting achievement, however, of Rilke's complex and challenging late poetry is that it does not repress modernity altogether, but turns the poet's lament about modern alienation and suffering into affirmative praise of those things that might help reorientate human experience towards oneness. For all their relative outspokenness about the evils of modernity, the late elegies frequently invoke 'earth', a topographical signifier in opposition to transcendence. In this geocentric turn, Rilke's poetry and aesthetics celebrate chthonic life, but under a different perspective than in his brief embrace of regional art around 1900. Against the false allure of pure transcendence, which is fundamentally unsayable and remains the preserve of the angel or Orpheus, they turn towards 'Hiersein' (being here), and as a result, the tone is no longer elegiac but becomes hymnic.[15] The emphasis, if hesitant, is on language:

> Are we perhaps *here* in order to say: House,
> Bridge, Well, Gate, Jug, Fruit Tree, Window, –
> at most: Column, Tower.     (KA II, 228)

Rilke's mythic poetry involves a return to saying the seemingly simple, elementary things associated with human life. But the listed items are connected in complex ways and even gesture towards transformation: a house signifies the centre of human existence and the mode of being at home; a bridge connects land and water horizontally, while a well links them vertically. A fruit tree links soil and air. A jug, made of clay or porcelain, links earth and water and contains the water necessary for the renewal of life. Gate and window suggest connections between interior and exterior, home and world, and column and tower suggest human culture as a form of desire to communicate with what is above.[16]

But even a myth-making poet such as Rilke, who placed poetry in an alternative time-space, recognised that modernist writing is of its culture and history. In an often-cited letter to his Polish translator Witold Hulewicz (13 November 1925), he wrote:

> For our grandparents a 'house', a 'well', a familiar tower, even their own clothing, a coat was still infinitely more, infinitely more intimate, and almost every object was a vessel in which they found humanity already present and to which they added a store of humanity. Nowadays empty, incurious things are forcing their way across from America, fake things, *substitute lives* [...]. A house, in the way it is understood in America, an American apple or a vine from over there has nothing in common with the house, the fruit, the grape into which the hopes and reflectiveness of our forefathers had made their way. [...] The vitalised, directly experienced things that *share knowledge with us* are in decline and cannot be replaced any more. *We are perhaps the last ones to have known such things.* (B II, 376–7)

Far from rejecting modernity, mythic modernism stresses its categorical difference to a dehumanising modernity that Rilke (along with many conservative writers and intellectuals in the 1920s) identifies with capitalist 'America'. Mythic modernism questions the alienation produced by modernity and cultivates lateness as a differential form of knowledge. Rilke persists in the idea that poetic language embraces difficult, experimental forms, not just to revitalise perception, as in the earlier phases, but now to disrupt modern myths such as the ones provided by global capitalism. To this end, Rilke defines poetry in a paradoxical way:

> The earth has no escape other than to become invisible: only within us can this intimate and lasting transformation of the visible into the invisible, into a state where we are no longer dependent on being visible and tangible, take place. (B II, 377)

The production of poetry (derived from *poiesis*, making) transforms the visible into the invisible, a purely linguistic entity: poetry transcends the experiential world. It retreats into a mythic time-space that involves a denial of vision, the interiorising and making invisible of chthonic life and the world of 'Dinge' to salvage them from the kinds of alienation produced by contemporary capitalism.

As this overview has suggested, Rilke's modernism is shifting and complex, and it situates itself in opposition to modernity. But Rilke's opposition to many of the social and cultural forms of modernity is active, not reactive or defensive, and the twin imperatives of 'learn to see' and 'transcribe the world into language' are key factors in shaping the various modernisms we find in his literary work.[17] But throughout his work, we find a fundamental tension. Rilke was fascinated by the energy and discontinuity of social change that could be observed in the metropolis, and by new thought and ideas. At the same time, he recoiled from what he perceived as the disorientation of metaphysical and artistic values, and developed an increasingly mythic concept of poetry and aesthetics to shore against the modern world. An active antagonist of modernity, he meant his poetry to offer the fullest account of human consciousness under the impact of modernity. Many of his poems work through this specifically modernist tension, often teasing out the dynamics of subject and object, deploying differential time-spaces and insisting on visual-cognitive movement and positionality (the way of arriving at a position, rather than having it), with the cumulative effect of opening up language and experience to the limits of expression.

Largely on account of his late work, Rilke has long been seen as a poet of 'Being' (in the Heideggerian, existentialist sense). Against that, recent studies have revealed the complex aesthetic, cognitive and epistemological issues his work raises. The very high value Rilke persistently placed on art and poetry, however, suggests how unwilling he was to reflect on art's institutionalised position within modern culture and the social conditions that place literature and art in that position. Rilke's modernism does gesture, intermittently, towards an art that is no longer autonomous and self-contained, but at the same time, it is also vulnerable to the typically modernist belief that cultural transformation can be brought about by formal innovations and revolutionary aesthetics alone.

To some, this places Rilke at a great distance from our contemporary situation. Whether or not he can indeed become a spiritual 'Führer' (leader or guide) into a world beyond modernity as Robert Musil was the first of many to suggest;[18] whether he represents a bridge between modernism and post-modernism; or whether he simply offers a progressive, non-reactionary critique of modernity – as well as betraying many of our own cultural and spiritual dilemmas and needs – such views of Rilke suggest the enduringly complex and contradictory ways in which his work is situated in a modernist culture whose issues refuse to be consigned to history.

## NOTES

1  Walter Benjamin, 'The Work of Art in the Age of its Technological Reproducibility' and 'The Storyteller' (both 1936), in *Selected Writings*, III, ed. Howard Eiland and Michael W. Jennings (Cambridge, MA, and London: The Belknap Press of Harvard University Press, 2002), pp. 99–133 and 143–66.

2  David Bathrick and Andreas Huyssen, 'Modernism and the Experience of Modernity', in Bathrick and Huyssen (eds.), *Modernity and the Text: Revisions of German Modernism* (New York: Columbia University Press, 1989), p. 7.

3  Fredric Jameson, *The Political Unconscious: Narrative as Socially Symbolic Art* (Ithaca: Cornell University Press, 1981), p. 42.

4  Stéphane Mallarmé, *Selected Prose, Poems, Essays and Letters*, trans. Bradford Cook (Baltimore: Johns Hopkins University Press, 1956), pp. 48–9; cited in Peter Nicholls, *Modernisms: A Literary Guide* (Basingstoke and London: Macmillan, 1995), p. 40.

5  Dorothea Lauterbach, 'Frankreich', in *RHB*, p. 177.

6  This emphasis was most likely a result of Rilke's Russian journey and his confrontation with Russian art (see *RHB*, pp. 106–7).

7  For useful overviews, see Dorothea Lauterbach, '*Die Aufzeichnungen des Malte Laurids Brigge*', in *RHB*, pp. 318–36, and George C. Schoolfield, '*Die Aufzeichnungen des Malte Laurids Brigge*', in Erika A. Metzger and Michael M. Metzger (eds.), *A Companion to the Works of Rainer Maria Rilke* (Rochester, NY: Camden House, 2001), pp. 154–87.

8  Angelika Corbineau-Hoffmann, *Kleine Literaturgeschichte der Großstadt* (Darmstadt: Wissenschaftliche Buchgesellschaft, 2003), p. 91.

9  For a psychoanalytic reading of these issues, see Andreas Huyssen, 'Paris / Childhood: The Fragmented Body in Rilke's *Notebooks of Malte Laurids Brigge*', in *Modernity and the Text*, pp. 113–41.

10  Cited in Walter Benjamin, 'On Some Motifs in Baudelaire', in *Illuminations*, trans. Harry Zohn (London: Fontana, 1992), p. 167.

11  For a summary of Rilke's reading of Baudelaire, see Lauterbach, *RHB*, pp. 76–9.

12  *RHB*, p. 78

13  Letter of 27 October 1915 in Rainer Maria Rilke, *Briefwechsel mit Regina Ullmann und Ellen Delp*, ed. Walter Simon (Frankfurt am Main: Insel, 1987), p. 90.

14  Eric L. Santner, *On Creaturely Life: Rilke, Benjamin, Sebald* (University of Chicago Press, 2006).

15  In her reading of the *Elegies*, Kathleen L. Komar pinpoints this geocentric turn to indicate Rilke's continued modernity and allure to today's readers. See her essay 'Rethinking Rilke's *Duino Elegien* at the End of the Millennium', in Metzger (eds.), *A Companion to the Works of Rainer Maria Rilke*, pp. 188–208.

16  Helmuth Kiesel, *Geschichte der literarischen Moderne: Sprache, Ästhetik, Dichtung im zwanzigsten Jahrhundert* (Munich: C. H. Beck, 2004), p. 221.

17  Manfred Engel, 'Rilke als literarischer Autor der Moderne', in *RHB*, pp. 507–28, especially pp. 509–13.

18  Robert Musil, 'Rede zur Rilke-Feier in Berlin am 16. Januar 1927', in Musil, *Gesammelte Werke*, ed. Adolf Frisé, 9 vols. (Reinbek: Rowohlt Taschenbuch, 1978), vol. VIII, p. 1240.

# 9

ROBERT VILAIN

# Rilke the reader

When considering Rilke's reception of the various literatures, ancient and modern, that were so familiar to him, we should expect a process of thoroughgoing assimilation and interiorisation rather than one of borrowing and imitation. A poem from *The Book of Images*, 'The Man Reading', shows how for Rilke the process of reading opens out the self, dissolving both the antitheses and contradictions of the external world and those between inner and outer life such that 'there outside' matches 'what I am living within' ('Dort draußen ist, was ich hier drinnen lebe', KA 1, 332). The incommensurability of existence ceases to be disconcerting to the individual experiencing it, who mysteriously feels more interwoven with it than ever. The act of reading is an act of self-discovery rather than a process of collecting data about someone, something or somewhere else.

The next poem in the collection is called 'The Man Looking', clearly intended to function as a partner to 'The Man Reading'. Both open with an evocation of tempestuous weather, the storm in the second 'a transformer' ('ein Umgestalter') rendering the natural world it touches ageless, the landscape 'like a verse in the Psalter', likening the visual to the verbal. Reading and seeing were not as distinct for Rilke as might be expected. He will have been more than aware of the dual aspect of the word 'Bild' – as in the title of the collection, *Buch der Bilder* – which can be translated as 'picture' or 'image', the former anchored in the visual world, the latter also used of verbal constructs. The figure in a poem entitled 'The Reader' in *New Poems* is also described in terms of 'seeing', his face lowered 'from Being into a second Being', a mere shadow of the figure familiar to others, unrecognisable even by his mother,

> lifting upon himself everything
> that was going on in the book below
> with eyes that, far from taking, givingly
> touched against the full and finished world.

alles auf sich hebend,
was unten in dem Buche sich verhielt,
mit Augen, welche statt zu nehmen, gebend
anstießen an die fertig-volle Welt.

(KA I, 581)

Rilke reminds us that reading is on one level an act performed with the eyes. A famous letter to Clara Rilke written during the composition of the *New Poems* describes the processes of *seeing* in a manner that overlaps strikingly with the account of *reading* that these two poems present:

> Gazing is such a wonderful thing, and one we know so little about. In gazing we are completely turned outwards, but at the very moment when we are most outward-turned things appear to happen within us that have waited longingly until they are unobserved, and whilst these things happen within us, without us, perfectly and strangely anonymously – their significance grows in the object outside, a convincing, strong name, their only possible name, in which we blissfully and reverently recognise what is happening within us.

Common to both processes is the fact that the reader or observer is not reflecting directly upon himself; and yet the self is nonetheless illuminated, informed and changed by the objects, persons or places observed. In very few instances are Rilke's experiences of reading the literary products of the various cultures he was interested in *not* linked in some way to the images he encounters of the landscapes, monuments and artefacts of the countries that nurtured them.

The exception, ironically, is his native literature, writing in German.[1] Rüdiger Görner aptly characterises the early Rilke's reading in German as 'essentially directionless' (*RHB*, p. 50), although there is, as he suggests, a crucial positive dimension to such a deliberately unprogrammatic approach, namely a very low risk of becoming derivative. In letters of 26 February and 17 August 1924 to the academics Alfred Schaer and Hermann Pongs, Rilke responded to requests for information about his earliest influences, recalling the support he had been shown by Detlev von Liliencron and musing on how the older poet's work must also have been important to him: he and the Danish writer Jens Peter Jacobsen are cited as the ones who had shown him 'in [his] immaturity and blinkeredness [ . . . ] how it was possible to use the thing that is closest and always with us to make the leap into the furthest distance' (B II, 340). At Jakob Wassermann's suggestion, he read Jacobsen's *Niels Lyhne* and his novellas in a popular translation by Maria von Borch. Richard Dehmel was 'hard and important'; Hofmannsthal was appreciated as 'the most unconditional of poets'; George's principle that 'words are magic' was an irresistible lesson (B II, 327); lesser poets such as Wilhelm von

Scholz and Emanuel von Bodmann served temporarily as models. Rilke sent his first collection, *Offerings to the Lares*, somewhat surprisingly perhaps, to Theodor Fontane, which suggests he may have known his poetry as well as the novels, and he also mentions Gerhart Hauptmann. However, he breaks off to say that the complex of stimuli represented by his journeys to Russia, his move to Paris and later visits abroad then renders any mere sequence of names an impossibility: individual writers give way to places and cultures. His student years, too, were important for his cultural grounding – he seems to have attended lectures on medieval German lyric in Berlin in 1905, and certainly knew Walther von der Vogelweide well enough for Samuel Fischer's publishing house to ask him to edit a volume of his verse in May 1901. He turned down the request, feeling 'too far away from him in my tone and the way I listen to love him justly', but recommended Otto Julius Bierbaum as editor instead because of his 'most intimate relationship' with the medieval poet (B I, 83).

Rilke was often sent large packages of books by friends and publishers, sometimes at his request, but also evidently unsolicited, too, which may account for the eclectic range of works he sometimes lists in his letters. He read individual texts in isolation and embarked on systematic attempts to cover the whole oeuvre only of important figures. Reading the whole of Kleist for the first time in Paris in 1913, for example, he was struck by the storminess of Kleist's life and works and was pleased that he had not been able to read him when younger because he would not have been ready (B I, 487 and 483–4). Equally, Kleist's essay 'On the Puppet Theatre' ('Über das Marionettentheater', 1810) directly influenced sections of the fourth *Elegy* – Rilke's creative responses to this reading are traceable, then, even if they are sometimes modest or even vestigial. But in contrast, it is not easy to reconcile Rilke's feverish activity in early 1922 – the composition of all *The Sonnets to Orpheus* – with a request to Kurt Wolff to set aside for him 'everything that appears by Franz Kafka', whose novel *The Castle* (*Das Schloß*) he regarded as 'one of the most important German books of our age' (B II, 221; *RHB*, p. 56).

There is a more consistently identifiable pattern to Rilke's reading of Goethe, who was naturally an important stimulus. Rilke had read *Faust* at school and the major novels as well as the autobiography *Poetry and Truth* (*Dichtung und Wahrheit*) in his late teens. There is some evidence that Goethe (amongst others) influenced Rilke's early collection *Lives and Songs* (1894). A further intensive period of concentration on his great predecessor seems to have been initiated by his friend and publisher at Insel, Anton Kippenberg, and his wife Katharina, from about 1908 onwards. His not entirely positive reception of the 'self-conscious' and, in love, overly 'conventional' Goethe is reflected in *The Notebooks of Malte Laurids Brigge* where Malte takes Bettina von Arnim's part against the 'greatest poet', seeing his lack of warmth towards her, his 'sad, embarrassed responses' to her inspirational passion as marking 'the boundaries of his greatness'.[2]

In 1904 Rilke confessed to Tora Holmström, 'I lack the appropriate organ to be able to derive much from Goethe' (B II, 201) and it took him several more years, the reading in July 1911 of another of Goethe's correspondences with a young woman (the 'Gustgen letters' to Augusta Louise zu Stolberg-Stolberg), and the 'annunciation, revelation' of a visit to Weimar with the Kippenbergs in August 1911,[3] to come to appreciate the poetic advantages of Goethe's more restrained and measured stance. However, by the time he came to start the *Duino Elegies* his reading of poetry including the *West-Eastern Divan* (*West-östliche Divan*), 'Harz Journey in Winter' ('Harzreise im Winter') and the 'Metamorphosis of the Plants' ('Metamorphose der Pflanzen') had aroused profound admiration. The presence of Goethe's 'The Diary' ('Das Tagebuch') has been detected in 'Seven Poems' ('Sieben Gedichte' – otherwise known as the 'Phallic Hymns'), and his reading of 'Euphrosyne' perhaps served to remind him of the power of the dactylic rhythms of the elegiac tradition that was to be of such metrical importance for the *Elegies*.

At about the same time Rilke also renewed his acquaintance with the works of Klopstock, who led the German literary revival of the late eighteenth century. Klopstock's elegy 'The Future Beloved' ('Die künftige Geliebte'), and the hymnic style of the Odes undoubtedly influenced Rilke's *Duino Elegies* as well. There are specific echoes of Klopstock (as well as Novalis and Hölderlin) in the poem 'Pearls roll away' (KA II, 38).[4] The *Elegies* also bear signs of a reading of Hölderlin, his linguistic and rhythmic virtuosity in particular, which Rilke came to value between 1912 and 1914 via his friend Norbert von Hellingrath. Hölderlin's visionary style was also a significant impetus behind the controversial 'Five Songs' that Rilke wrote in the first days of World War One – he confessed to Hellingrath on 24 July 1914, Hölderlin's 'influence on me is great and noble, as only that of the richest and those with greatest inner power can be' (B II, 542). Hölderlin meant more to Rilke than visionary fervour, however; Judith Ryan suggests convincingly that his 'powerful articulation of the function of poetry in a time of intellectual and social upheaval' and the intimate connection in his work between creativity and 'death, loss and suffering' may have supported Rilke's own attempts to set his creative power against the loss of political and cultural coherence that he perceived in the world around him.[5]

A thorough and constantly developing familiarity with literature in German from the middle ages to his own age was underpinned by a strong interest in classical antiquity, initiated by six years of classical studies at school then boosted by a reading of Nietzsche's *The Birth of Tragedy* (*Die Geburt der Tragödie*) in 1900. Reading notes suggest that Nietzsche confirmed Rilke's sense of the importance to art primarily of myth and music ('the great rhythm in the background'; KA IV, 161). At every stage of his life he was fascinated by the artefacts and artworks of classical Greece and Rome that he found in museums and archaeological sites. Some find their way into the *New Poems*, including 'Early Apollo' and the 'Archaic Torso of Apollo' that open each of the two parts, but these are joined by works that pick up motifs from literature, notably from Ovid's *Metamorphoses* ('Orpheus. Eurydice. Hermes'). Another of the *New Poems*, 'Alcestis', has specific echoes of Euripides' drama of the same name which Rilke is thought to have read in Ulrich von Wilamowitz's 1906 translation.[6] The *New Poems* also contain a sequence on the Greek poet Sappho and the connection between love and poetry (KA I, 451–2), although these are also linked to Rilke's reading of Baudelaire's *Flowers of Evil* (*Les Fleurs du mal*); Sappho stands as an example of the ideal of 'possessionless love' in *Malte* (KA III, 621–3). *The Sonnets to Orpheus* also testify to Rilke's knowledge of classical myth, of course, mediated in this case by the charismatic Alfred Schuler's lectures on the cultic religion of Orphism and its interpretation of human life as a mere blip in the greater continuum of existence that is death.[7] By this point the nature of Rilke's interest in classical antiquity has shifted, in Nietzsche's terms, from an attraction to Apolline clarity in 1906–7 to a darker, more obviously Dionysian approach in 1922.

Specific areas of Rilke's literary interest in cultures outside Germany and Austria were often awakened or at least reinvigorated by his travels. Rilke had been familiar with Russian literature since his youth – writing on 12 February 1894 to an unknown recipient, 'For how long have Tolstoy, Zola and Turgenev been as prophets to me, seeming to usher in a rapturous new age'[8] – and he had already studied aspects of Russian culture in Munich in 1896. However, Russia only became of intense importance to him in the period of his two visits there in mid-1899 and mid-1900, visits that marked a 'turn into what was truly my own self' ('Wendung ins eigentlich Eigene'; B II, 342). His appreciation of Russian literature was shaped and extended by his relationship with Lou Andreas-Salomé, the daughter of a Russian army general, born in St Petersburg, whom he met in 1897, and by the critic Akim Volynsky with whom he worked in Munich in the same year.[9]

Rilke learned Russian in preparation for his journeys there with Lou, and although never by any means fluent, was eventually able to communicate competently both orally and in writing. He produced eight original poems in (somewhat faulty) Russian and several translations of Russian literature

into German, including in 1899–1900 no less a work than Chekhov's
*The Seagull* (which he sent to the author, receiving no reply[10]), parts of
Dostoevsky's *Poor Folk* and poems by Lermontov, as well as a controver-
sial version of the twelfth-century epic *The Lay of Igor's Campaign* in 1904.
As far as his reading was concerned, he was familiar with at least selected
works by most of the great nineteenth-century writers – Pushkin, Tolstoy,
Dostoevsky, Turgenev, Gogol, Chekhov and Lermontov – as well as others
of lesser international renown, such as Aleksandr Sergeevich Griboedov,
Aleksei Koltsov, Afanasy Fet and Ivan Goncharov. A letter to Sofiia
Nikolaevna Schill of 29 August 1900 includes an extract from a list of
his books of Russian literature with several other names, too, including the
village- or peasant-poet Spiridon Drozhzhin, who was particularly important to Rilke as a 'natural focus for [his] profoundly apolitical aesthetic
search'.[11] He did not appear to have much knowledge of the so-called Silver
Age of Russian poetry, the age of Symbolism and Futurism, of Akhmatova,
Blok, Mandelstam and Pasternak – despite the fact that this was the very
period of Rilke's own flowering as a great poet.

Perhaps because of the slight sense of incoherence that attaches to these
lists of names, and because there is little evidence of a study of Russian writing *en bloc*, the importance of Slavic literature for Rilke's own development
as a poet has been understated by many critics. Rilke's experience of Russia
and its literature generated some of the issues that *The Book of Hours* deals
with – particularly in the figure of the Icon painter in the first book, 'Of
Monastic Life' – quasi-theological explorations of the nature and existence
of God and (in conjunction) the self and the relationship of the self to both
art and religion. But there are Russian themes, too, in *The Book of Images*
(linked to the Battle of Poltava, Ivan the Terrible and medieval epic) and
poems such as 'Storm' and 'Charles XII' reflect the young Rilke's idealised
impressions of the 'mythic vastness of the Russian plains'.[12] The six poems
entitled 'The Tsars' treat themes of history, heredity, inheritance and the
influence of the past (the generation of the fathers) on one's current identity
that will be developed more extensively in *Malte*, and prefigure one of the
key themes of the fifth *Duino Elegy*, that of 'Bleiben', lasting or duration.

The famous 'white nights' of St Petersburg offered Rilke a unique example
of one of the transition times that fascinated him, the indecisive twilight
of the very short period each day when the sun goes down. He evokes
it in the poem 'Night Ride' as the point when 'this city / ceased to be.
Suddenly it admitted / that it had never existed' (KA 1, 551), suggesting
that it produces a state in the observer akin to mental instability. The same
effect of almost delirious sleeplessness that results from a radical uncertainty
about time peculiar to the 'white nights' features in *Malte*, too: one of Malte's

neighbours in the then Russian capital 'saves' the precious time that he has left by reciting verse, Pushkin and Nekrasov, because doing so provides 'something stable that one can look at, inwardly of course' (KA III, 577). *Malte* has a further Russian connection: there exist two versions of what was possibly an alternative ending for the novel that focus on the figure of Tolstoy. Rilke had visited Tolstoy twice, in late April 1899 and early June 1900, and had for a while considered him a kind of father-figure. He always regarded him as a great artist despite vehemently rejecting the deep suspicion of art that lies at the heart of Tolstoy's aesthetic, and he regarded Tolstoy's brand of morality and religion as naïve. He had already attacked Tolstoy's *What is Art?* in 1898 (KA IV, 114–20) and the final notes for *Malte* offer a polemicising reformulation of his views on Tolstoy's betrayal of art. In these drafts Tolstoy was to have functioned as an articulation of the opposite of Malte's credo, that the artist's highest and only allegiance is to art.

The next phase of Rilke's interest in foreign literatures and cultures was an intense preoccupation with Scandinavia, or 'the North' as he usually referred to it. Again, a journey played an important role: in June 1904 he travelled via Copenhagen and Malmö to Borgeby gård near Lund to stay with Hanna Larsson and Ernst Norlind; before returning to Germany in December, he and his wife Clara even made an unsuccessful attempt to settle together in Copenhagen. But Rilke's interest predates this visit. He had seen performances of Ibsen in Prague in the late 1890s, which may have affected his own dramatic writings (Strindberg, in contrast, was not to become significant for him until much later, the winter of 1911–12). His account of the five Worpswede painters written in 1902 links them to Scandinavian literature: 'Books from the North were read', we learn, '[Bjørnstjerne] Bjørnson in particular', but supplemented by stories and novels such as 'Mogens' and *Niels Lyhne* by Jacobsen (KA IV, 333), encouraged especially by Clara, who felt a special affinity with the Nordic lands. Rilke knew the work of many other Scandinavian writers (including Edith Nebelong, Herman Bang and Sigbjørn Obstfelder), as his reviews of German translations testify. His interest in the educational philosophy of Ellen Key prompted a complex, long-lasting and chiefly epistolary relationship with her. Rilke learned some Danish in order to read Kierkegaard in the original and translated, amongst other things, Jacobsen's *Songs of Gurre* (*Gurre-Lieder*) and essays by the philosopher Hans Larsson. Rilke's interest in Kierkegaard was to last until at least the outbreak of the First World War and may have had an impact on the existential questioning of the *Duino Elegies* composed by 1914.

Poetry from the period of Rilke's journey reflects his passion for the Scandinavian landscape. Later recollections, such as 'In a Foreign Park' and 'The Apple-Orchard' from *New Poems* (KA I, 479 and 582), use topographical details to suggest affinities between the processes of nature and those of poetic composition. But a sequence of four poems from the *Book of Images* (KA I, 285–7) that were actually written during Rilke's visit has a more overtly existential focus, developing dynamic imagery of wind and storm to suggest the opening out of the self to the elements. The movements of cloud formations offer a glimpse of infinity – 'a gate into such distances / as perhaps only birds can know' ('Evening in Skåne'). In 'Storm' the poet loses contact with everything except the skies and lying on his back beneath them, '[his] eyes are open like pools / and in them the same fleeting movements take flight' (KA I, 286). Overall, however, there is relatively little poetry directly inspired by the Scandinavian experiences, virtually none with literary sources, and the major receptacle for literary stimulus is *Malte Laurids Brigge* once more. Bang and Jacobsen provide names and models for relationships, the latter being also an important source for some of Malte's reflections on the nature of death; Ellen Key and two of her friends are the models for the three Schulin sisters. In various places, too, the novel transposes Rilke's thoughts on Scandinavian authors previously published in reviews and applies them to Malte himself. The theme of marriage, Rilke maintained in a 1903 review of Gustav af Geijerstam's novel *The Comedy of Marriage*, was particularly well understood by Nordic writers: Malte, too, writes a drama called *Marriage* (KA IV, 466), and his critique of his own verse at this period as insufficiently reflective of the importance of interiorising the processes of remembering and forgetting echoes a review by Rilke of novels by Bang.[13]

The prospect of another major journey, to Egypt from January to March 1911, initiated the systematic study of ancient Egyptian literature, helped by some of the leading contemporary scholars including Friedrich Wilhelm Freiherr von Bissing and Georg Steindorff. He paid particular attention to a work from the twelfth Dynasty, 'A Dispute over Suicide' (otherwise known as the 'Dialogue of a Man Tired of Life with his Soul') and to the so-called 'oldest book in the world', *The Teachings of Ptah-Hotep* written more than 2000 years BCE (see KA II, 103). A few of Rilke's poems can be linked to this period of Egyptian enthusiasm – including 'Tears, tears breaking out of me', 'It was in Karnak' and the so-called 'Phallic Hymns' from late 1915 (KA II, 71, 174–6 and 136–8) – but its most significant poetic effects are found in parts of the *Duino Elegies*. Motifs from the 'Great Hymn to the Sun' of Pharaoh Amenophis IV-Akhenaten can be detected in the eighth, but literary influences are quickly supplanted by those of travel: the Temple at Karnak is mentioned in the sixth and the seventh; the transformation of the visible into the invisible in the ninth is exemplified by the

Egyptian rope-maker and the potter, both – like the poet – crafting their raw materials into shapes that embody their own intellectual designs; and Rilke's late-night confrontation with the Sphinx and the ideas on the hereafter of the *Egyptian Book of the Dead* are central to the tenth. It is true that the specifically identifiable lyric products of this journey are relatively few (KA II, 694), but the effect it had on 'unblocking' a crisis in his literary creativity should not be underestimated. The journey to Egypt enabled Rilke to restart the process of transforming the experience of *seeing* into the practice of *saying*, not immediately (as had been the case for Goethe visiting Italy) but only gradually – in other words the *Elegies*, whilst in no sense a direct poetic transposition of this journey, were essentially facilitated by it.[14]

Rilke's literary interest in Spain was boosted by a journey there, too, via Toledo, Cordoba and Seville to the Andalusian city of Ronda, between 28 october 1912 and 19 February 1913. Spain also seems to have contributed to the project that became the *Duino Elegies*, albeit only modestly, with the rewriting in Ronda of an idea conceived in Duino as the first thirty-one lines of the sixth *Elegy*. Rilke read *Don Quixote* in Ronda in a translation by Ludwig Tieck, but letters from the period show that his reading during his visit was nonetheless heavily weighted towards German-language fiction (Thomas Mann, Annette Kolb, Jakob Wassermann, Ricarda Huch and the four volumes of 'German Prose' edited by Hofmannsthal). The 'best evenings' were spent reading *Studies* (*Studien*) by Adalbert Stifter, who became 'a particular object of love and edification', offering Rilke 'immaculate accommodation and secure gratification in his proportionate world' (B I 494).

The journey to Spain resembles the visit to Egypt in that a dominant theme of Rilke's letters is wonderment at the way the cultural artefacts produced throughout history by these very different civilisations are embedded into the natural world leading to 'a correspondence between space and time' (*RHB*, p. 422), and 'The Spanish Trilogy' written in Ronda in January 1913 develops a concept that reflects these observations. The first poem is virtually a prayer for the self and a sequence of ordinary things and feelings (such as clouds, a river, light, sleeping vagrants or 'imprecision') to be mystically united: what they have in common is something 'welthaft-irdisch', something combining for a brief epiphanic moment the qualities of earthliness with an intimation of the essence of life itself (KA II, 42–3). It is the figure of the shepherd in the second poem of the trilogy who seems to have the capacity to perpetuate this inspiring combination: he 'has / nothing but world, has world in every look upwards, / in every inclination forwards' (KA II, 43). He has 'within his being' the call of the bird filling space with its song, a symbol for Rilke of a rare moment of access to 'Weltinnenraum', the interiorisation of the world into a space within the self. There is little that would identify these poems as topographically Spanish, but they are no less products of the experience of Spain and its culture for that.

This experience was not primarily a literary one, although it was certainly a 'reading' of Spain in Rilke's extended sense of that term. His experience of Italy was different in that he visited this part of Europe (Florence, Rome and Venice in particular, but southern Italy and Capri, too) much more frequently and no single journey triggered an intellectual investigation. Castle Duino, although politically part of Austria, also belongs amongst Rilke's Italian experiences. Rilke reported that Dante was said to have stayed in one of the earlier castles that once occupied the Duino site (KA II, 607–8), and it was in Duino, in October 1911, that he and Princess Marie von Thurn und Taxis began to read and translate *La Vita nuova* together.[15] He had known this and the *Divine Comedy* since at least the early 1890s (translating part of the *Inferno* in 1893–5 and Sonnet 24 from *La Vita nuova* in 1898); his lecture 'On Modern Lyric Poetry' from the same year dates modern lyric from 1292, the composition of *La Vita nuova* (KA IV, 61–2). The 1907 poem 'To the Poet: / Vita N:A' apostrophises Dante simply as 'Lord', virtually deifying him and praising him as the poet who has perfectly transferred his own experience of Beatrice via his verse. Dante remained important to Rilke as a model for a version of 'possessionless love'.

Rilke spoke and read Italian more than adequately, often translating from it. He made a version of Giacomo Leopardi's poem 'Infinity' ('L'infinito'), for example, immediately before embarking on the *Elegies* in January 1912, and a poem by Gabriele d'Annunzio in 1913, but for the most part stuck to the great authors of the middle ages and the Renaissance, Dante, Petrarch and Michelangelo, and planned versions of poems by the sixteenth-century Venetian poet Gaspara Stampa. He also read the poems of Lorenzo the Magnificent. Rilke's interest in Michelangelo was perhaps strongest, inspired in part by Rodin's love of the sonnets of a fellow sculptor. The earliest translations, from 1912 and 1914, are connected with Rilke's attempts to break out of the creative crisis that was associated with the *Duino Elegies*. He wrote to Marie von Thurn und Taxis in February 1914, for example, that he was translating Michelangelo 'pour le salut de mon Âme' – for the salvation of his soul – but sent, too, one of his own poems, 'a fragment, recently sprung from my heart, inadvertently, unexpectedly' (B I, 512).

Rilke was thus perfectly familiar with the classics of Italian literature but there is little evidence that he read more widely – when he first went to Venice his reading matter was Goethe's *Italian Journey* (*Italienische Reise*) rather than anything 'local'. There is no shortage of poetry and prose that reflects his journeys and experiences there: the 'Florentine Diary', for example, Venetian passages in *Malte*, a group in *New Poems* including 'Late Autumn in Venice' and 'Venetian Morning', as well as others there recollecting Capri ('Song of the Sea') and Rome ('Orpheus. Eurydice. Hermes' and 'Roman Sarcophagi'); Michelangelo is the subject of one of Rilke's *Stories of the Dear Lord* (KA III, 390–4). And it was via Venice that Rilke's only really sustained engagement with the literature of the Anglo-Saxon world came about, English being as he said 'the language most remote and alien to me'.[16] This, a translation of Elizabeth Barrett Browning's *Sonnets from the Portuguese*, came about after a visit in 1903 to the memorial to Robert Browning in Ca' Rezzonico (itself prompted by reading Ellen Key's account of the Brownings' history).[17]

French literature was much more important to Rilke than any other, and the language preoccupied him so much that he spent his last years writing poetry in it. He wrote to Eduard Korrodi when his first French poems were published, of his 'wish to be more visibly connected [ . . . ] with France and the incomparable Paris, which represent a whole world to me in my development and my memory' (20 March 1926; B II, 432). Rilke had lived in Paris almost continuously from the end of August 1902 until the outbreak of war, although he only returned there after the end of hostilities for relatively short periods in 1920 and 1925. The city of Paris and the experience of living there are central to his poetic development, literally changing the way he conceived of his own life. He described 'life' in Russia as 'lying open before me like a picture book'; in Paris, by contrast, he knew himself to have been 'drawn in' by life and to be participating in its pain, its threats and its joys (B II, 328). This is one of the dominant themes of *Malte Laurids Brigge*, the relationship of the protagonist's subjectivity to an experience of the city that renders traditional, stabilising or normative conceptions of life impossible to sustain.

Rilke spoke and wrote French before coming to Paris – French had been used at home during his childhood – and his work as Rodin's secretary naturally improved it. He translated a few poems by Baudelaire, Verlaine, Mallarmé and Anna de Noailles over the years, and rather more by Maeterlinck, before turning to the sixteenth-century poet Louise Labé in 1913 and to Paul Valéry in 1921–3. Letters indicate that Rilke was reading eclectically during the whole of his time in Paris – Villon, Montaigne, the Goncourts, Francis Jammes and André Maurois all feature: 'I read,' he wrote, 'despite the fact that the language makes me sad, with its ability to do everything' ('mit ihrem Alleskönnen'; B I, 141). Rilke loved Proust's immense novel *In Search of Lost Time* (*A la Recherche du temps perdu*), obtaining each volume as it appeared, annotating some in a manner that suggests a very careful reading. He was fascinated by the use of reminiscences, memories and child-hood associations as the organisational principle of the narration – akin to his own procedure in *Malte* – by Proust's investigation of the interaction of time and subjectivity, and above all by his celebration of the 'privileged moment' as the locus for fusing inner and outer experience. Flaubert (whom he preferred to Balzac) was also a particular favourite, but generally he seems to have had a preference for contemporary or recent writers. The list of those whose works we know he read has more than fifty names (*RHB*, p. 76).

Rilke's interest in French-language writing predates his arrival in France. He was an unusually persistent admirer of the work of the Belgian Symbolist dramatist Maurice Maeterlinck from the late 1890s on, for example, and his own drama bears the signs of Maeterlinckian mysteriousness (notably in *The White Princess*). More importantly, however, Rilke drew from Maeterlinck's allusive, quasi-mystical, inwardly-turned writings confirmation for his own feeling that the heyday of imitative art, of Naturalism and its aspirations to objectivity, was well and truly over. External action was less important to Maeterlinck than the depiction of an individual soul's unfolding and the evocation of 'the power of gentle experiencing' (KA IV, 123), and for a while Rilke saw in this the future of drama. Since Rilke did not pursue this genre with any vigour, Maeterlinck's influence is less obvious than it might have been, but his revelation of possibilities for a language of silence and the power of the ineffable were a major stimulus for what Rilke termed communication 'behind words'.[18]

An interest in Maeterlinck paved the way for perhaps the most impor-tant of Rilke's French interests, his study of Baudelaire and the Symbolists, which he undertook by way of preparation for his *Rodin* monograph. Of Rodin's response to Baudelaire's verse he writes that 'there were places that stepped out of the writing, did not seem written but shaped instead, words and groups of words that had melted together in the hot hands of the poet, lines that felt like bas-reliefs and sonnets that carried the burden of a timid thought like columns with complicated capitals' (KA IV, 413) – again superimposing visual, plastic imagery on the act of reading. Once more, reading served as a tool in managing a creative crisis, this time the loss of stability in the years before the successful breakthrough to the *New Poems*. A letter to Lou Andreas-Salomé of 18 July 1903 tells of how Rilke, unable to sleep, reached for his 'favourite book', Baudelaire's *Little Poems in Prose* (*Petits poèmes en prose*) and for 'At One in the Morning' ('A une heure du matin') in particular, which made its way into *Malte* (KA III, 491). Baudelaire's aesthetic in this volume is not a self-abasing confession of decrepitude and collapse but a celebration of how art can transform the transitoriness of the ordinary and ugly into beauty and permanence. Despite widely varying poetic practices Baudelaire and the Symbolists shared a belief in the essential beauty of the world and in art's unique capacity to realise it. By 1907 a different view prevails for Rilke; the presence of the ugly in poetry is part of 'seeing what is, what is *valid* alongside all other things that are' ('das Seiende zu sehen, das, mit allem anderen Seiende, *gilt*'). Baudelaire is seen as a key element in 'the whole development towards objective saying' that is seen to culminate in Cézanne (*Letters on Cézanne*; KA IV, 624) and which was a prerequisite for the composition of the *New Poems*.

Rilke was enormously widely-read, probably with a greater range, if with a less systematic approach, than his famously learned contemporary Hugo von Hofmannsthal; he learned several languages in order to be able to read literature in the original. But in sharp contrast to Hofmannsthal, it is very difficult to pin down just how Rilke's reading affected his own creative production. One can sometimes see how a given work 'requires' a knowledge of certain predecessors – how the *Elegies*, for example, presuppose some familiarity with the German and classical elegiac traditions – but rarely is it possible (and even more rarely is it important) to identify a clear source, an influence or a precise stimulus for an image, a paragraph or a stanza. With the exception perhaps of some of the French literature with which he was familiar, his reading often becomes incidental to his travels or his environment. More often still it is conflated with, even supplanted by, the beloved processes of seeing and looking that travel, nature or art provoke. The similarities that Rilke posits between reading and seeing in his poems on the subject are in effect a means of subordinating the former to the latter. Hofmannsthal needed his reading in order to write; Rilke did not, and it may be this high degree of literary independence that guaranteed his perpetual creative originality and thus in turn his lasting value to the literature of the twentieth and twenty-first centuries.

## NOTES

1 Although born in Prague, Rilke never mastered Czech well enough to be confident in reading or speaking.
2 Quotations from KA III, 598 and B II, 313 (letter of 5 September 1908 to Sidonie Nádherný von Borutin). See also B I 306–14.
3 Letter of 28 September 1911 to Hedda Sauer in Rainer Maria Rilke, *Briefe*, ed. Karl Altheim, 2 vols. (Wiesbaden: Insel, 1950), vol. I, p. 314.
4 See Judith Ryan, *Rilke, Modernism and Poetic Tradition* (Cambridge University Press, 2000), p. 124.
5 Ryan, *Rilke*, p. 99. See also pp. 148–9 for an account of how Rilke criticises Hölderlin's notion of patriotic poetry.

6 See Ernst Zinn, 'Rainer Maria Rilke und die Antike. Eine Vortrags-Folge', in Michael v. Albrecht (ed.), *Viva Vox: Römische Klassik und deutsche Dichtung* (Frankfurt am Main: Lang, 1994), pp. 315–78 (esp. pp. 321–3).

7 See for example a letter to Marie von Thurn und Taxis of 18 March 1915 (B 1 566).

8 Ingeborg Schnack, *Rainer Maria Rilke: Chronik seines Lebens und seines Werkes*, 2 vols. (Frankfurt am Main: Insel, 1990), vol. 1, p. 26.

9 Konstantin M. Asadowski, 'Sur les traces du Vieil Enthousiaste: A. Volynski – L. Andreas-Salomé – R. M. Rilke', *Etudes germaniques*, 53.2 (1998), pp. 201–11.

10 Ralph Freedman, *Life of a Poet: Rainer Maria Rilke* (New York: Farrar, Straus, and Giroux, 1996), p. 110. The text of this translation has since been lost.

11 Konstantin Asadowski (ed.), *Rilke und Russland: Briefe, Erinnerungen, Gedichte* (Frankfurt am Main: Insel, 1986, p. 191; Anna A. Tavis, *Rilke's Russia: A Cultural Encounter* (Evanston, IL: Northwestern University Press, 1994), p. 53.

12 Patricia Pollock Brodsky, 'Russia in Rilke's *Das Buch der Bilder*', *Comparative Literature*, 29 (1977), 313–27 (here p. 8).

13 See *RHB*, 120; KA III, 466–8 and KA IV, 551–2.

14 See Paul Bishop, '"An solchen Dingen habe ich schauen gelernt": Rilke's Visit to Egypt and the *Duineser Elegien*', *Austrian Studies*, 12 (2004), 65–79.

15 For a description of their working methods, see Donald Prater, *A Ringing Glass: The Life of Rainer Maria Rilke* (Oxford: Clarendon Press, 1986), p. 197. None of their versions have survived.

16 Letter to Hermann Pongs of 21 October 1924, quoted from *RHB*, p. 461.

17 Rilke intended at one point to include a reflection on Oscar Wilde in *Malte* (see *RHB*, p. 319), and he translated two of Shakespeare's sonnets, but he was otherwise uninterested in English literature.

18 This was a phrase he had intended to use as the title for a trilogy of novellas eventually called *Die Letzten* (*The Last Ones*) (see KA III, 844).

# 10

HELEN BRIDGE

# Rilke and the visual arts

While Rilke's poetry is well known to English-speaking audiences through numerous translations, his writings on art are less frequently acknowledged. Rilke himself, who tended to play down literary influences on his work, referred regularly and enthusiastically to the inspiration he had found in visual art. In the decades around 1900 it was not uncommon for German-speaking writers to take an interest in the visual arts. Hugo von Hofmannsthal, Hermann Bahr, Eduard von Keyserling and Rudolf Borchardt were amongst those who took up a tradition already well established in France, and combined writing about art with a literary career.[1] Rilke went further than any other German writer in using ideas from the visual and plastic arts to shape his poetry. The years between his first long stay with the artists of Worpswede in 1900 and his excitement about Cézanne in 1907 mark a continuous development in his understanding of the visual and his ideas about artistic form. The three longer pieces of art criticism (on Worpswede, Rodin and Cézanne) which he produced in this period represent distinct stages in this development, while the two volumes of *New Poems* published in 1907 and 1908 contain the results of his reflections on the relationship between poetry and visual art, and on the potential of painting and sculpture to provide models for a linguistic art form.

Worpswede was not the first focus of Rilke's interest in art. In the second half of the 1890s he had studied art history, albeit somewhat half-heartedly, in Prague, Munich and Berlin, while rather more enthusiastically following the latest developments in the German art scene. In a number of art-critical essays written for journals such as *Ver Sacrum* and the *Wiener Rundschau*, he shows his familiarity with the ideas and art of Jugendstil, with Arnold Böcklin and Max Klinger, who dominated contemporary discussion of modern German art, and with French Neo-Impressionism. Besides engaging with the contemporary art scene, Rilke informed himself about the history of art by visiting galleries and exhibitions, and reading the most popular art history of the 1890s, Richard Muther's *The History of Modern Painting*, as well as other art-historical studies.[2] Under the influence of Lou Andreas-Salomé he undertook intensive studies of the Italian Renaissance and of Russian art, complementing his reading with a stay in Florence and two trips to Russia. His move, in August 1900, to Worpswede, a village near Bremen where a colony of artists had been resident since 1889, not only brought his first experience of extended personal contact with artists, but laid the foundation for a shift away from the eclecticism of his artistic interests in the 1890s, and towards a focus on one particular strand of development in modern art, a characteristically French one.

## Worpswede

Given his familiarity with the German art scene in the 1890s, Rilke must have known about 'the Worpsweders' who, on exhibiting as a group at the Munich Glass Palace in 1895, had gained sudden fame and commercial success, and become a regular subject of discussion in art journals.[3] His move to the village was the result of a chance encounter in Florence in 1898 with one of the Worpswede artists, Heinrich Vogeler. Vogeler was the youngest of the painters who had exhibited in Munich, and the style and content of his work, inspired by Jugendstil and fairy tale, distinguished him from the other artists, who concentrated largely on landscape painting in the Barbizon tradition. When Rilke's relationship with Lou Andreas-Salomé became strained during their second trip to Russia and he desired a peaceful environment where he could devote himself to his Russian studies, he took up Vogeler's long-standing invitation to stay in Worpswede, hoping he would able to 'belong to the past' in the seclusion of the North German village.[4]

To Rilke's surprise, Worpswede immediately confronted him with new experiences, ideas and sources of inspiration. During his first stay there he experienced a new and exciting sense of community in the company of artists: social gatherings on Sundays in the Barkenhoff, Vogeler's artistically renovated farmhouse, provided him with opportunities to read his work to an appreciative audience and to discuss art and literature with a party which usually included the artists Clara Westhoff, Paula Becker and Otto Modersohn, as well as the writer Carl Hauptmann. A second source of inspiration turned out to be the landscape: in his diary Rilke comments repeatedly on the peculiar atmospheric effects of the flat North German moorland environment. He is struck by the intensity of the colours, even when the sun is not shining (T, p. 210). And the apparent isolation of things in this landscape caused him to rethink the monistic world-view he had held until now, whereby all things had been part of a whole:

> One really does learn to see new things here. Besides the sky and landscape a third element asserts itself as an equal: the air. Things always seemed to me like arms and ends, connected with the great body of the earth; but here there are so many things that are like islands – alone, light, with the incessantly moving air flowing around them on all sides. (T, p. 223)

The combined effect of regular conversations with artists, particularly Paula Becker and Clara Westhoff, and the experience of this unusual landscape, meant that Rilke came to feel he was learning nothing less than a new way of seeing. After a group visit to a private art collection in Hamburg at the end of September 1900, where Rilke admired paintings by Arnold Böcklin, Charles-François Daubigny, Jean-Baptiste Corot and Alfred Stevens, he writes in his diary, 'I feel as if I'm only now learning to look at pictures. Can it be that, until now, I have still been seeing some things in a novelistic way or with regard to their lyrical properties, which I have sometimes (in Leistikow, for example) taken to be painterly values?' (T, pp. 263–4). The distinction here between a 'novelistic' or 'lyrical' way of reading a painting – that is, one that assimilates the visual to a literary model, focusing on narrative content or atmosphere – and an alternative mode of seeing which would do justice to the purely visual quality of a painting, gives a clear indication of the direction in which Rilke wished to develop his understanding of art at this stage, even if it is questionable whether he had actually already completed the transition he describes.

The circumstances in which Rilke came to write his monograph on Worpswede in spring 1902 were very different from those in which he had first discovered the village and its inhabitants in 1900. The three marriages of 1901 (Rilke and Clara Westhoff, Paula Becker and Otto Modersohn, and Heinrich Vogeler and Martha Schröder) had put an end to the regular social gatherings of summer 1900; the relationship between the Modersohns and the Rilkes had become strained; and for Rilke a nomadic way of life had given way, temporarily at least, to domesticity and the duties of a husband and father. When the financial support he had been receiving from his uncle Jaroslav and cousins ended in January 1902, he urgently needed to find ways of earning money. The commission from the art publishers Velhagen & Klasing to write a book on Worpswede for their popular series of art monographs, which Gustav Pauli, director of the Kunsthalle in Bremen, had helped to obtain for Rilke, represented first and foremost a means of securing an income for his family. As a commissioned piece of work for an established series, the monograph's content and form were largely laid down by the publishing house. The subject matter was to be the original group of painters who had exhibited at Munich in 1895; in the event one, Carl Vinnen, did not want to be included, which left Fritz Mackensen, Otto Modersohn, Fritz Overbeck, Hans am Ende and Heinrich Vogeler. The exclusion of Paula Modersohn-Becker and Clara Westhoff cannot be interpreted as a failure on Rilke's part to appreciate the value of their art. (In fact, at this point he was not familiar with Modersohn-Becker's paintings.) By 1902 a standard format had developed for publications on the art of Worpswede: without exception, the focus was on the original group of 'Worpsweders'. In writing an introductory monograph for a fairly conservative commercial series, Rilke was expected to follow this pattern.

Rilke's letters suggest that he had mixed feelings about his subject matter. To Gerhart Hauptmann, for example, he described his work as 'only half pleasure, and half drudgery'.[5] This lack of real enthusiasm was no doubt partly due to the constraints of the commission. Furthermore, by 1902 tensions between the painters had put an end to the group identity which made their fame in 1895, making the task of writing about them as a group a difficult one. Despite the constraints within which he had to work, Rilke managed to use the monograph project to explore his own ideas about art and landscape, so that the text can be read as offering an insight into what he had gained from his time in Worpswede. On 26 June 1902 he wrote to Arthur Holitscher that the task gave him the opportunity 'to say a thing or two about artistic creation', and that the end product can hardly have been what Velhagen & Klasing or their readership were expecting (SW VI, 1276). It is in the lengthy introductory section preceding the separate discussions of the five painters that he goes furthest in pursuing his own ideas. His general reflections here on the relationship between man and the natural world, and on the function of art, provide the framework within which he discusses the painters' work, and reveal key aspects of his own ideas on art at this stage.

Rilke's starting point is the idea of a fundamental difference between humankind and nature:

> For let us just admit it: landscape is something alien for us and one is terribly alone amongst trees in blossom, and amongst streams flowing past. Alone with a dead person, one is far less vulnerable than when alone with trees. For however mysterious death may be, a life which is not our life and is without compassion for us is even more mysterious. (KA IV, 308)

While children, according to Rilke, enjoy a sense of unity with nature, this is lost in adulthood. It is the task of the artist and his art to recreate this lost unity: 'art [ . . . ] is the medium in which man and landscape, figure and world encounter and find each other' (KA IV, 311).

The conception of nature as alien is a significant modification of Rilke's early neo-Romantic world view and his tendency to regard everything in the world as a pretext for the expression of subjective feeling. It is a first step away from the aestheticising quality of Jugendstil, towards a form of art which, like Baudelaire's poetry, is able to create something beautiful out of the ugly and the alien. The mode of seeing which he had, in September 1900, identified with a focus on 'painterly values' and opposed to 'lyrical properties', is now closely associated with the idea of landscape. Rilke suggests that painting a portrait means 'seeing a human being like a landscape' (KA IV, 312), and he identifies this 'conception of the object as a landscape' in the works of Rembrandt and Böcklin (KA IV, 313).

Although Rilke begins, in *Worpswede*, to formulate the idea of a way of seeing which treats its object as something unfamiliar and alien to man and language, he is not consistent in applying this insight, often tending to treat painting and poetry as essentially similar. Throughout the monograph, and especially in the chapter on Modersohn, he uses the terminology of language and literature to describe artistic style and mood in painting. At this stage the purely visual quality which he has begun to perceive in painting does not lead him to new ways of using language to denote visual reality. Many of the poems inspired by Worpswede – such as 'Atmosphere in the Barkenhoff' (SW I, 375),[6] 'The Bride' (about Martha Schröder; KA I, 263), or 'I know how to listen to you: a voice goes' (SW III, 703–4) – are responses to experiences and people. The visual impressions of Worpswede are often central to these poems: 'The red roses were never so red' (SW III, 688) conveys the intensity of the colours of the landscape on a rainy evening, while 'A girl, white and before the evening hour' (SW III, 697) describes the strong contours of a figure against the landscape, as in a Millet painting. In this poem Rilke formulates the idea of words becoming pure 'contour' in a way which parallels the transformation of human beings into purely visual silhouetted shapes, and carries this idea over into the form of the poem: the play with sounds ('Konturen nur', 'abends haben', 'Wiesenblumen . . . Waisenknaben') emphasises the 'contours' of the words of the poem alongside their semantic essence. In most of Rilke's poems at this stage visual qualities are, however, evoked only semantically, as subject matter. A number of poems – contained in the volume *In and After Worpswede* – respond to works of visual art, usually Vogeler's. Far from evoking the 'painterly values' Rilke had begun to appreciate in Hamburg, these poems offer subjective interpretations of the situations and atmospheres depicted, with very little attention to the specifically visual quality of the paintings. It is not until after his move to

Paris that the specifically visual medium of art begins to have a formative influence on Rilke's poetics and poetic practice.

## Rodin

Viewed retrospectively, in the context of Rilke's career as a whole, one of the most important outcomes of the time in Worpswede was an intensification of his interest in sculpture – in the sculpture of Rodin in particular. The only Worpswede artist about whose work in progress Rilke writes in his diary is Clara Westhoff. (Whether this is because he did not see any of the painters' work in progress, or because it made less of an impression on him, remains a matter of speculation.) Not only did he admire Westhoff's work, but she told him about her experiences of working with Klinger and with Rodin, and they discussed the latter's work. In the entry for 21 September 1900 Rilke records the thoughts about Rodin which he shared with Westhoff: he emphasises the isolation and the permanence of the sculptures, which separate them from the transient world of the viewer. Of particular importance is the self-containment of a sculpture: in order to maintain its 'sacred existence as stone', it must not 'look out from itself, out from the cycle of its laws to the viewer who happens by chance to be standing opposite it at this moment' (T, p. 245). Although Rilke's interest in Rodin predates his aquaintance with Westhoff, the determination to go to Paris which he expresses in his diary entry for 27 September seems to have been inspired by conversations with her and Becker: 'I must definitely go to Paris after Christmas to look at pictures, visit Rodin and catch up on the countless things from which I have become estranged in my isolation' (T, p. 264).

As it turned out, Rilke did not go to Paris until September 1902. In spring of that year, he agreed to write a second commissioned monograph, this time on Rodin and for a series edited by Richard Muther, with whom Rilke had been in contact since 1899, and under whose supervision he was considering writing a doctorate on art history. Rilke's excitement about this project, even before arriving in Paris, forms a marked contrast to his attitude to the Worpswede monograph. In letters to Alfred Lichtwark and to Arthur Holitscher at the end of July 1902, he enthuses about the 'eminent greatness and magnificence' of Rodin's work, describing how it transforms 'a great inner world' into sculptural form.[7]

Rilke's admiration for Rodin was at once personal and aesthetic. His idealisation of him as a lonely 'master' (the term he uses to address the sculptor) devoting every waking hour to his art clearly has elements of myth: Rodin was a sculptor for the industrial age, employing numerous assistants and the working practices of a factory production line to create his works; his work also often came second to entertaining visitors and pursuing erotic adventures.[8] Nevertheless, during his time with Rodin in autumn 1902 Rilke learnt two kinds of lesson from him. At a personal level, Rodin (or, at least, Rilke's image of him) served as a role model and example of disciplined artistic working-practices. The comment he made to Rilke in a conversation reported in a letter to Westhoff on 2 September 1902 – 'Oui, il faut travailler, rien que travailler' (Rilke and Rodin, *Briefwechsel*, p. 49) – is one that made a great impression on Rilke and is repeated to a number of his correspondents. As he makes clear in a letter to Lou Andreas-Salomé on 10 August 1903 (B I, 154–9), it is his own inability to work constantly that makes him dwell on this idea. The differences between writing a poem and making a sculpture mean that this ideal is not easy for a poet to adopt. Yet the shift of emphasis away from dependence on inspiration and towards artistic creation as an active and disciplined process of forming material was one that Rilke could follow in his own work.

The contact with Rodin and his work also produced insights of a more specifically aesthetic nature, and these form the basis of the discussion in the monograph, which Rilke wrote in November and December 1902. Because of the three-dimensional physicality of sculpture, Rodin's work enabled Rilke to develop a conception of artistic form as something which exists alongside the objects of the real world, but is distinct from them. Using the term 'thing' ('Ding') or 'art thing' ('Kunstding') to refer to a sculpture, he emphasises its independence from ordinary objects, as well as its special, permanent status outside the flux of time (KA IV, 410–11). Sculpture, in Rilke's analysis, is able to give visible expression to human emotion, not just through the 'allegory and semblance' offered by poetry or painting, but by actually transforming inner phenomena into a physical form. For this reason it has an especially important role to play in the modern world, whose problem is that nearly all its conflicts lie 'in the realm of the invisible' (KA IV, 408).

As a physical objectification of such conflicts and emotions, Rodin's works – according to Rilke – attain a quality of self-contained independence. He compares the sculptures to a fountain or a walled medieval town – they exemplify an aesthetic ideal based on perpetual motion which is held in balance within the art object and never reaches outside it: 'However great the movement of a sculpture may be, even if it comes from infinite distances, from the depths of the sky, it must return to the sculpture; [ . . . ] it [a sculpture] should refer to nothing that lay beyond it, see nothing that was not within itself; its environment must lie *within* it' (KA IV, 418). The autonomy of the sculpture as an artistic form means that its wholeness does not necessarily correspond to whole objects in the real world. For example,

Rodin's statues without arms are, as visual entities, perfectly complete: 'One stands before them as before something whole, complete, which allows no addition. The feeling of something unfinished comes not from simply looking, but from ponderous reflection, from petty pedantry, which says that a body needs arms' (KA IV, 421). Recalling the Impressionists' tendency to cut parts of trees off with the picture-frame, Rilke makes the point that an artistic whole does not necessarily have anything to do with the organisation of the real world, since it involves 'new unities, new unions, relationships and equilibria' (KA IV, 421). The ideas here represent a significant step towards an understanding of artistic form based on a purely visual mode of seeing, which aims at creating 'painterly values', rather than a seemingly transparent representation of reality.

One of the most intriguing aspects of Rilke's understanding of Rodin is his idea that the expressive dynamism of a sculpture is contained in its surface.[9] This surface, he argues, consists of 'an infinite number of encounters between light and the thing' (KA IV, 411). He describes surface as 'the basic element' of Rodin's art and his world. This emphasis on surface rather than depth goes hand in hand with the absence of any 'grand idea': rather than starting with such an idea and trying to realise it in artistic form, Rodin builds his work on 'a small conscientious realisation'. An underlying idea throughout Rilke's discussion of the sculptor is that his visible plastic forms have nothing to do with 'ideas' or, by extension, language and preconceived meaning. In Rilke's understanding, Rodin works with a non-conceptual, visual language of body and gesture, and his sculpture becomes a model for the ideal Rilke had first identified in Hamburg in 1900. Thus, even when a literary or historical subject matter provides the initial inspiration for a sculpture, Rodin's creative process, he argues, quickly leaves this subject matter behind, in order to create something 'objective and nameless' (KA IV, 430). In other words, the 'content', or 'meanings', of a sculpture emerge as an almost unintended consequence of its form; the sculpture is not a vehicle for a preconceived 'content'.

After completing the monograph Rilke maintained contact with the sculptor, and in September 1905 he returned to Paris, taking up an invitation to stay with Rodin at Meudon. The following month he wrote a lecture on him, which he gave in Prague and Dresden, and then in Elberfeld, Berlin and Hamburg in summer 1906. Withholding the name 'Rodin' until almost half-way through the lecture, Rilke talks about *Dinge*, expressive surfaces, Rodin's process of creating such a surface, and the movement created by the effects of light on the surface. His understanding of Rodin and his work has not fundamentally changed since 1902. In November 1905, Rodin offered Rilke a post as his secretary, which he gratefully accepted. By spring 1906, however, the duties associated with this arrangement had become a burdensome distraction from Rilke's own work. In May, Rodin suddenly dismissed Rilke, apparently over a trivial matter. While Rilke was upset about this unexpected end to their working relationship, in letters from this time he insists that his respect for Rodin as an artist is undiminished. This was shortly to change. By the time he came to revise his lecture on the sculptor in June 1907 for inclusion as the second part of a new edition of the monograph, he regarded his ideas on him as belonging to the past, commenting in a letter to Westhoff that he could not take 'certain shifts of perspective' into account, since they would destroy much of the existing text, and this was not the moment to write anything new about Rodin (Rilke and Rodin, *Briefwechsel*, p. 200). When Rilke saw some of Rodin's drawings at an exhibition in Paris in October 1907 he was surprised to find his view of them transformed, commenting – again to Westhoff – that what he had written only a couple of months previously, when revising the lecture, now barely seemed valid. Now he is disturbed by the deliberate symbolism of the drawings. In other words, Rodin's work is much more dependent on linguistic and literary meaning, on preconceived ideas, than he had believed.

An important, but sometimes overlooked, influence behind the shifts in Rilke's attitude to Rodin in 1906 and 1907 is the history of art which had displaced Muther's *History of Modern Painting* in the popularity stakes: Julius Meier-Graefe's *Modern Art* of 1904. Rilke, who had been acquainted with Meier-Graefe at least since his arrival in Paris in 1902, knew this work probably by May 1906, and in December of that year recommended it enthusiastically to Sidonie Nádherný von Borutin.[10] While admiring Rodin, Meier-Graefe ends his chapter on the sculptor by expressing the view 'that he by no means represents our possible degree of perfection' and anticipating 'a further development that will go far beyond Rodin'.[11] Rilke will have found in Meier-Graefe's work an endorsement of his own aesthetic ideals, first espoused during his time in Worpswede and elaborated in the writings on Rodin. Meier-Graefe sees the essence of art in its specifically visual and aesthetic qualities, rather than in any 'literary' qualities derived from a particular subject matter. In his praise for modern French painting as the supreme manifestation of such 'painterly' qualities, he undoubtedly played an important role in opening Rilke's eyes to the work of new artists, most importantly Cézanne, in the course of 1907.

## Cézanne

As Rilke gradually became aware of the gap between his own aesthetic ideals and Rodin's sculpture, with its strong literary and symbolic qualities, his attention shifted to modern painting, which promised to come closer to a purely visual ideal. In late 1906 and 1907 he engaged with Manet and van Gogh, but it was the retrospective exhibition of Cézanne's paintings at the 'Salon d'automne' in October 1907 that most inspired enthusiasm in him and provided him with the opportunity to reflect in depth on a modern painter's work. That month he visited the exhibition almost daily, and recorded his impressions in a series of letters to Westhoff, later published (posthumously) as *Letters on Cézanne*.

The qualities Rilke admires in Cézanne's work are essentially similar to those he thought he had perceived in Rodin's in 1902. Despite the two-dimensional nature of painting, he sees Cézanne as making 'things' compa-rable to Rodin's sculptures in their air of permanence and self-containment. Whereas the Impressionists captured fleeting appearances and the effects of atmospheric conditions, dissolving the distinction between objects and the space around them, in Cézanne's paintings objects have a solidity and integrity which appeal to Rilke. This is presumably what he has in mind when he comments that Cézanne's painted apples are inedible, 'they become so thinglike and real, simply indestructible in their stubborn presence' (KA IV, 608). The paintings convey an objective way of seeing the world which focuses on purely visual qualities, without relating these to conceptual knowledge. As the painter Mathilde Vollmoeller told Rilke when they visited the exhibition together, '[Cézanne] sat before it like a dog and simply looked' (ibid., 614): the image of a dog encapsulates the lack of partiality and con-scious intention in this way of looking, a kind of naivety, even innocence, of gaze. The intentional symbolism which Rilke had recently realised is central to Rodin's work, is absent from Cézanne's. He contrasts Cézanne's work with 'atmospheric painting' (he may well have had the Worpswede painters in mind): whereas the painters of atmosphere paint 'I love this here', Cézanne paints 'here it is', using up his love for the object in 'anonymous work' which produces 'pure things' (ibid., 616). In its approach to all subject matter, even the most ugly, with the same objectivity, Cézanne's painting is closely related to Baudelaire's poetry: Rilke was delighted to discover that Cézanne knew the poem about a rotting corpse, 'A Carcass' ('Une Charogne'), by heart (ibid., 624).

It is not just the idea of an objective approach to things that provides continuity between Rilke's writings on Rodin and his letters on Cézanne. Reflecting on the painter's work also allowed him to develop further his ideas about artistic form. Just as Rodin's sculptural surfaces had presented themselves to Rilke as a model of an autonomous aesthetic form, it is the autonomy of the colours in Cézanne's paintings that fascinates him. There is, though, an important difference here. Whereas a sculpture occupies the same space as the real object or person which serves as its model, and its surface is at once artistic form and a representation of reality, Cézanne's work is remarkable for the way it separates artistic form from representation: colour serves both to represent objects and to emphasise the two-dimensional materiality of the picture surface. This allows for a rather more abstract conception of artistic form, as something independent of both the subject-matter of a work of art, and the task of representing reality. In art history Cézanne marks a point of transition between nineteenth-century figurative painting and the abstract constructivism which began with Cubism. Precisely this duality in his work appealed to Rilke. With Mathilde Vollmoeller's help, he conceived of the relationship between 'thing' and colour in the paintings as one of balance: 'It's as if they were placed on scales: the thing on one side, and the colour on the other; never more, never less than is required for the scales to balance' (ibid., 614). Within a broad framework of representational painting (after all, Cézanne does still paint recognisable objects), Rilke was fascinated by the movement towards abstraction and the independence of form and medium. Towards the end of his month of visiting the exhibition, he reached the conclusion that the effect of Cézanne's paintings derives from the autonomous interaction of colours on the canvas: 'No one before [Cézanne] ever demonstrated so clearly the extent to which painting takes place among the colours, and how one has to leave them completely alone, so that they can have it out among themselves. Their interaction with each other: that is everything in painting' (ibid., 627–8).

The *Letters on Cézanne* make it clear that Rilke was concerned with the paintings not merely for their own sake; rather, his interest was determined by the insights he hoped to gain for his own work. He talks of 'personal inner reasons' that make him particularly receptive to these paintings, which would not have captured his attention so much had he encountered them only a short time earlier: 'It is the turn in this painting which I recognised because I myself had just reached it in my work, or at least had come close to it' (ibid., 622).

## New Poems

So the same basic ideal remains at the heart of Rilke's thoughts on visual art, from the stay in Worpswede, through the encounter with Rodin, to the experience of Cézanne's paintings. This ideal involves an objective way of looking at the world and transforming it into artistic form which is purely visual, rather than dependent on ideas, or 'literary' modes of meaning. While Rilke only articulated this ideal in a fairly sketchy way while in Worpswede, after his move to Paris in 1902 he elaborated it further, and he becomes much more consistent in applying it to the works of art he writes about. From 1902 onwards his insights into visual art also began to have a real influence on his poetics. The first poem later to be included in the first volume of *New Poems* was 'The Panther' (KA I, 469), probably written in November 1902. For the next six years Rilke wrote poems of a kind he felt to be 'new', and this newness had much to do with the influence of the visual arts. It may seem paradoxical that inspiration for poetry should come from an emphatically non-literary artistic ideal, but precisely his awareness of the differences between poetry and sculpture or painting enabled Rilke to make his reflections on these arts productive for his own poetic development.

The theme of vision is important in *New Poems*; the collections contain a number of poems which are – or seem to be – based on paintings, sculptures or pieces of architecture. The most important result of the encounters with Rodin's and Cézanne's work, however, is a new approach to writing poems, which transfers principles of these artists' practice to the medium of language. A number of the most well-known poems in *New Poems* have been termed *Dinggedichte*: poems about things (whether objects, plants, animals or human beings), but also poems which attempt to create linguistic equivalents to things by using the material qualities of language – for example, sound and syntax. While not all of the *New Poems* are *Dinggedichte*, these poems most clearly demonstrate Rilke's new discipline in using language. Rather than expressing subjective feelings inspired by the object, as was the case in his earlier poetry, including the poems written in Worpswede about works of art, the aim is now to create a self-contained object in poetry. This implies an attempt to use language in a way which approximates to a sculptor's use of a plastic medium, or a painter's use of paint on a canvas. In the form of the poem, the objective reality of an object and subjective perspectives on it are interrelated, so that the precise, often emphatically visual, description of the object becomes at once an embodiment of aspects of inner life.

'The Carousel' (KA I, 490) provides a clear example of how these poems realise objects in linguistic and poetic form, rather than merely describing them. The repetition of the line 'and now and then a white elephant' at ever-decreasing intervals as the poem progresses conveys the visual reality of the merry-go-round as it speeds up, from the perspective of a stationary observer. Similarly, the increasing velocity is conveyed by the modulation of descriptions of colour, from a conventional attributive use of adjectives ('a fierce red lion'), via a grammatically correct but semantically odd attribution ('a little blue girl') and an adverb ('reitet weiß ein Junge'; literally 'a boy rides whitely'), to the independence of colour from any object signalled by nominalised adjectives ('a red, a green, a grey'). The merry-go-round is not, however, simply a visual object described from the perspective of an observer. For in its association with 'the land / that lingers long before it disappears', it is also a concrete expression of the experience of childhood.

Following the publication of the second volume of *New Poems* in 1908, Rilke continued to watch developments in the art world closely, often discussing visual art at length in his correspondence. Never again, though, did he publish art criticism; nor did visual art ever again have the formative influence on his poetry it had had between 1902 and 1908. Despite his fascination with the more abstract tendencies in Rodin's and Cézanne's work, he remained at best ambivalent about the development of non-figurative modes of art at the beginning of the twentieth century, tending to regard the loss of the object in art as a symptom of the abstract quality of modern life which so disturbed him. His admiration for Picasso and his interest in the work of the painter Paul Klee were exceptions to a general dismissal of modern art. Picasso famously provided inspiration for the imagery in the fifth *Duino Elegy*, while certain aesthetic parallels – never acknowledged by Rilke himself – are apparent between Klee's work and Rilke's late poetry. Neither of these artists provided a role model in the way Rodin and Cézanne had. By 1908 visual art had fulfilled and reached the end of its function for Rilke as a source of aesthetic models.

## NOTES

1 See Heide Eilert, '"...daß man über die Künste überhaupt fast gar nicht reden soll": Zum Kunst-Essay um 1900 und zur Pater-Rezeption bei Hofmannsthal, Rilke und Borchardt', in Andreas Beyer and Dieter Burdorf (eds.), *Jugendstil und Kulturkritik: Zur Literatur und Kunst um 1900* (Heidelberg: Winter, 1999), pp. 51–72.
2 Richard Muther, *The History of Modern Painting*, trans. Ernest Dowson, George Arthur Greene and Arthur Cecil Hillier, 3 vols. (London: Henry, 1895–6).
3 For an insightful analysis of the Worpswede artists' colony, its context and its contemporary reception, see Nina Lübbren, *Rural Artists' Colonies in Europe 1870–1910* (Manchester: Manchester University Press, 2001), pp. 118–36.
4 Rainer Maria Rilke, *Tagebücher aus der Frühzeit*, ed. Ruth Sieber-Rilke and Carl Sieber (Frankfurt am Main: Insel, 1973), p. 240. Subsequent quotations will be included in the text as T with a page reference.
5 Letter to Gerhard Hauptmann, 1 May 1902, in Rainer Maria Rilke, *Briefe aus den Jahren 1892 bis 1904*, ed. Ruth Sieber-Rilke and Carl Sieber (Leipzig: Insel, 1939), p. 218.
6 This poem, otherwise known as 'Von den Mädchen II', is given this title in Rainer Maria Rilke, *In und nach Worpswede: Gedichte mit Bildern von Heinrich Vogeler* (Frankfurt am Main and Leipzig: Insel, 2000), p. 15.
7 Rainer Maria Rilke and Auguste Rodin, *Der Briefwechsel und andere Dokumente zu Rilkes Begegnung mit Rodin*, ed. Rätus Luck (Frankfurt am Main and Leipzig: Insel, 2001), pp. 33–4.

8 For a helpful analysis of Rilke's relationship with Rodin which makes the elements of myth in his view of the sculptor clear, see Michaela Kopp, *Rilke und Rodin: Auf der Suche nach der wahren Art des Schreibens* (Frankfurt am Main: Lang, 1999).

9 For a discussion of this and other aspects of Rilke's studies of Rodin, see Georg Braungart, *Leibhafter Sinn: Der andere Diskurs der Moderne* (Tübingen: Niemeyer, 1995), pp. 242–82.

10 Rainer Maria Rilke and Sidonie Nádherný von Borutin, *Briefwechsel 1906–1926*, ed. Joachim W. Storck with Waltraud and Friedrich Pfäfflin (Göttingen: Wallstein, 2007), p. 13. Rilke refers to a publication by Meier-Graefe in a letter to Ellen Key on 28 May 1906.

11 Julius Meier-Graefe, *Modern Art: Being a Contribution to a New System of Aesthetics*, trans. Florence Simmonds and George W. Chrystal, 2 vols. (London: Heinemann, 1908), vol. II, p. 19.

# II

## PAUL BISHOP

# Rilke: thought and mysticism

There is a long tradition of treating Rilke as a philosophical poet. Perhaps the most prominent of those who have done so is Martin Heidegger, for whom Rilke was, in Hölderlin's phrase, 'a poet in time of need'. But Heidegger is not alone. One of the first books by Otto F. Bollnow, the philosopher of vitalism, was an in-depth study of Rilke (1951). The phenomenologist Hermann Schmitz derived the title of one of his books, *The Inexhaustible Object* (1990), from one of *The Sonnets to Orpheus* (II: 6), explaining his entire philosophical project with reference to this text. And to the list of those who have offered significant readings of Rilke, one should add a range of such philosophers, theologians and critics as Hans-Georg Gadamer, Gabriel Marcel, Franz Josef Brecht, Fritz-Joachim von Rintelen, Romano Guardini, Käte Hamburger, Maurice Blanchot, and Hans Urs von Balthasar.

It is true that Rilke was never a philosopher in his own right, and it would be a mistake to read him on the purely propositional level. But it would equally be mistaken to assume that, because Rilke's ambitions were aesthetic, his work has no philosophical dimension, or that his conception of what it means to be a poet does not have philosophical implications. In his essay of 1902 on the great Belgian Symbolist Maurice Maeterlinck, Rilke specifically problematised the relationship between the task of the philosopher (the search for truth) and the task of the poet (the search for beauty), for in his view these two activities are now more closely linked than ever before (KA IV, 217). As we shall see, Rilke was right about this, not least in the case of his own work.

It is difficult to know the exact extent to which Rilke was familiar with the European philosophical tradition, for he underplayed his knowledge of philosophical texts. Nevertheless, it is possible to sketch an outline of his knowledge of European philosophy, and identify some of the figures he had read. At the university in Prague in 1895, Rilke attended lectures on art history, on literature, and Anton Marty's lectures on philosophy. One of his early poems, 'When I attended University' in *Offerings to the*

*Lares*, gives us some idea of his early attitude to the subject (KA 1, 32). In 1896, Rilke matriculated as a student of philosophy in Munich, whilst in 1899 and 1900 it is thought he attended lectures given in Berlin by the cultural philosopher and sociologist philosopher, Georg Simmel, with whom he remained in contact for several years (one of his first biographers, Joseph-François Angelloz, interprets this friendship as a desire on Rilke's part for philosophical culture).[1] In two long letters to Lou Andreas-Salomé (12 and 13 May 1904; B 1, 170–92), Rilke outlined his expectations of university education in general and scholarship in particular, drawing up an ambitious programme of work for himself. He wanted, he wrote, to hear 'real things, new things, to which everything intuitive in me says "yes"'; he had no interest in 'the nature of philosophical systems', but he wanted to learn 'a few great and simple certainties, that are there for everyone, I should like to gain and earn them'. Not surprisingly, Rilke never completed his degree.

And so Rilke kept reading throughout his life, remarkably widely and astonishingly eclectically. In 1905, for instance, he undertook, together with Jakob von Uexküll (who became a pioneering figure in the semiotic approach in theoretical biology), a detailed study of the works of Immanuel Kant, especially the first *Critique*. Rilke also studied – if sometimes, and under-standably, with difficulty – various texts by the contemporary French thinker Henri Bergson, including *Matter and Memory* (1896), *Creative Evolution* (1907) and *Mind Energy* (1919). In the works of this philosopher, who opposes intuition to intellect, Rilke found 'something we all need and for which we are, in fact, quite urgently prepared'.[2] To judge from another early poem, entitled 'Nevertheless' (KA 1, 33), he enjoyed at least some familiarity with the writings of Arthur Schopenhauer (who was the only philosopher Rilke actually named, when asked about his philosophical interests, in his letter of 21 October 1924 to Hermann Pongs). And over many years Rilke engaged with the Danish philosopher Søren Kierkegaard, as his correspondence with Ilse Erdmann of 1915 shows.[3] He even translated some of Kierkegaard's letters to his fiancée, after he had learned Danish in order better to appreciate the writings of Kierkegaard (as well as those of the novelist, Jens Peter Jacobsen).

Nevertheless, undoubtedly the most important philosophical figure for Rilke was, as for so many writers and artists of the turn-of-the-century generation, Friedrich Nietzsche. Although numerous critics have rightly suggested the importance of Nietzsche for Rilke, it has proved harder for all of them (including more recent commentators on this subject) to pin down the exact nature of this Nietzschean influence. We know that Rilke read the second *Untimely Meditation*, 'On the Advantages and Disadvantages of History for Life' (of which one can detect resonances in the early essay, 'Bohemian

Walking-Days'), as well as *The Birth of Tragedy*, on which he drafted some suggestive comments in 1900 (KA IV, 161–72), and *Thus Spoke Zarathustra*. In these marginalia Rilke shows himself to be a sympathetic, if critical, reader of Nietzsche. Rilke agreed, for example, with Nietzsche's admission ('Attempt at a Self-Criticism', §6) that he had relied too much on Kant and Schopenhauer, but he also believed that Nietzsche's encomium of Wagner detracted from the book (KA IV, 170). Yet Rilke's reaction and response to Nietzsche go much deeper, as is evidenced in his writings by echoes of the Delphic rhetoric of Zarathustra. This subterranean presence of Nietzsche in Rilke's writing can be explained in part by the mediating influence of Lou Andreas-Salomé, but arguably it is also because Rilke took seriously Nietzsche's declaration in *The Birth of Tragedy* that 'the world is justified only as an aesthetic phenomenon'.

Of his contemporary philosophical contacts, the closest he entertained was with Rudolf Kassner, a prolific cultural philosopher with a distinctly mystical bent, whose work, particularly his 'intellectual physiognomics' ('Physiognomik der Ideen'), elaborates a characterological approach to culture. Although each had already become aware of the other, the two men first met in Vienna in the autumn of 1907. Rilke regarded Kassner as no less than 'a spiritual child of Kierkegaard',[4] and soon after finishing *The Notebooks of Malte Laurids Brigge* he read in some detail Kassner's *On the Elements of Human Greatness* (1911). In Kassner's 'From the Sayings of the Yogi' Rilke found a phrase (which, as it turns out, Kassner had actually formulated with the poet in mind) to use, in modified form, as the motto to a poem written in 1914, 'Turning-Point' (KA II, 100–2). He paid a further tribute to Kassner by dedicating the eighth of the *Duino Elegies* to him, and echoes of Kassner's ideas can be heard throughout this text. For Countess Marie von Thurn and Taxis, with whom both men were close friends, Rilke was the *Dottor Serafico*, and Kassner the *Dottor Mistico*, and Kassner's anti-rational – not to say, mystical – leanings would most likely have proved attractive to Rilke.

For, despite professing a 'rabid anti-Christianity',[5] Rilke was not insensible to the charms of the external apparatus (as well as the internal mindset) of organised religion, as the monks, candles and icons of 'The Book of Monastic Life' in *The Book of Hours* amply demonstrate. The cultural achievements of religion must have seemed too obvious to ignore, however much he agreed with Nietzsche's proclamation of 'the death of God'. On his visit to Algiers and Tunisia in 1910, Rilke was impressed by the Christian and the Islamic culture of North Africa, recalling in Tunis that the birthplace of St Augustine was nearby, and he tried to translate part of Augustine's *Confessions*. In Kairouan, he was moved by the presence of Mohammad, and his interest in Islam was – like Goethe's – intense. As far as religious, theological and mystical literature are concerned, we know that, in addition to the Bible, Rilke read various apocryphal texts; the *Golden Legend* by Jacob of Voragine; the hagiographies by the Spanish Jesuit, Pedro de Ribadeneira; the *Book of Visions and Instructions* by Angela of Foligno; St Augustine's *Confessions*; St John of the Cross, Meister Eckhart, Teresa of Avila and Catherine of Siena.

Less well-known, perhaps, is that Rilke maintained a strong interest in spiritism, which came to the fore in turn-of-the-century Europe, arguably in response to the crisis of liberalism, the decline of organised religion and the ascendence of materialism. Now, occultistic tendencies were particularly strong in the Schwabing district of Munich where, during his stay in 1896–7, Rilke came into contact with Carl du Prel, one of the leading spiritists, whose *The Riddle of Humankind* and *Spiritism* he duly read. In a letter to du Prel, Rilke placed the search for an alternative to materialism, and for poetic inspiration, at the centre of his interest in spiritism, and, a couple of days later, he sent du Prel a small poem as a testimony of, so he said, his discipleship (SW III, 556).[6] Several years earlier, Rilke had been interested in the parapsychological study, *Urania* (1889), by the French astronomer Camille Flammarion, and likewise he was fascinated by the work of the psychiatrist and occultist Albert von Schrenck-Notzing (1862–1929). In 1912 he participated in several séances held by Marie von Thurn und Taxis in her castle in Duino, and made transcriptions of what the visiting spirits said and did. And the occult episodes in *Malte*, he told Pongs (21 October 1924), had drawn on childhood experiences in Prague, as well as on what he had experienced and heard of in Sweden. (Rilke added that he had decided to make Malte Danish, because ghosts only really belonged to the atmosphere of Scandinavian countries.)

Did any of these apparently 'fringe' interests impact on his work? Possibly; according to Thomas Laqueur, Rilke 'faked belief to get over writer's block'.[7] And if we are to believe Rilke's correspondence, the poems in the short cycle 'From the Literary Remains of Count C. W.' (1920/1921) were the product of 'automatic writing', when an aged gentleman in eighteenth-century clothes materialised in front of him one evening in Schloss Berg. Is this a whimsical conceit? Or a variant of the topos of inspiration he used to describe to Marie von Thurn and Taxis the composition of the first *Elegies* one bright, windy day at Duino? On that occasion, Rilke had 'stood still and listened. "What is that?" he whispered. "What is coming?"'[8]

This account raises the question: is there a sense in which Rilke himself was a *homo religiosus*, even a mystic? It is a matter of historical record that some critics – Feodor Steppuhn, for example, Eva Wernick, and Simon Frank – have indeed regarded him in this light. Erich Heller went so far as to describe

Rilke as 'the St Francis of the Will to Power',[9] and Ronald Gray highlighted how, time and again, Rilke returned in his poems to the person of Christ – albeit in an entirely unorthodox manner.[10] Today's critical discourse is less interested in making confident assertions of this kind, although it would be hard to deny that, in stylistic terms, at least, Rilke has much in common with the German mystical tradition. On the level of biography, moreover, one text appears to record experiences that could be interpreted as mystical.

In a short piece entitled 'Experience' (1913), Rilke attempted to capture in prose just one such intuitive event that had happened the previous year in the garden of Schloss Duino. Reclining against the fork of a shrub-like tree, Rilke felt 'completely received into nature, in an almost unconscious contemplation' (KA IV, 666–8).[11] The philosophical vocabulary of the numinous – as Rilke's contemporary, the theologian, Rudolf Otto, called it – in this enormously evocative and richly suggestive passage is extremely telling, and his account includes many phenomenological details associated with the mystical experience by another contemporary thinker, William James. There is a strangely occult overtone, too: if Rilke himself felt like a ghost, then he also expected to see other ghosts, such as the daughters of Marie von Thurn und Taxis – Polyxène and Raimondine – who had died when they were young. Above all, what this experience gave Rilke was a vision of a different quality of perception, at once more distant and yet more involved, at once so far away and yet so close. Rilke's contemplation of nature – accompanied, we should note, by a cultural object, a book – induces in him an apparently transcendental experience, altering his perception of the external world *and* of himself as the subject of that perception. In the rest of this essay, and in a letter to Marie von Thurn und Taxis of 26 November 1915, Rilke recalled analogous experiences on the island of Capri, and in Saonara. These experiences conform to Bergson's distinction between the essentially selective nature of analysis and the direct knowledge yielded by intuition, in which the mind pays attention to itself as well as focusing on the material object.

Through his 'intense sensibility to such borderline experiences', J. B. Leishman believed, 'Rilke reached his characteristic conception of "the Whole", and of death as the other, the unilluminated side of life.'[12] But we could also regard his experiences as falling under the category of what Michel Onfray has termed *hapax existentiels* – that is, radical or foundational experiences such as the conversion of St Augustine, the mystical visions of Blaise Pascal, or Nietzsche's intuition of the Dionysian in the revelation of the doctrine of the eternal recurrence.[13] And if we recall the distinction made by Paul Valéry between existential experiences and mystical / religious ones,[14] Bergson's concept of 'intuition',[15] and Georges Bataille's notion of 'interior experience',[16] we might regard such *hapax existentiels* as precisely that – not so much mystical as existential; not religious, but aesthetic. Such, arguably, was the case with Rilke.

A figure who is insufficiently recognised as having played an important role in Rilke's intellectual and poetic development is the 'cosmic' poet, Alfred Schuler (1865–1923). Thanks to Schuler, Rilke became acquainted with the work of Johann Jakob Bachofen, whose work concentrated on the funerary reliefs of the ancient world. And along with Rudolf Kassner and Erwin Rohde, Schuler was one of the main sources of Rilke's interest in Orphic mystery-cults, reflected in *The Sonnets to Orpheus*. (In Rilke's correspondence there are several strong hints at a connection between the thought of Schuler and the *Sonnets*, to the extent of remarking that he would have been one of the few who could have properly understood them.) In the eyes of his contemporary, the vitalist philosopher Ludwig Klages, Schuler was nothing less than a reincarnation of a visionary past, and this was precisely the effect he had on Rilke who, like so many others (including Werner Deubel and Walter Benjamin), was bowled over by Schuler – although few can have gone so far as Rilke did when he allegedly remarked to Hedwig Jaenichen-Woermann, 'Schuler is a mountain, and I am a just a small, wretched thing.'[17] When he learned of Schuler's death in 1923, Rilke placed a bunch of narcissi on the altar of an abandoned country church near Muzot where no services were held, thus 'returning it to all the gods, and always full of open, simple homage'.[18]

Although Rilke's first encounter with Schuler might have taken place in 1914, his real impact on Rilke began in March 1915, when the poet attended at least three of his privately given lectures on *The Essence of the Eternal City*, the first of which was entitled 'On the Open and the Closed Life'. The terminology of 'open' and 'closed' anticipates Bergson's related distinction in *The Two Sources of Morality and Religion* (1932) between 'open' and 'closed' morality, for Schuler declares that 'in the open life there is no religion', 'in the open life there is no property', 'it is the great festival day of life / and where there is celebration / festival / happiness / there also is the open life'.[19] Just such an existential insight into 'the open life' had been intuited by Rilke, according to Angelloz, during his time with the French sculptor, Auguste Rodin.[20] In Rilke's own writings, the vocabulary of 'openness' is used in the eighth *Duino Elegy*, a text which Hans Urs von Balthasar has described as 'one long variation' on the philosophy of Schuler's friend and biographer, Klages.[21]

As well as in *The Sonnets to Orpheus*, Schuler's presence makes itself felt in what might be termed Rilke's 'phallic theology'. Early in 1914 Rilke read the manuscript of Lou Andreas-Salomé's *Three Letters to a Little Boy* (1917), a kind of fictional sexual (and emotional) primer, based in part on Freudian principles. Rilke responded with enthusiasm.[22] One passage in particular, he told her – in the second letter, where she discusses how plants 'hold up their sexual organs to the air and the sun, and directly endeavour to make themselves more noticeable by their smell and their colour, and to become more appealing to the eye'[23] – had reminded him of the ancient sculpture he had seen in Egypt, 'this laying bare of the secret, which is utterly, and in every place, so secret, that one does not need to hide it'. Remembering the suggestively-shaped, massive pillars of the great hypostyle hall in the temple complex at Karnak, at the centre of which lies the Temple of Amun-Re, dedicated to the king of the gods, the divine father, the creator of the universe (who, according to legend, grabbed his phallus with his hand and masturbated the world into existence), Rilke wondered whether 'perhaps everything phallic [ . . . ] is only an interpretation of what is humanly at-home-and-hidden ('heimlich-Geheim') in the sense of the open-and-hidden ('offen-Geheim') in Nature' (B I, 523). When he added that he could not recall the Egyptian divine smile, without thinking of the word 'pollen' – those tiny seeds containing the male genetic cells of the plant, which fertilise and stimulate fruition in the same flower or another, when the wind or an insect pass them on – Rilke's unspoken (but clearly implied) logic associates the self-pollinating sufficiency of the flower with the divine smile of Amun, the masturbating and world-creating deity.[24] Rilke's choice of the flower, especially the rose, as a poetic motif takes on a new dimension of meaning in the light of these associations.

Inspired by the sexual message of Lou Andreas-Salomé's *Three Letters*, in 1915 Rilke completed the 'Seven Poems' (KA II, 136–8), a cycle of poems in praise of the phallus, an ecstatic exploration of the realms of sexuality and death, carried out to a degree of intensity at which an earlier poem, 'On Marriage' (KA I, 357), had only hinted. Whereas such poems as 'The Swan' and 'The Flamingos' in the *New Poems* already displayed, as Kassner noted, a 'sublimated phallicism',[25] the topos of rising (*steigen*) and falling (*fallen*), which occurs in at least two early poems (KA I, 163 and 280), brings the *Elegies* to their conclusion (*Elegy* X, 110–13), and is, moreover, explicitly associated with the sexual in a one-line fragment from 1922, 'This is the silent rising ('Steigen') of the phalluses ('Phallen')' (KA II, 282). In his letters to Franz Xaver Kappus, published as *Letters to a Young Poet* (1903), Rilke had discoursed at length on the themes of sexual pleasure, motherhood, and love relationships; in his 'Letter from the Young Worker' (1922), he argued equally strongly for a resacralisation of sexuality and an emancipation of the erotic. Elsewhere, he demonstrated a preoccupation with female sex-organs in such poems as 'Tombs of the Hetaerae' and 'Orpheus. Eurydice.

Hermes' in the *New Poems*; while showing, in the third *Duino Elegy*, an insight of veritably psychoanalytic proportions into 'the dark river-god of the blood', the 'inner jungle' and 'primal forests', of passionate, sexual lust. Not surprisingly, it has been suggested that Rilke 'may have learned much from emancipated German (or Russo-German) ladies who were steeped in the erotic movement in Germany at the beginning of the century'.[26] Thus Rilke sought to make good a lack of which he spoke at length in a letter to Rudolf Bodländer (23 March 1922): 'The terrible thing is that we do not possess a religion in which these experiences, literal and palpable as they are (: because: at the same time so ineffable and so untouchable), may be taken up to God, to the protection of a phallic divinity' (B II, 244). For Rilke, politics matters a good deal less than the (inter)personal. 'Little by little one will have to recognise that *here*, not in the social and the economic, our contemporary great fate lies – in this repression of the act of love into the periphery; the power of the individual who sees clearly is worn out by trying to move it back into his *own* centre' ('die *eigne* Mitte'). Thus where the Austrian art historian Hans Sedlmayr, in his polemical study of 1948, *The Lost Centre*, would use the term to mean a loss of 'heart' (in the sense, say, of Pascal and Augustine), Rilke understood the centre in a far more literal – and physiological – sense, but referring to a lower portion of the body.

Elsewhere in Rilke's correspondence we find further philosophical reflections, which provide insight into the intellectual context within which he produced his works, both lyric and prose. In one of his early letters to Rodin, for instance, the young Rilke recalled how he had posed the great artist the simple, if fundamental, question – 'how should one live' – and been told in reply – 'doing work'.[27] If Rilke's poetic productivity, then and later on, shows he took this advice to heart, another letter, written during the period when he was Rodin's secretary, reveals how Rilke gave this programme a specifically hedonist twist, when he summarised his own ambitions as being 'to live, to exercise patience, to work, and to miss no opportunity for pleasure'.[28]

An even more dense set of philosophico-theological reflections can be found in Rilke's letter to Lotte Hepner of 8 November 1915 (B I, 599–605). Later Rilke published the letter, together with another text, 'Letter from the Young Worker', in the form of a short work entitled *On God* (1933). In his letter to Hepner, Rilke claims that the central problem in *Malte* had been '*this*: how is it possible to live, when the elements of this life are completely incomprehensible to us? When we are constantly inadequate in matters of love, indecisive in making decisions, and incapable in the face of death – how is it possible for us to be at all?' Using these questions as a starting point, Rilke developed an argument which, some fifteen years later, he still regarded as valid for publication: if we are looking for a philosophical text in the corpus of Rilke's writings, this letter is it.

As Rilke expands on his theme, he introduces the curious notion of approaching the gods from behind – curious, that is, until one remembers the biblical passage in Exodus, where Moses is permitted to see only the backside of God (Exodus 33:18–23). Like Moses, then, we can only see the backside of the gods; but at least this means, Rilke suggests, that our face and the divine countenance are facing the same direction. Rilke goes on to provide an anthropological-cum-psychological explanation of the notion of divinity, arguing that, from the earliest times, human beings have believed in gods as an expression of aspects of themselves they did not understand, and that 'the history of God' represents 'a part of the human temperament which remains similarly untrodden, a part forever deferred, set aside, in the end neglected [ . . . ], until it gradually turned, where it had been repressed, into a tension'. And so it is, Rilke continues, with death, which we both experience and don't experience. In the course of history, however, death became increasingly conceived as the enemy of life and happiness, and so, in Rilke's eyes, death and God became the Other, as opposed to which the One was life – our life. Yet the result was a forgetfulness of death and God, as 'so-called progress became the main event in a world caught up in itself, which forgot that, whatever it got up to, it was always already surpassed by God and by death'. For God and death are not just 'mere ideas', he insists, but from the very outset are part and parcel of Nature. 'If a tree blossoms, then death blossoms in it just as much as life does, and the fields are full of death.' Thus death, in the form of temporality, is really something in which we are always situated. In a sequence of striking images, Rilke writes that 'death is at home everywhere around us, and it looks at us out from the cracks in things'. But love, says Rilke, which engages us in 'a game of what's close and what's distant', ushers us into 'an infinite consciousness of the Whole'. And because lovers do not live 'in some detached here-and-now', he says, 'they take possession of the enormous assets of their hearts, and of them one can say that God becomes real to them and death can do them no harm: *for they are full of death, inasmuch as they are full of life*'.

The essence of Rilke's philosophy, if it can be called one, lies in his project for a restoration of the erotic and an investment of life with aesthetic significance. In other respects, Rilke lacked any kind of political programme, despite an instinctive inclination towards authoritarianism, probably acquired from frequenting aristocratic circles. The 'Five Songs' bear witness to Rilke's initial enthusiasm for the First World War, and in 1919 he devoured Oswald Spengler's *Decline of the West* (although, at that time, there was hardly anyone who did not). For a while, albeit from the safe distance of a Swiss sanatorium, he was an admirer of Mussolini. In a letter to Pongs (21 October 1924), Rilke, rather irritably, rejected the suggestion there were 'social' aspects to his work. 'To change, to improve the condition of a human being,' he wrote from Muzot, 'means to exchange the difficulties in which he is experienced and practised for other difficulties, which he might find even more puzzling' (B II, 358). Claiming for himself 'the justified impartiality of artistic expression', he concluded that, 'in a world which tries to dissolve the divine in a kind of anonymity, the sort of humanitarian overestimation that expects from human assistance what it cannot give, inevitably gains ground'. In a way, of course, Rilke is right: poetry cannot feed an empty stomach.

Is there a sense in which Rilke's actual poetic work can be said to have a dimension that is philosophical, or even mystical? There is a long tradition in German literature of writing *Gedankenlyrik* ('intellectual poetry') or *Lehrdichtung* ('didactic poetry'), exemplified by the work of Barthold Brockes, the protestant scientist poet Albrecht von Haller, Johann Peter Uz, or Friedrich Klopstock, which looks back to such classical antecedents as Horace, Ovid and Lucretius. (Rilke's near-contemporary, Bertolt Brecht, revived the Lucretian tradition in his 'Didactic Poem on the Nature of Human Beings' ('Lehrgedicht von der Natur des Menschen'), which included a rendering of the *Communist Manifesto* into classical hexameters – a greater contrast with Rilke is almost impossible to imagine.) Such works as Uz's 'Theodicy', Brockes' collection *Earthly Delight in God*, and Haller's 'Thoughts on Reason, Superstition, and Unbelief' offer a clearly set-out set of doctrinal tenets, much as such later texts as Schiller's patient explanation of the function of art in 'The Artists' ('Die Künstler') or Goethe's exhilarating exposition of his scientific views in 'The Metamorphosis of Plants' ('Die Metamorphose der Pflanzen') do. Evidently, such explicit philosophical statement is not to be found in Rilke's lyric work (with some important exceptions – see, for example, *Sonnets*, I: 18 and II: 10; or such didactic poems as 'So long as you catch the things you throw yourself' (KA II, 195–6), 'Just as nature leaves to creatures' (KA II, 324–5), or 'Written for Karl Count Lanckorónski' (KA II, 410)). Yet often Rilke's poems are not just philosophical in their choice of vocabulary or rhetoric; if we look more closely, a fundamental philosophical conviction emerges from his texts.

'Why is there something rather than nothing?' This is – as Leibniz pointed out, and as Heidegger reminded us – the fundamental philosophical question. And it is to this 'somethingness' that Rilke – to this extent, participating in Goethe's project of engaging in 'objective thought' ('gegenständliches Denken') – turns his attention. Sometimes, this 'something' may turn out to be a 'nothing': such is the mystical experience of the *via negationis*, to which the poems in *The Book of Hours* allude. Elsewhere, the 'thingness' of a particular something forms the centre of Rilke's preoccupations: hence the development in his hands of a kind of poem in which Eduard Mörike and Conrad Ferdinand Meyer likewise excelled – the *Dinggedicht*. In Rilke's oeuvre, some of the best-known examples of this kind of text – 'The Mountain', 'The Panther', 'The Carousel' – are found in the *New Poems*. Rilke's approach in these texts might well be described as phenomenological: his concern is with the appearance of these objects, with our relation to and our interaction with them. What, to the 'workaday attitude', is simply another statue of Apollo in a gallery, is, to the 'festive attitude', a call for radical self-transformation ('Archaic Torso of Apollo').[29] Or another example: for the farmer, an orange is a fruit, part of his crop; for the grocer, it is a commodity, to be weighed and sold; but for the lyrical subject, it is the starting-point of a series of sensuous and reflective experiences: 'Wait a moment..., that tastes good', is how Rilke begins a sonnet, which enjoins the women of hot, sunny climes to 'dance the orange' (*Sonnets*, I: 15).

At the same time, Rilke can be seen to insist on the nothingness that lies at the heart of some- or anything – the nothingness that 'lies coiled in the heart of being, like a worm', as Sartre darkly put it.[30] For what is revealed is, in medieval terms, the quiddity – the 'thingness', for want of a better expression – of a thing. Hence his concern, well expressed in *Malte*, with experiences of alienation, loneliness and isolation. Nothingness results from the lack of, so to speak, ontological depth (there is no 'why' for things being there). Nevertheless, this very lack of depth draws the attention of the poet to the surface of things – like Nietzsche's ancient Greeks, Rilke is 'superficial – *out of profundity*' (*The Gay Science*, Preface, §4). For there are – this was Nietzsche's message, which Rilke well understood – only things, in the sense of appearances, *phenomena, Erscheinungen*; there is no meaning that stands 'behind' them. Why is there is a something? – is a question Rilke cannot answer. What is a thing's (aesthetic) mode of being? – is the question he can, and does, explore.

This focus on the existential aspect of our experiences is highlighted in Rilke's insistence that external objects be in some way interiorised: 'Nowhere, beloved, can the world exist, but within' ('Nirgends, Geliebte, wird Welt sein, als innen') (*Elegy* VII, 50). Rilke speaks of outwardness as diminishing to the point of disappearance ('Und immer geringer / schwindet das Außen'; 51–2); the house that once stood now exists in our mind, as an object of our vision; over time a temple becomes (externally) invisible, but it is – along with its pillars and statues – (internally) rebuilt (52–4, 57–62). In the gaze of the angels – mythical avatars of the divinity that Rilke acknowledged as the source of fecund life itself – even the great architecture

of the world – 'pillars, pylons, the Sphinx' ('Säulen, Pylone, der Sphinx') –
become redeemed ('gerettet'), as their essentially phallic nature is revealed
in the angelic, poetic vision ('Anschaun'; 70–4). To such intuitive interiorisation of our experience of the world Rilke gave the name 'celebration'
('Rühmen'), both in the seventh *Elegy* and in the *Sonnets*: 'To give praise,
that's it!' ('Rühmen, das ists') – such is the task of Orpheus himself, 'the one
whose task is to praise' ('Ein zum Rühmen Bestellter' I: 74).

   Now, although Rilke himself expounded at length the philosophical aspect
of the *Duino Elegies* in his programmatic letter – written some time after
their composition – to Witold Hulewicz (13 November 1925), all such
discussion will remain at the level of mere abstraction, if it fails to attend to
Rilke's use of language and poetic devices. In a line, for example, like 'deinem
erkühnten Gefühl die erglühte Gefühlin' from the seventh *Elegy* (line 9), his
characteristically intricate patterning of sounds captures the intertwining of
subject and sensation in an ever-intensifying phonetic repetition of *g, l* and *ü*.
This goes hand in hand with the extraordinary, even disturbing, imagery that
unsettles us from our conventional view of the world (the youthful dead that
glide towards the visitor of a church in Rome or Naples in *Elegy* I, the gaze
of the dead onlookers at the lovers together on the carpet (*Elegy* v), or the
emergence from their graves of the little girls who have died (*Elegy* vii) and
the powerful, oracular rhetoric that Rilke deployed to such startling effect
(*Elegy* I, 1–25; *Elegy* x, 106–13)). Rilke's language is not only a medium,
but a component of his meaning.[31] And to argue for a coherent outlook in
Rilke's work, whether as something that is present from an early stage or
as something that gradually emerges, should never lead us to overlook the
aesthetic specificities of a particular text.

   To return to an idea mentioned at the beginning of this chapter, one
might argue that what Rilke proposes in his writing is an 'inexhaustible
object'. The poem in which he uses this phrase (*Sonnets*, II: 6) is addressed
to a rose, by means of which Rilke also associates himself with a tradition that includes Angelus Silesius's mystic epigram 'The rose does not
ask why' ('Die Rose ist ohne warum') (*The Cherubic Pilgrim*, Book 1,
no. 289) and Goethe's poem 'As the most beautiful you are known' ('Als
Allerschönste bist du anerkannt') from the cycle *Chinese-German Times of
Year and Day* (*Chinesisch-deutsche Jahres- und Tageszeiten*), no. 10). In
his sonnet Rilke reminds us that, in antiquity, a rose was 'a chalice with
a simple rim'. According to Hermann Schmitz, such a schematic representation typifies the views of the atomists (such as Leucippus and Demo-
critus), who applied the characteristics of being (as set out by Parmenides)
to the atoms: only what is ungenerated, imperishable, unchangeable is real.
All other characteristics of objects are thus relegated to the category of

'secondary qualities', and dismissively ascribed to the perceiving subject; so begins, Schmitz argues, the reductionist world-view which admits as valid only what is identifiable, measurable and manipulable. But, Schmitz suggests, what Rilke wants to say is 'that, *for us*, the rose is (once again at last) the complete, uncountable rose', and that '*we* can once again accept the incalculable, where it momentarily manifests itself, [ . . . ] as a chaotic manifold of meanings not susceptible to calculation, by virtue of which situations and impressions are significant'.[32] In other words, for Rilke the object of aesthetic perception can be attained only if we transcend our conceptual grasp on reality, thereby allowing the beautiful particular, endowed by aesthetic perception with universal significance, to recover its status as an individual entity of sheer artistic value.

Perhaps it is no coincidence that, as well as Heidegger and the existentialists, it is thinkers working in phenomenological traditions associated with vitalism who have demonstrated a notable interest in Rilke. In his lecture 'On Modern Lyric Poetry' (1898), Rilke defined art as 'the endeavour of the individual' to 'come to an understanding with all things', so that, 'through this constant dialogue', he or she may 'approach the last, gentle sources of all life' (KA IV, 65). Rilke's 'prayer' in his 'Florentine Diary' (1898) constitutes nothing less than a vitalist celebration of 'sacred life'.[33] In Rilke's evocation (in the opening poem of 'The Book of Pilgrimage' in *The Book of Hours*) of the rising sap that falls back into God (KA I, 201), Angelloz senses an intuition of a vital energy that is circulating in the world, analogous to Schopenhauer's Will or Bergson's *élan vital*.[34] Writing to Ellen Key on 3 April 1903, Rilke expressed his love of and his belief in life, 'not the life that constitutes time, but that other life, the life of small things, the life of animals and the great plains', a life that 'persists through the centuries, apparently without sympathy, and yet in the balance of its forces full of movement and growth and warmth'.[35] Even in his last days, amid intense pain and suffering, he was able to tell Nanny Wunderly-Volkart: 'Never forget, my dear, life is something marvellous'.[36] Consideration of Rilke from a philosophical perspective can thus reveal a different Rilke from the mournful, gloomy figure that he is sometimes presented as being. We discover instead a cheerful, joyous Rilke, who seeks to increase our sense of vitality, to enhance the keenness of our appreciation of life. After all, as Rilke himself put it, 'art is just one way of living' (KA IV, 547).

## NOTES

1 J.-F. Angelloz, *Rainer Maria Rilke: L'Evolution spirituelle du poète* (Paris: Paul Hartmann, 1936), p. 132.

2 Letter to Marie von Thurn und Taxis, 13 June 1914 in Rainer Maria Rilke and Marie von Thurn und Taxis, *Briefwechsel*, ed. Ernst Zinn, 2 vols. (Frankfurt am Main: Insel, 1986), vol. I, p. 201.

3 See Clive H. Cardinal, 'Rilke and Kierkegaard: Some Relations between Poet and Theologian', *Bulletin of the Rocky Mountain Modern Language Association*, 23 (1969), 34–9.

4 Letter to Lou Andreas-Salomé, 7 February 1912 (B I, 397).

5 Letter to Marie von Thurn und Taxis, 17 December 1912 (B I, 447).

6 Letters to Carl du Prel, 16 and 18 February 1897.

7 Thomas Laqueur, 'Why the Margins Matter: Occultism and the Making of Modernity', *Modern Intellectual History*, 3 (2006), 111–35 (p. 116).

8 Donald Prater, *A Ringing Glass: The Life of Rainer Maria Rilke* (Oxford: Clarendon Press, 1994), p. 204.

9 Erich Heller, *The Disinherited Mind* (Harmondsworth: Penguin, 1961), p. 115.

10 Ronald Gray, *The German Tradition in Literature 1871–1945* (Cambridge University Press, 1965), p. 255.

11 Rainer Maria Rilke, *Duino Elegies*, ed. and trans. J. B. Leishman and Stephen Spender (London: Chatto and Windus, 1975), p. 153.

12 Ibid., p. 156.

13 Michel Onfray, *L'Art de jouir* (Paris: Grasset and Fasquelle, 1991), p. 27.

14 Paul Valéry, *Oeuvres complètes*, 2 vols. (Paris: Gallimard, 1957–1960), vol. I, pp. 814–16.

15 Henri Bergson, *La Pensée et le mouvant* (Paris: Presses Universitaires de France, 1962), pp. 27, 29.

16 Georges Bataille, *L'Expérience intérieure*, second edition (Paris: Gallimard, 1954), p. 15.

17 Gerhard Plumpe, *Alfred Schuler: Chaos und Neubeginn – Zur Funktion des Mythos in der Moderne* (Berlin: Agora, 1978), p. 210.

18 Letter to Clara Rilke, 23 April 1923 (B II, 301).

19 Alfred Schuler, *Cosmogonische Augen: Gesammelte Schriften*, ed. Baal Müller (Paderborn: Igel, 1997), p. 223.

20 Angelloz, *Rainer Maria Rilke*, p. 190.

21 Hans Urs von Balthasar, *Apokalypse der deutschen Seele*, vol. II: *Im Zeichen Nietzsches* [1939], second edition (Einsiedeln and Freiburg: Johannes, 1998), p. 88.

22 Letter to Lou Andreas-Salomé, 20 February 1914 (B I, 521–4); see also her response of 1 March 1914 ('It was clear to me: you should have written these three little-boy-letters').

23 Lou Andreas-Salomé, *Drei Briefe an einen Knaben* (Leipzig: Kurt Wolff, 1917), p. 37.

24 See Sandra Kluwe, *Krisis und Kairos: Eine Analyse der Werkgeschichte Rainer Maria Rilkes* (Berlin: Duncker and Humblot, 2003), pp. 212 and 214.

25 See Rudolf Kassner's letter to Anton Kippenberg, 13 March 1912.

26 Raymond Furness, *The Twentieth Century 1890–1945* (London and New York: Croom Helm and Barnes and Noble, 1978), p. 137.

27 Letter to Rodin, 11 September 1902, in Rainer Maria Rilke and Auguste Rodin, *Der Briefwechsel und andere Dokumente zu Rilkes Begegnung mit Rodin*, ed. Rätus Luck (Frankfurt am Main and Leipzig: Insel, 2001), p. 53.

28 Letter to Arthur Holitscher, 13 December 1905 (B 1, 207).
29 Bernd Jager, 'Rilke's "Archaic Torso of Apollo"', *Journal of Phenomenological Psychology*, 34 (2003), 79–98.
30 Jean-Paul Sartre, *L'être et le néant* (Paris: Gallimard, 1976), p. 56.
31 See Elsie Weigand, 'Rilke and Eliot: The Articulation of the Mystic Experience', *The Germanic Review*, 30 (1955), 198–210 (p. 198).
32 Hermann Schmitz, *Der unerschöpfliche Gegenstand: Grundzüge der Philosophie*, second edition (Bonn: Bouvier, 1995), p. 2.
33 *Tagebücher aus der Frühzeit*, ed. Ruth Sieber-Rilke and Carl Sieber (Frankfurt am Main: Insel, 1973), p. 69.
34 Angelloz, *Rainer Maria Rilke*, p. 149.
35 Rainer Maria Rilke, Ellen Key, *Briefwechsel* (Frankfurt am Main: Insel, 1993), pp. 26–27.
36 Prater, *A Ringing Glass*, p. 405.

# 12

ANTHONY PHELAN

# Rilke and his philosophical critics

In a groundbreaking essay in 1966, Käte Hamburger noted that the interest of philosophers in Rilke's work is no accident. Her point is carefully formulated: it is not that the answerable style of Rilke's poetry makes it sympathetic to philosophical interrogation, but rather that by avoiding explicitly conceptual forms it is able to respond in its own terms to philosophical positions.[1] In this essay I focus on engagements with Rilke's poetry in the philosophical work of Heidegger and Maurice Blanchot; and, responding to them, in the criticism of Paul de Man.

## Stefan Zweig – Robert Musil

Long before this philosophical interest, however, Rilke's poetic vision provoked sophisticated responses among his contemporaries. Perhaps the most penetrating early account of the *New Poems* is Stefan Zweig's review in the *Literary Echo* (*Das literarische Echo*) at the end of 1908. Observing a transition from musicality to plasticity via certain painterly qualities in *The Book of Images* (1902, 1906), Zweig finds a new strength and immediacy in poems that present 'a singular thing, like a drop of water held up as a mirror against the sky, an object that a single second enriches with all the life of its surroundings, a shard of the everyday set in its place within the inordinate'.[2] Much here is prescient. The sound effects of Rilke's verse will become a crucial consideration for de Man's critique, for instance. Zweig notes how an inert object or a fragmentary moment is seen as a richly social event, illustrated by his only quotation from the poems. The final stanzas of 'The Square' suggest, Zweig claims, that a lifeless agglomeration of houses acquires a certain vitality from the human life that animates the square. Rilke's description personifies the inert buildings by imbuing them with the social and historical life of the Flanders town. What Zweig evidently neglects is the poem's sense of space, and the way it reverses and inverts the force of familiar ideas in the rhetorical pattern called chiasmus: past and present, fullness and emptiness. This also matches the formal qualities of the poem: a group of six lines leads, after a single line in brackets, to two quatrains. 'The Square' is an inverted sonnet, beginning with two tercets (six lines), pivoting on the 'additional' bracketed line, and concluding with the two quatrains (eight lines) we would normally expect at the start. (The poem 'Late Autumn in Venice' has a similar inversion written into its syntax.) Zweig, however, emphasises the interpretative activity of Rilke's new poetry: '. . . he grasps [things] only as images, as the constant mutual recollection of things, and so the whole of life round about him becomes one vast unity ('Zusammen-schluß'), an eternal self-interpretation, a mutual meshing' (p. 46).

This mutual interaction among the poems is also a perpetual deferral of interpretation ('Sicherläutern', 'Aneinandererinnern'). If we take this account seriously, the meanings of things are found both within the network of deferred memory as an interplay of significances, but also in their insertion into what Zweig calls 'das Ungeheure', the *inordinate*. When Rilke uses this word, it is generally in the colloquial sense of 'tremendous' or 'huge'; but in *The Notebooks of Malte Laurids Brigge* it takes on aspects of existential terror. Here Zweig seems to anticipate the modern sense of a Sublime, not unlike the Terrible ('das Entsetzliche') in *Malte*, that takes its place alongside the angels and the characteristic spatial terms of the *Duino Elegies* in Rilke's metaphysical vocabulary. Zweig's sense of the existential place of each singular object within the space of the inordinate in the project of the *New Poems* uncannily anticipates Rilke's reflections on consciousness and language in the *Elegies* – just as Zweig's identification in Rilke's poetic personality of something like the insatiability of an intrepid Alpine climber (p. 46) looks ahead to poems not yet written: the ninth *Duino Elegy* and 'Exposed on the mountains of the heart'.

Zweig understands this aspect of Rilke's middle poetry as a whole vision of the world. His emphasis on an endless interplay in the process of consciousness is taken up in a different way by another literary author responding to Rilke. In the commemorative address he delivered in Berlin about a month after the poet's death at the end of 1926, Robert Musil asserts the seriousness of Rilke's claim to be a great poet before addressing the difficulty presented by the poet in terms of the 'affect' of his poems. And here it is Zweig's insight into the interplay of phenomena that dominates; Musil refers principally to the poetry up to *New Poems*, although he may allude to the *Elegies* also. His claim is that Rilke's poems are never dominated by their ostensible theme:

> It is never the thing itself that constitutes the content of the poem, but always something like the incomprehensible existence of these perceptions and things,

their incomprehensible proximity to one another and invisible interwovenness, that triggers and guides the lyrical affect.

In this mild lyrical affect one thing becomes a metaphor ['Gleichnis'] of another.[3]

Musil's sense of contiguity and interconnectedness sketches the rhetorical tension between metonymy and metaphor. Proprieties are breached and properties become universal ('Die Eigen-schaften werden zu Aller-schaften!', p. 1237). To illustrate his case that any one thing can become the 'Gleichnis' of any other, Musil offers an off-the-cuff example to show that 'here metaphor becomes serious to a very high degree' (p. 1237): imagine, he says, a writer who compares a particular November evening with a soft woollen shawl; another writer might equally well compare an unusually soft woollen fabric with a November evening. The very same sense of the commutative structure of simile and metaphor is critically important when Ulrich, the central figure of Musil's novel The Man without Qualities (Der Mann ohne Eigenschaften, 1930–2) and his sister Agathe recognise that all experience, anything that can be articulated in language at all, 'everything that has a name leans on everything else in regular series and perspectives ("in Hinsichten", "in Fluchten"), as a link in large and incalculable unities, one relying on another...' (IV, 1090).[4]

Musil's point at the end of the commemorative address is that instead of determining to mean either one thing or the other in the comparative structure of simile, it might be possible to say both – which, he asserts, is what Rilke had always done, weaving things together like a tapestry (VIII, 1238): while we may see things separately, we may equally focus on the background to the woven fabric ('Untergrund'), and if we do so 'strange relations arise between [things]' (p. 1239). These relations are witness to the instabilities that Zweig had sensed, but they also point to the labile realm of 'feeling as a whole, upon which the world rests like an island' (p. 1240). In an envoi, Musil paraphrases this feeling as the 'mobility of sense'. Such sense arises independently of any ideological commitments to give shape to what Musil calls spiritual or intellectual powers – taking Rilke's work well beyond a poetry of emotion or ideas.

## Martin Heidegger

In a recognisable way, Musil, like Zweig, is both elaborating a sense of the metaphoric connections that sustain Rilke's verse, but also anticipating Käte Hamburger's insight that Rilke responds to questions that might be viewed as the territory of European philosophy: language, consciousness and reality.

In particular, the unifying ground ('Untergrund') which Musil names as a variety of *feeling* on which the world rests like an island anticipates some of the structures evident in Martin Heidegger's philosophical responses to Rilke.

Initially, in his Parmenides lectures given in the winter of 1942–43, the existential philosopher Heidegger is highly critical of Rilke, but nevertheless appears to address exactly those aspects of the poetic project that Musil and Stefan Zweig celebrate: the endlessly connected nature of human experience. Towards the end of his lectures Heidegger identifies what he thinks is a mistake in the way Rilke conceives the idea of 'the Open' ('das Offene') in the first lines of the eighth *Duino Elegy*: 'With all its eyes the creature sees / the Open'. Heidegger's complaint is that this use of the notion of openness is identical to its use in a phrase like 'the open sea', by which we would mean that all limits or boundaries had disappeared.[5] Instead Heidegger wants to insist that the idea of openness is not accessible as a sense of extension that could be traversed or measured step-by-step: it is not some kind of 'gigantic container' (p. 222; tr. p. 149). But in Rilke's imagination, 'the Open' is 'the limitless, the infinite wherein living beings breathe and unrestrainedly dissolve into the irresistible causal nexus of Nature' (p. 233; tr. p. 157). This constant progress from being to 'being within the realm of beings' ('innerhalb des Seienden', p. 226; tr. p. 152 [modified]) offers another account of what Zweig calls the mutual interaction and intertwining of things in the vast integration of life we encounter in Rilke's poetry. Heidegger's emphatic objection is that this progress through things, creatures, beings is additive and extensive but cannot point us to the real nature of existence: what he calls 'the Free of the clearing of Being in distinction from all beings' (p. 226; tr. p. 152).

Although Heidegger had taken Rilke's description of the interior wall of a demolished house in *Malte* as an example of the way in which language can disclose a profound reality, and called this an elemental coming-to-expression, Rilke's status is still relativised in his major essay 'Wozu Dichter?' ('Why Poets?'), originally delivered, to a very select audience, for the twentieth anniversary of Rilke's death in 1946. Heidegger's title is from Friedrich Hölderlin's ode 'Bread and Wine' ('Brot und Wein'): 'what are poets for in a destitute time?' the poem asks ('Wozu Dichter in dürftiger Zeit?'). Hölderlin's question asks simply what poets are for in a needy, desolate time – and Heidegger wants to measure Rilke's insights by that standard.

For Heidegger, Rilke's 'valid' poetry is concentrated in the *Duino Elegies* and *The Sonnets to Orpheus*. The times are destitute 'not only because God is dead, but because mortals scarcely know or are capable even of their own mortality'.[6] And so the question arises: does Rilke give adequate expression to this condition? The date of Heidegger's text, as well as his development of Hölderlin's idea of the time's destitution, reveals this crisis as an aspect of modernity itself. The context of his thinking is provided by 'modern science and the total state' (p. 290; tr. p. 217) along with a relationship to commodities that Heidegger calls Americanism ('dieses Amerikanische'), themes which find their echo in Rilke – in poems such as *The Sonnets to Orpheus* II: 10 or in the letter Heidegger quotes (13 November 1925) in which Rilke describes 'empty indifferent things, sham things, counterfeit life' intruding from America (p. 291; tr. p. 218). Caught between very recent memories of a total state, the rise of technology and American mass-production, Heidegger seems to be in shock, casting about for the poetic word which can at least still point towards everything that seems, since the Greeks, to have been lost. Rilke, too close to the contemporary world if we think of *Malte*, of many of the *New Poems* and of the urbanism that prevails in *Duino Elegies* V and X, must be subordinate to Hölderlin. Only this poet of the loss of gods can guarantee a timeless alternative to the failure of Heidegger's own engagement with a contemporary 'total state' in the form of the Nazi regime.

The key term connecting the two poets, for Heidegger, is once again 'the Open'. Heidegger interprets the opening lines of the eighth *Duino Elegy* 'With all its eyes the creature sees / the Open' ('Mit allen Augen sieht die Kreatur / Das Offene') in the light of one of Rilke's occasional poems addressed to Helmuth Freiherr Lucius von Stoëdten: 'Wie die Natur die Wesen überläßt / dem Wagnis'; much of his account of Rilke's understanding of the Open is written as an elaborate commentary on this poem:

> As Nature leaves its creatures to the daring
> of their blunt drive to pleasure, chooses none
> to protect among earth-clods or boughs: so we
> are no more cherished by the primal
> ground of our being; *it dares us*. Only we
> go *with* this daring, further than plants or beasts,
> and will it; sometimes we dare even more
> (and not because we're drawn by selfishness)
> than life itself dares, just a breath's span more daring...
> This gains us, in our unprotectedness,
> a safe place there, just where the gravity
> of pure forces takes effect; in the end, what
> shelters us is our exposure, and, when we saw it turn
> threatening, that we faced it towards the Open,
> so that we might affirm it somewhere in
> the furthest round, where law impinges on us.[7]
>
> (KA II, 324)

In Heidegger's reading, Rilke sees two critically important movements at the start of his poem. First, something *like* 'Nature' but called instead the primordial ground ('Urgrund') of our being simply dares or *ventures* human beings in a way that leaves us without protection. Human beings, however, are different from the 'earth-clods' or branches (different from the mineral and the merely organic) because they share the will of the *Urgrund* – and are at times bolder ('wagender') than life itself. Heidegger understands this human willing as concentrated in technological construction which attempts to provide *artificial* protection for human beings in their 'unshieldedness'. In this way humans actively resist the 'pure relation' to Being as our primordial ground. Because we objectify our condition, stepping away from it, all things become for us mere objects that might be useful in the struggle against our sense of being existentially without protection. However, there is a second step in the poem: Rilke's claim that it is possible to be 'more daring / by a breath' means that (some) human beings go beyond the ground of the *Urgrund* willed for us by Nature, as it were, and into the *Abgrund* – the abyss of Being. Here, in free fall, it is possible for humankind to be returned to proper vulnerability to the Open where Being alone provides the order or orbit of our existence. In this way, Heidegger glimpses the possibility of a movement beyond the impasse of technology and its systematic reification and ruination of any human relation to Being.

What gives Heidegger pause, once more, is the idea at the very end of Rilke's poem that we are able to affirm our unprotectedness 'in the furthest round' or circumference ('im weitsten Umkreis'). Puzzled by the phrase, Heidegger finds Rilke's letter to Countess Sizzo-Norris-Crouy of 6 January 1923 illuminating.[8] Here the poet's words of condolence and encouragement speak of death as being like the dark side of the moon – not the opposite of life 'but rather its complement toward perfection, toward full measure, toward the real, whole, and full sphere and globe of Being' (p. 302; tr. p. 226). For the philosopher this fails to begin an understanding of the sphere of being from its central disclosure or opening towards a *boundless* circumference; instead it limits the sphere of life to a bounded totality that could be enumerated, but which is guaranteed some meaningful unity in human consciousness – and for Heidegger that leaves Rilke still caught up in the metaphysical tradition he wants to break away from.

In one sense, Heidegger grasps the characteristic structures of Rilke's poetic imagination very precisely in this critique. Like Zweig and Musil, he recognises the way in which, through metaphor and simile, otherwise unique objects, the *things* of the '*Ding*gedichte', are entirely dependent on each other when we come to perceive and understand them; the world as experienced is mutually inter-articulated. And second, these verbal metamorphoses often accomplish a spatial reversal: in the *New Poems* architectural and topographical poems, such as 'The Tower' in Furnes, 'The Steps of the Orangerie' in Versailles, or the canal-side bar and its inverted reflection in 'Quai du Rosaire', de-naturalise our perceptions of space, movement, and stillness, to generate the enlarged space of poetic imagination. In later poems, above all in the *Duino Elegies*, the rise and fall of the Belgian tower become the explicitly moralised dimensions of a larger world: indeed, if there is a lesson to be drawn from these poems, it seems to be this –

> and we, who think of happiness
> *rising*, would be touched
> by a sense that almost dismays us
> when a happy thing *falls*.
> (KA II, 234)

What is sketched here, nevertheless, also entails and invites pathos; and so it is easy enough to identify the space in which these relations and movements take place as the ground that 'provides for' them. Such provision is what Heidegger seems to understand by one of the fundamental words ('Grundwort') he identifies in Rilke's use of 'Bezug'. In *The Sonnets to Orpheus* I: 12, the living out of human life in 'signs and figures', quite distinct from the clock-time that only seems to shape it, leads to a profound recognition:

> And though our element's a mystery
> we somehow still act out of what it marries –
> antennae seeking out other antennae
> as the empty distance carries...[9]

> Ohne unsern wahren Platz zu kennen,
> handeln wir aus wirklichem Bezug.
> Die Antennen fühlen die Antennen,
> und die leere Ferne trug...

The place in which human beings find themselves is unknown, and yet our action is the issue of a relation that is real enough: in an insect image suggesting a sector of human being beyond the usual scope of perception and rationality, our antennae reaching out discover that 'the empty distance carries' ('die leere Ferne trug') – what seemed empty distance can nevertheless bear our weight and sustain the relationship of what is related ('aus wirklichem Bezug'); its apparent void was deceptive ('trug' from both 'tragen', to carry, and 'trügen', to deceive). Yet what sustains all of this, in the sonnet's final lines, is the earth itself that 'bestows'. This generosity takes us beyond all calculation and anticipation. However much the farmer undertakes,

> The sower
> Can't reach down to where the fattening seed
> is turning towards summer. The Earth *bestows*.

The transformation of the seed (or the act of sowing) into the temporality of the season is simply a gift.

It has been pointed out that the interiority conjured in so many of Rilke's poems is not a space of human consciousness. *Weltinnenraum* (literally 'worldinnerspace') is rather 'a realm of poetic figuration freed from the referentiality of ordinary language'.[10] This commitment to a different dimension of language is also what Heidegger seeks towards the end of his difficult essay, when the risk bolder than life's itself in Rilke's poem to von Stoëdten is identified as nothing less than the language of the poet, venturing beyond the merely communicative towards the place where 'Song is being' (*The Sonnets to Orpheus* I: 3, Paterson).

## Maurice Blanchot

Maurice Blanchot's essay 'The Work and Death's Space' in his 1955 collection *The Space of Literature* takes up many of Heidegger's themes. Blanchot considers a number of texts that address the poet's understandings of his task, through which he can explore the relations between writer and work, the calling of art, and its end, figured as Death. Blanchot's limpid style offers a striking counterpoint to Heidegger's idiom; more importantly his essay contrives a grave set of harmonious movements in close relation to the patterns of Heidegger's thought.

It is perhaps worth making two thematic statements. First, Blanchot sees in writing and its completion, its 'end', a deep solitude. The solitude of the artist, on which Rilke himself insisted in life, and which informs moments of the *Duino Elegies*, is only the beginning of this deepening isolation: 'He who writes the work is set aside; he who has written it is dismissed.'[11] The separation between the author and the work which has been written and completed is absolute and unmitigated. It is for this reason that the work, understood as that to which the author as a *writer* (and therefore not as a reader) ultimately has no access, no relationship, partakes in the other unknowable dimension of human existence, Death itself. Blanchot wants to insist that the very nature of the activity of writing poetry is irretrievably concealed in the same way. The poet never knows what his or her own action is. Art, Blanchot points out with reference to Clemens Brentano's Romantic novel *Godwi* (1801), consumes an entire life and annihilates its author.

Rilke provides a signal case of this relationship between writing and death, though not initially where we might expect it. *The Book of Hours*, after all, develops a line of thought about 'the rich death' and 'the little death' until, in a sustained sequence of poems, running from 'For Lord, the great cities are' through to 'The last sign, let it happen to us' (KA 1, 234–9) and anticipating the *Duino Elegies*, death and above all *authentic* death ('der eigne Tod') becomes a decisive criterion for Rilke's critique of the modern world. The principle that attributes such significance is approached in Blanchot's essay through Rilke's 'Requiem for Wolf Count von Kalckreuth' (KA 1, 422–6), who had committed suicide. Echoing Heidegger's sense that it is utter human vulnerability that gives access to a more profound kind of safety, Blanchot returns to Rilke's language of maturity and ripeness: there are, he says, two kinds of 'distracted death' – 'the one in which we have not matured, which does not belong to us, and the one which has not matured in us and which we have acquired by violence' (p. 153; tr. p. 121). Such distorted relations to the event of death can be found in many of Rilke's texts, from *The Book of Hours* to the world of Paris that haunts Malte Laurids Brigge. If Malte's characteristic anxiety ('Angst'; Blanchot's 'angoisse') is derived from the overwhelming anonymity that modern, urban life and its crowds impose on the individual, the extreme form of that anonymous existence takes shape in the 'mass-produced' death that Malte finds in the city's hospitals. On the basis of a retrospective biographical identification of this experience with Rilke's own experience during his earliest stay in Paris, Blanchot explains *The Book of Hours* texts that envisage an authentic death as a flight from such anonymity, but also from the neutrality of a death that can never be possessed or personalised. The story of Malte's grandfather, Chamberlain Brigge, in Denmark turns death into a carefully crafted achievement: like a work of art, brought forth by a kind of terrible male act of birth ('The great death which each one carries within / That is the fruit around which all things turn', Rilke writes in *The Book of Hours*: KA 1, 236).

In imagining an aristocratic death through the figure of Chamberlain Brigge, Rilke, as Blanchot is quick to point out, is not simply fantasising some kind of personal survival – a life *through* death, if not quite life after death. Rather he recognises the ineluctable reality of that death and thus seeks to expand life towards it, in some sense to include it. And yet the tension between the anonymity of death and the desire to make it 'my own' in an act of opening and appropriation continues. Blanchot cites one of the most extraordinary passages from *Malte* as testimony to the impersonal sense of death 'which is the excess of our strength, which exceeds it' (p. 167;

tr. p. 131). After scanning the ways in which readers in the Bibliothèque Nationale in Paris seem to live in their books, and noticing the mysterious world of signs inhabited by the street people of the city, Malte encounters a dying man in the dairy where he has gone to eat. The man faces that moment 'when everything will have lost its meaning' (KA III, 489). Safely returned to his chilly room, Malte acknowledges how much he wants 'to remain among the meanings that have become dear to me' (KA III, 490). The loss of meaning, or the radical reconfiguration of meaning beyond the self, is hence understood in the context of mortality when Malte notes that another time, the time of 'another exegesis' will dawn, 'leaving not one word resting on another' (KA III, 490). This remarkable text appears something like one fifth of the way through *Malte*, which for Blanchot indicates the need to live or to write *beyond* death; or perhaps to avoid the full recognition of what has been seen: 'Everything conspires to suggest that Rilke hid the end of the book at the beginning, in order to demonstrate to himself that after this end something remains possible' (p. 168; tr. p. 131).

In conscious human imagination there appears to be a prospect beyond the limit fixed by death; and yet, as Blanchot reads it, the very possibility of imaginative representation traps us in a relationship in which we are forced to observe ourselves and so turn away from the realm-beyond which we thought could be accessed in this way. In these pages Blanchot offers a subtle reading of the first pages of the eighth *Elegy*, in counterpoint, once again, to Heidegger:

> This we call Fate: to be in opposition
> and nothing else and always opposite.

> Dieses heißt Schicksal: gegenüber sein
> und nichts als das und immer gegenüber.
>
> (KA II, 225)

For Blanchot's reading, it is the human condition to be delivered over to a world of representations and deprived of any presence other than our own. In being thus turned away from things and back in upon ourselves we are trapped in a bad kind of extensive space, where at best any one thing necessarily supplants another, and in the bad interiority of consciousness itself. It is hence Rilke's insight that intimacy (subjective interiority) and the exteriority of space can be known as one and the same: this is what the 1914 poem 'It beckons us to feeling' calls *Weltinnenraum*, the inner space of the world. Such a coincidence of interior and exterior, which Blanchot identifies with Rilke's notion of openness, can only ever be utterly uncertain – because any glimpse we may catch of it is bound to be figurative and so return us to secondary representations: 'for all mirroring is already that of a figurative reality' (p. 176; tr. p. 137). Like the confidence generated from the sheer vulnerability of human beings in Heidegger's essay, for Blanchot the constant deflection of consciousness (in both senses) opens up the possibility of a return. Yet this, it emerges, will be possible not as a reversal of interiority, but as its intensification, in an abandonment of all desire to possess or to represent: a kind of mystical non-attachment.

For Blanchot this remains, critically, a *literary* process: Rilke's 'tasks are essentially those of the poetic word' (p. 178; tr. p. 138); the intensity of *Weltinnenraum* has to do with how language works to produce meaning. The higher meanings Rilke refers to in his famous letter to Hulewicz, the Polish translator of the *Elegies*, are gained by abandoning representations. This can seem very close to Edmund Husserl's attempts to capture pure perception through what he called phenomenological reduction; Blanchot recognises the similarity, in an anticipation of Hamburger's argument, but insists that Rilke must be understood in a different way. For the intensification of the inwardness of human consciousness and imagination draws all the supposed objects of our awareness into interiority in order to free them from human exploitation, so that their meanings change. The process of (re)naming invoked in the ninth *Elegy*, and the unimaginable invisibility of the world that follows upon it, can then be identified with the poet's project of translation within this inner space of the world (*Weltinnenraum*) that is the space of the *poem itself*.

Language draws visible things into its realm of invisibility. This human power is also the point at which human beings step into a space utterly beyond the self. Language takes us into a dimension to which we have no relation, just as the writer's work *written* is beyond any *reading* the author might undertake. And for Blanchot, as in Rilke's own mythology, Orpheus – the godlike hero who enters the realm of Death to recover Eurydice, but whose creativity is at one with her loss – is the supreme figure of a poetic life known ultimately in its relation to death, its *other* relation: 'der andere Bezug' when writing carries identity beyond 'itself' into metamorphosis and dispersal, like Orpheus torn apart by the Maenads. Blanchot thus brings Rilke close to a high Symbolist understanding of the almost-nothing that is the poem. The inaccessibility of the poem enacts the unknowable certainty of death, and both are traced through the figure of Orpheus. In this way Blanchot can follow a continuous line of thought in Rilke, leading from the idea of *The Book of Hours*, and most fully presented in Chamberlain Brigge, that each individual might achieve a death proper to them, through the *New Poems* and their commitment to visibility, the gaze and the work of sight, to the occultation of Malte's death in the novel, and the acknowledgment of death as the un-ownable and of the poem as the space of the *in*visible. In a final turn of Rilke's thinking, and of Blanchot's essay, the things – objects or places – that dominate in the *New Poems* can be reclaimed, but now in the disinterested celebration that offers them to the Angel of the *Elegies*. Blanchot returns to Rilke's poem for von Stoëdten, and identifies 'the gravity . . . of pure forces' which is 'repose in the web of influences and the balance of movements' (p. 198; tr. p. 151). But rather than seeing this, as Heidegger suspects, as a distortion of the Open into a plenitude marked and enclosed by limits, Blanchot construes the *locus standi* of the poet as the intersection of infinite relations, risked in affirmation, for which Rilke finds a metaphor in the wide open anemone of *The Sonnets to Orpheus* II: 5. In the spirit of Heidegger's semantics, Blanchot can hear in Rilke's use of the word 'Entschluß' (decision, resolution) an un-closing ('ent-schließen') so total that the poet must confront the indeterminacy of being itself – 'at the intersection of infinite relations, at the place opened and as if void where foreign destinies cross' (p. 201; tr. p. 153).

Blanchot has a very high view of the work of poetry. Rilke's task, as he says, is essentially poetic, and towards the end of his essay, in a reflection on *The Sonnets to Orpheus* I: 5, it is Rilke's 'poetic experience' that leads to absolute abandonment to the realm outside the self, where

> *Orpheus*, we say
> wherever the true song is manifest.
> He comes and goes.

The quest for an authentic, personal death, canvassed in *The Book of Hours* and still contemplated in Chamberlain Brigge, can be surpassed – but not in some transcendence for which Orpheus might serve as the divinity. The final human vulnerability lies in the unavoidable necessity of Orpheus's disappearance:

> But though his constant leaving is a torment,
> leave he must, if we're to understand.

Poetry itself, on Blanchot's reading, emerges in this necessary absence; and so it is no surprise that his final reflections draw Mallarmé into the argument. Yet, for Rilke, this relation to negativity is the very thing that sets language free for celebration.

## Paul de Man

Yet negativity is perhaps not so easily contained. Paul de Man's essay on Rilke presents one of the most sophisticated readings of the poetry.[12] Written for a French translation of the poems in 1972, in *Allegories of Reading* (1979) it serves as the first demonstration of de Man's theoretical focus: the divergence between grammar and referential meaning, identified as 'the figural dimension of language' (p. 270). De Man can take up Blanchot's understanding of Rilke's task as essentially poetic by radicalising it: the apparent pathos of the poet's existential engagement with Death is misleading once we attend closely to the mechanism of his writing. In spite of his accessibility to biographical readings, through his private correspondence or its resonance with any reader's personal experience, 'Rilke is less interested in his own person than one might gather' (p. 21). What's more, the range of his themes – whether places, objects, or characters – is also a false trail: for between the reader and this colourful immediacy there is always interposed 'the screen of language that controls its own representational mastery'. De Man insists that when Rilke writes of the 'home of the sayable' in the ninth *Duino Elegy*, he cannot avoid referring to the text of the poem itself: the claim made in the largest movement of the work, from Duino to Orpheus, its task of converting loss into celebration, lament into praise, entrusts to language *in the poetic text* a salvific power which in de Man's reading will prove unreliable.

In this respect, de Man acknowledges in Heidegger's paper, 'Why Poets?', a predecessor for his own scepticism; but he also holds that Rilke's own poetic language puts into question the very claims its seems to make. First, de Man points towards the sound effects, euphony and pattern, that undeniably dominate Rilke's technique in *The Book of Hours* (and beyond) so that 'the meaning of the poems is the conquest of the technical skills which they illustrate by their success' (p. 31). The monastic subject of these poems is hence no more than a subterfuge, a mask for their obsession with their own linguistic resources. From *The Book of Hours* de Man moves to a poem in *The Book of Images* which provides the model for the crucial theme of his analysis. 'At the Edge of Night' (KA 1, 283) seems to present the interior of a room in relation to the nocturnal landscape: the lyric voice presents itself as a violin string resonating across this unified space. De Man identifies in the imagery of the violin, its body, strings and F-holes, not a mode of expressivity through the lyric voice, but an exemplary model of the structure of metaphor, relating the interiority of feeling and experience to some external object (as in 'My love is like a red, red rose'). This, de Man claims, guides Rilke's choice of images; and the fact that the poem derives this pattern from a musical instrument usefully links the function of metaphor with the acoustic qualities identified in *The Book of Hours*. The universality that Musil had sensed in the poetry is effectively shown to be a quality of its recurrent means.

If subjective interiority moves into external 'expression', simultaneously the externality of things and their mystery is drawn into the inner imaginative world of the lyric voice: this yields a structural principle central to de Man's exposition. The figure of *chiasmus*, taken beyond its usual definition as a feature of syntax, becomes the determining factor in Rilke's 'reading' of the world, which extends to the *New Poems* and beyond. The autobiographical motivation of so many of the poems from Rilke's middle period is shown to be the mask of a *rhetorical* practice: the things that preoccupy the poetry 'are conceived in such a way as to allow a reversal of their categorical properties, and this reversal allows the reader to conceive of properties that would be normally incompatible (such as inside/outside, before/after, death/life...) as complementary' (p. 40). Rilke becomes a poet obsessively and repeatedly investigating and displaying the structure of metaphorical and therefore of poetic language itself.

De Man's reading makes 'Orpheus. Eurydice. Hermes', in *New Poems*, central to Rilke's enterprise as a whole. The loss of the beloved and the abandonment of desire turns out to be the very thing that makes the poet's power of lament possible – a world of lament 'in which / everything was there once more' ('in der / alles noch einmal da war'; KA 1, 502): that *alles* must be taken seriously; a world figured as poetry or, at any rate, as elegy. The paradoxical result is that the power of poetic language actually depends on the loss of the very thing it seems to be about, ultimately of the belief that the poem's referent is the source of its meaning. This language no longer has any purchase on the world at all: the loss of the object, however loved, means for de Man's nihilistic account that at the centre of the poetry there is a necessary void, around which its patterns of sound and figuration move emptily. The rise and fall of the *Elegies*, Orpheus's coming and going in the *Sonnets*, the understanding of an inner truth different from outward appearances in *New Poems* are no more than variations on a recurrent pattern of chiasmus. And in the end Rilke has to concede that his project of Romantic coherence is a subterfuge – like the stars in *The Sonnets to Orpheus* I: 11, such structured constellations are illusory: 'Even their starry union is a lie.'

NOTES

1 Käte Hamburger, 'Die phänomenologische Struktur der Dichtung Rilkes', in *Philosophie der Dichter: Novalis, Schiller, Rilke* (Stuttgart: Kohlhammer, 1966), pp. 179–275 (p. 179).
2 Donald A. Prater (ed.), *Rainer Maria Rilke, Stefan Zweig: Briefe und Dokumente* (Frankfurt am Main: Insel, 1987), p. 45. Translations are my own unless otherwise stated.

3 See Robert Musil, *Gesammelte Werke*, ed. Adolf Frisé, 9 vols. (Reinbek bei Hamburg: Rowohlt, 1981), vol. VIII, pp. 1229–42 (p. 1237).
4 Robert Musil, 'From the Posthumous Papers', trans. Burton Pike, in *The Man Without Qualities*, trans. Sophie Wilkins, editorial consultant Burton Pike, 2 vols. (London: Picador, 1995), vol. II, p. 1185 (modified).
5 Martin Heidegger, *Parmenides* [Gesamtausgabe vol. 54], ed. M. S. Frings (Frankfurt am Main: Klostermann, 1982), p. 226; English trans., *Parmenides*, by André Schuwer and Richard Rojcewicz (Bloomington and Indianapolis: Indiana University Press, 1992).
6 Martin Heidegger, 'Wozu Dichter?', in *Holzwege* (Frankfurt am Main: Vittorio Klostermann, [1950] 2003), pp. 274; English trans., *Off the Beaten Track*, trans. and ed. Julian Young and Kenneth Haynes (Cambridge University Press, 2002), p. 204.
7 This version is from the vigorous discussion of Rilke's philosophical interpreters by Anthony Stephens, 'Cutting Poets to Size – Heidegger, Hölderlin, Rilke', *Jacket* 32 (Spring 2007), at httpi//jacketmagazine.com/32/stephens-heidegger.shtml.
8 Heidegger misdates the letter to 26 January: see *Materialien zu Rilkes 'Duineser Elegien'*, ed. Ulrich Fülleborn and Manfred Engel (Frankfurt am Main: Suhrkamp, 1980), pp. 280–4 and B II, 263–9.
9 Don Paterson, *Orpheus. A Version of Rilke's 'Die Sonette an Orpheus'* (London: Faber and Faber, 2006), p. 14.
10 Véronique Fóti, *Heidegger and the Poets* (New Jersey, London: Humanities Press, 1992), p. 37. See also Michel Haar, *The Song of the Earth*, trans. Reginald Lilly (Bloomington and Indianapolis: Indiana University Press, 1993).
11 Maurice Blanchot, *L'Espace littéraire* (Paris: Gallimard, 1968), p. 10; English trans., *The Space of Literature*, by Ann Smock (Lincoln and London: University of Nebraska Press, 1982), p. 21. Further references to this version appear in the text.
12 Paul de Man, 'Tropes (Rilke)', in *Allegories of Reading: Figural Language in Rousseau, Rilke, Nietzsche and Proust* (Newhaven, CT, and London: Yale University Press, 1979), pp. 28–56.

# 13

KAREN LEEDER

# Rilke's legacy in the
# English-speaking world

This chapter will trace the vigorous, if sometimes curious, afterlife of the poet in the English-speaking world, with a view to exploring the phenomenon that the writer John Bayley called 'Rilke-in-English', and also in order to turn the spotlight back on Rilke and ask what this reception reveals about him and his work.[1] It is an intriguing paradox that Rilke, who had little affinity for Anglo-Saxon culture and indeed demonstrated a marked hostility towards many aspects of it, should have become in America today 'the most popular German literary export to the country outside of Goethe'.[2] The history of his reception in Germany and Austria had been fraught: inevitably bound up with the need to come to terms with Fascism after the Second World War. Although Rilke himself was not a Nationalist and was not favoured by the regime, he was much emulated during the Third Reich and his works were often distorted to suit the dominant mood. After 1945 his reputation suffered, with poets suspicious of his aloof aestheticism at a time when the political credentials of poetry were uppermost. Indeed his quasi-mystical inwardness was so out of tune with the prevailing post-war tone that critics failed to identify any kind of Rilke-school in the emerging voices after 1945 and the poet Hilde Domin even complained of a Rilke 'black-out'.[3]

Rilke was in the end too formative a poet in the German language for other poets to ignore him for long. By the 1970s, and certainly by the centenary of his birth in 1975, it was clear that his influence had continued working at a subterranean level and now emerged onto the scene as a decisive voice. This was demonstrated in a famous sequence of (marginally satirical) poems by the Austrian concrete poet Ernst Jandl, 'The ordinary Rilke', included in one of the many volumes which marked this centenary, but also in countless essays discussing the renewed interest in Rilke by noted poets and critics.[4] That interest has continued pretty much uninterrupted since then in Austria, Germany (East and West) and in the Berlin Republic and is today as strong as ever. Indeed the German-language reception of Rilke would have furnished an extensive study in itself and goes beyond the scope of this volume. 'A Little Blue Girl' ('Ein kleines blaues Mädchen'), a recent essay on Rilke's poem 'The Carousel', by one of the most remarkable German-language poets to have emerged over the past few years, Durs Grünbein, will have to stand here as a single and rich example.[5]

By contrast, after his death, Rilke enjoyed a much more unequivocal welcome in English-speaking cultures. Not only was he translated early, frequently and well; some of those translations have even come to exist as definitive works in their own right. The translation by J. B. Leishman and Stephen Spender of the *Duino Elegies*, published by the Hogarth Press in 1939, is a case in point. It has become a literary landmark and still remains for many the first contact with this most extraordinary and contradictory work. Today translation of Rilke has become something of an industry in itself. But more significant still: a galaxy of prominent poets and novelists have attested to the importance of Rilke for their thinking and have been demonstrably inspired by him in their work. That list is often surprising, including names one would not immediately link with Rilke, such as Ernest Hemingway or the Scottish Nationalist and Communist Hugh MacDiarmid (Christopher Murray Grieve). For all that many writers attest to certain personal affinities with Rilke, it could be argued that the extraordinary extent of the reception owes its existence to the fact that Rilke represents something largely absent in English poetry, but not beyond its reach. Rilke epitomises the German poetic tradition, and within it the apotheosis of the German language. As the poet and translator Michael Hofmann puts it: Rilke is 'the poet in whom its persuasions, abstracts and music are most triumphantly effective'.[6]

Rilke embodies the paradigm of the itinerant or homeless poet, both literally as his biography attests, but also in literary terms. He does not belong securely to any individual national literature, and especially not to the despised German tradition, with which he saw himself 'linked only by language' ('The Testament'; KA IV, 710). Despite his many travels in Europe, North Africa and Russia, Rilke never visited England or the United States of America. The English language remained alien to him despite desultory attempts to learn it in order to read Keats and translate Elizabeth Barrett Browning's *Sonnets from the Portuguese*, and his friendship with the ardent Anglophile Rudolf Kassner. Despite Kassner's encouragement, Rilke harboured a bizarre and lasting aversion for English culture too and confessed that England itself lay outside the magic circle of his nature and its experiences and possibilities.[7] America, moreover, represented an alien world for him, a symbol of everything that was repugnant. As the Austrian poet

Nikolaus Lenau stated in a passage that Rilke alludes to in one of his letters
(5 June 1896, to Rudolf Christoph Jenny):

> America has no wine, no nightingale [ . . . ] brother, these Americans have the
> souls of shopkeepers, they are dead to all life of the mind, as dead as mutton.
> The nightingale is in the right not to visit these fellows. It seems to me seriously
> and profoundly significant that America has no nightingale. It seems to me like
> a poetic curse.[8]

America not only lacked the nightingale and the inspiration for the lyrical
mood, it was for Rilke the land of the machine, of mass production, of
'gold-lacquered din' (*Elegy* x; KA II, 230): a region fundamentally inimical
to poetry. It seemed to him devoid of what he called the 'Laric' value (from
'Lares et Penates', the Roman house-gods), which objects in daily use had in
the time before mass-production. Nothing in America could be considered
'real', as Rilke argues in a famous letter to his translator Witold Hulewicz,
in the same way that the thousands of inanimate objects that went into his
own poetry were real for him.

> But now empty indifferent things are forcing themselves upon us from America,
> mere semblances of things, mere dummies of life. . . . A house in the Amer-
> ican sense, an American apple or one of the vines, have *nothing* whatso-
> ever in common with the house, the fruit, the grapes, into which the hopes
> and the pensiveness of our forefathers had been transfused. [ . . . ] The lived
> and living things, the things *that share our thought*, these are on the de-
> cline and can no more be replaced. *We are perhaps the last to have known such
> things.*
> (B, II, 376–7)

In the light of this marked hostility towards everything American, it is amaz-
ing that Rilke should have enjoyed such a sustained and vigorous reception
both there and in England – the latter perhaps less vigorously despised by
him, but certainly no more cherished – right up to the present day. Moreover,
that reception has reflected and been marked by the needs of the historical
moment to the extent that very different emphases have emerged – very
different versions of Rilke.

### Rilke in time of war

When the first English translation of Rilke's *Duino Elegies* appeared, it was
reviewed in the United States by W. H. Auden. Having mentioned Rilke's
growing influence on the diction and imagery of contemporary English-
language poetry, he concludes that Rilke 'is probably more read and more

highly esteemed by English and Americans than by Germans'.[9] In 1946, in similar vein, Stephen Spender stated in a talk on the BBC Far Eastern Service that Rilke's work had been considered by most English poets as deeply as that of Eliot himself.[10] Other poets of the 1930s–1950s most strongly influenced by him were W. H. Auden, Sidney Keyes, Alun Lewis, Edith Sitwell, Stephen Spender, Cecil Day-Lewis, and Hugh MacDiarmid. Given Rilke's general political abstinence, it is noteworthy that the reception of him in England in the 1930s and beyond was for the most part initiated by the 'pink' (to use the jargon of the times), that is politically engaged, but not necessarily Communist, writers. More importantly his work was ultimately placed under the sign of death and war.

Auden's own works are marked by a large number of reminiscences and conscious borrowings from Rilke. He clearly learned a great deal of his craft from his model before very vocally rejecting the poet outright. In *Poems* (1928) Auden is already practising the 'Rilkean sonnet' form which would dominate his work in the 1930s. Both Auden's architectural imagery (buildings, fountains, aqueducts, etc.), along with his images (the doll, child, animal, rose, mirror), recall Rilke and are invested with Rilke's symbolic value. But in particular it is the expression of 'human life in terms of landscape', that fascinated Auden in Leishman and Spender's translation of the *Duino Elegies*, the 'Paysage Moralisé' (to borrow the title of one of Auden's own poems), that offered Auden a model of how to balance abstraction with the concrete ('Rilke in English', p. 135). The sonnet sequence 'Sonnets from China' (1939) contains a number of direct allusions, which suggest that as a poet at least Rilke is also offering a kind of creative inspiration.

> To-night in China let me think of one,
>
> Who for ten years of drought and silence waited,
> Until in Muzot all his being spoke,
> And everything was given once for all:
>
> Awed, grateful, tired, content to die, completed,
> He went out in the winter night to stroke
> That tower as one pets an animal.[11]

By the time of *New Year Letter* (1941) the emphasis had changed as the relationship has been forced by the pressure of historical events into an ironical mode. Although there are a number of (sometimes unacknowledged) quotations, especially from the *Duino Elegies* and *Letters to a Young Poet*, Rilke's metaphysics of the spirit seems less urgent than the realities of the moment. Ironic versions of the acrobat, angel and hero figure appear and Rilke himself becomes an emblem of a kind of distasteful, life-denying abstinence. Auden's reference to 'RILKE, whom *die Dinge* bless / The Santa Claus of loneliness' (p. 204) is dismissive enough (if difficult to pin down exactly), but a later comment in the same poem makes Auden's stance clear. Here the Devil, friend of 'all vague idealistic art / That coddles the uneasy heart' (p. 214) champions Rilke:

> He puts a RILKE in my hands.
> 'You know the *Elegies*, I'm sure,
> *–O Seligkeit der Kreatur*
> *Sie immer bleibt im Schosse–* womb,
> In English, is a rhyme to tomb.'
> He moves on tiptoe round the room,
> Turns on the radio to mark
> Isolde's *Sehnsucht* for the dark.
>
> (p. 213)

Significant here is the sense that for him Rilke's 'creatureliness' represents a morbid longing associated most closely with German Romanticism. For Auden now, the technical inspiration once drawn from the poet has been succeeded by a rejection of his aesthetics of death. Later, it is true, Auden will cite 'boredom' rather than 'disapproval' as the reason he no longer reads Rilke;[12] and later still he attacks the poet (like Rilke) 'who comes to think of himself as the god who creates his subjective universe out of nothing' and dismisses his work, for all his craft, as 'false and unreal' (*The Dyer's Hand*, p. 76). However, at this point (1941), Rilke's poetry represents the antithesis of both the mundanity and also the vitality of life. For Auden, writing in the midst of the reality of death and war, this seemed too great a price for poetry.

Rilke as a poet of death also characterises the work of Sidney Keyes, a soldier and poet killed aged twenty in North Africa.[13] Keyes' original editor Michael Meyer documents a sustained and profound engagement with the German poet in his work. At one point Keyes was planning a series of elegies with pain as the central motif, to be based on the *Duino Elegies*, and a sonnet sequence based on *The Sonnets to Orpheus*, but also wrote enthusiastically about *The Lay of the Love and Death of the Cornet Christoph Rilke* and reported reading the novel *Malte*. Keyes' poem 'Prospero' (pp. 1–3), for example, written at the age of sixteen, is in many ways a pendant to Rilke's 'The Spirit Ariel' and documents a very similar understanding of death. Keyes' fragment 'Shall the Dead Return?' (pp. 7–8) recalls Rilke's 'Requiem for a Friend', and his 'Gilles de Retz' (pp. 20–1), one of the poems from the projected sequence of elegies, celebrates a love without possession, drawn directly from Rilke. Keyes made only one translation from Rilke, 'The Poet', but the poem which best reveals Rilke's influence on Keyes is 'The Foreign Gate', written between February and March 1942 (pp. 57–66). The motto for the poem comes from the sixth *Elegy* and echoes of phrases or thoughts appear in all the six sections. The engagement culminates, however, in the fifth section of the work

> Were I to mount beyond the field
> Of battle and the lovers' wood to the high-pillared house
> Where the great sit, in stone unmoved yet knowing
> The world's minute catastrophes;
> Judged and yet unjudging, presences of fame
> And still perfection; were I to speak out clear
> In that high house, a voice of light might answer.
> Once a man cried and the great Orders heard him:
> Pacing upon a windy wall at night
> A pale unlearned poet out of Europe's
> Erratic heart cried and was filled with speech.
> Were I to cry, who in that proud hierarchy
> Of the illustrious would pity me?
> What should I cry, how should I learn their language?
> The cold wind takes my words.                    (p. 64)

That gate here is the gate of death; Rilke 'the pale unlearned poet out of Europe's / Erratic heart'; and the cry that initiates the *Duino Elegies* returns here as a bleak and unheard echo: 'The cold wind takes my words.' As a whole the poem encourages the acceptance of death in accordance with Rilke's notion of submission. In a letter to Richard Church of January 1943 Keyes comments:

> As to the question of my symbolism: the best clue I can give you is to say that I believe the greatest and most influential poets in the last 100 years or so to be Yeats and Rilke. These two brought back reports from a kind of Ultima Thule of Romanticism, which suggest that there is even more – much more – to be discovered there; and that a starting point of my quest is to therefore synthesise this information.                    (p. 121)

A number of critics have seen this synthesis, the linking of the symbolism of continental writers with current English practice, as the significance of Rilke for English literature. However, there is also another side to Keyes' reaction which is worth noting here. In an article, 'The Artist in Society', written at the time of 'The Foreign Gate', Keyes claims it is the function of the poet 'to give to his [the poet's] audience some inkling of the continual fusion of finite and infinite, spiritual and physical, which is our world

[ ... ] to express the eternal meaning which resides in the physical world, and show the relationship between the eternal and its physical counterpoint' (p. 121). This enterprise certainly bears all the hallmarks of Rilke. But in Keyes' work that balance between the objective and the abstract or spiritual, the same balance that had troubled Auden in Rilke, has moved ever further towards the deathly. In a diary entry of the same period he dwells on the treatment of death during the centuries and comments that it has been left to 'necrophilious Germany' to provide Rilke, the ultimate 'Poet of Death' in the twentieth century. In a letter to John Heath-Stubbs of 20 February 1943, he dwells on the conception of death as a creature we bear within us and the necessity of making our own terms with it. But crucially he also recognises the danger of such a death-wish, and in the same letter comments on the 'hopeless infatuation' of the German nation with death: 'the persistent death wish in German poetry; it finds its highest form [ ... ] in Rilke's conception' (p. 123). Keyes is far from 'the degenerate Romantic who wooed death' (p. 122) that his editor fears he might be taken for. However, the Rilke that one encounters in his work, as in that of Auden and others, at this time, is a Rilke born of a uniquely emphatic, and perhaps uniquely distorting, historical moment.[14]

## Rilke in America: poet of inwardness

Rilke's reputation in the USA emerged with a certain time lag and long after his reputation in Europe was well established. Although the generation of modernism – Wallace Stevens, T. S. Eliot, Ezra Pound, William Carlos Williams – had taken cognisance of him, they remained largely detached. And after 1945 Rilke's 'Art for Art's sake' aesthetic took some time to find wider favour among writers struggling to establish their relevance in a politicised climate. Ironically perhaps, given the political suspicion which met Rilke in Germany after the war, it was not until the Cold War generation that Rilke found himself championed in America. His reputation was not uncontested. Archibald MacLeish warned against an aesthetic 'sealed and unventilated [ ... ] which sooner or later stifles the birds', though conceding that if something could come from this type of writing it would be from the pen of Rilke.[15] In his poem 'A Stimulant for an Old Beast', John Berryman makes a rather more pointed attack: 'Rilke was a *jerk*'.[16] It was rather through Robert Lowell, Randell Jarrell and Robert Bly, also prominent translators of Rilke, that the poet came to have such a central place in the American literary imagination. All three approached Rilke through a markedly biographical perspective, both in their translations and in their own poems. This 'elective affinity' allowed them to process aspects of their own personality, but also to introduce a new note into American poetry. Bly, in a famous statement of 1963, expounded upon the tendency of the century to dissipate its energies in destructive outward motion, and the fundamentally 'wrong turning' that American poetry had taken in not resisting that direction and not embracing the inwards movement he saw documented in the best of European poetry and painting.[17] Drawing on Rilke's early poetry, and especially the *New Poems*, showed him and the others how to develop a different voice. Lowell, for example, attempted to come to terms with the legacy of his forebears and especially his father through his engagement with Rilke. His version of Rilke's 1906 poem 'Portrait of My Father as a Young Man' (KA 1, 483) preserves the situation and the reflection on mortality of Rilke's poem, but personalises it:

> All the rest lies curtained in itself,
> and so withdrawn, I cannot understand
> my father as he bleaches on the page –
> Oh quickly disappearing photograph
> in my more slowly disappearing hand![18]

> Und alles andere mit sich selbst verhängt
> und ausgelöscht als ob wirs nicht verständen
> und tief aus seiner eignen Tiefe trüb –,
> Du schnell vergehendes Daguerreotyp
> in meinen langsamer vergehenden Händen.

There are several striking interventions: the play on the word 'withdrawn' (of the curtain) which is absent in the German, and the introduction of the first-person 'I cannot understand' (plural and more abstract in German), both serve to intensify the absence in the striking 'bleaching' of the next line. The words 'my father' do not appear anywhere in the German poem.

Jarrell's work with Rilke is even more sustained, including a preoccupation with transformation, childhood, exclusion, certain metaphors (windows, animals) and a very profound engagement with the inner life of marginal, exiled figures, especially women. Most of the poems in his cycle 'The Woman at the Washington Zoo' which was placed before his Rilke translations in the volume of the same name (1960) are seeking some form of transcendental escape from their situation. For example, the first three – 'The Woman at the Washington Zoo', 'Cinderella' and 'The End of the Rainbow' – all depict women who are neglected, isolated, ageing or unwanted. In this all of them are, as Jarrell put it himself, a 'distant relation' of the female speaker in the poem whose title he borrowed from Rilke, 'Seele im Raum' ('Soul in Space'; KA ii, 156), and suffer the same fate as the figures in the poems Jarrell translated at this time ('Faded' (KA i, 542); 'The Widow's Song' (KA i, 326)).[19] They are abandoned and forgotten. In the first and title poem of the cycle Jarrell depicts a middle-aged civil servant who feels herself cut off from the world around her. The first section introduces her and characterises her by the things that constitute her existence:

> The saris go by me from the embassies.
>
> Cloth from the moon, cloth from another planet.
> They look back at the leopard like the leopard.
>
> And I. . . .
>    This print of mine, that has kept its color
> Alive through so many cleanings; this dull null
> Navy I wear to work, and wear from work, and so
> To my bed, so to my grave, with no
> Complaints, no comment: neither from my chief,
> The Deputy Chief Assistant, nor his chief –
> Only I complain. . . . this serviceable
> Body that no sunlight dyes, no hand suffuses
> But, dome-shadowed, withering among columns,
> Wavy beneath fountains –[20]

The speaker is overwhelmed by the objects around her upon whose existence she leaves no imprint. Indeed the speaker does not occupy the subject position at all in the first three lines: she is the object that others pass by. When a first-person subject finally does emerge, it dissolves immediately in a series of dots to be followed by further objects that characterise her dilemma. The edging out of the subject, the bombardment of nouns, the use of objects to illustrate inner states and the interest in loneliness and ageing are all recognisable from Rilke. As the poem continues the speaker's body is described as:

>                    small, far-off, shining
> In the eyes of the animals, these beings trapped
> As I am trapped but not, themselves, the trap,
> Aging, but without knowledge of their age,
> Kept safe here, knowing not of death, for death –
> Oh! bars of my own body open, open!

It is difficult to imagine a passage that so echoes Rilke; it embodies the sense, found especially in the *New Poems* and the *Duino Elegies* but also elsewhere, that human beings are trapped by their acute consciousness of life (and death) and are thus unable to experience it simply and fully.

Robert Bly took this engagement with inner states even further and is the poet whose preoccupation with Rilke is marked by a unique longevity and intensity. His 'The Night Journey in the Cooking Pot' charts his first encounter with Rilke's work and the discovery of a new kind of poetry within himself.

> I float on solitude as on water...there is a road...
> I felt the road first in New York, in that great room
> reading Rilke in the womanless loneliness.
> How marvellous the great wings sweeping across the floor,
> inwardness, inwardness, inwardness [...][21]

The poem contains the three words (solitude, road and inwardness) now synonymous with Bly, who lived as a virtual recluse in New York during the period 1951 to 1954; but of course the great significance is that they emerge in the study of the Austrian poet. Indeed during this time Bly also translated twenty-four poems from Rilke's *Book of Hours*, marking what he called his own time of 'Innigkeit' or inwardness.[22] From the beginning what Bly understood by the word 'Innigkeit' was not a Romantic indulgence in the self, but rather the search for something that had been repressed in contemporary culture (as he expresses in the 'Wrong Turning' essay). Within the self he hoped to discover the profound interrelatedness of human existence and the natural world and to work at the internalisation of the 'Things of this World' (ibid., p. 4). For him the key is what he calls 'Gott-natur' which he defines as 'divine instinctuality' but also 'non-human nature'. It is these he wishes to bring together within the work of art and thus rescue things from city culture by dint of 'seeing' so intently as to bring creation to a deeper sense of being.[23]

However, this focus on the inner-self has, particularly in recent years, been trivialised, simplified and commercialised to the point where Rilke has been reinvented as 'a high Priest of Narcissism', who has earned his place alongside workout videos and gourmet cookbooks.[24] His presence in Hollywood movies and even in pop culture has already been documented. In her trawl through recent 'American Rilkeana', Kathleen L. Komar discovers that this use of Rilke has become more widespread and perhaps even more surprising. She traces Rilke's place as self-help guru, especially (and paradoxically) on matters of love and sexual fulfilment; as 'an icon of [...] New Age Awakening'; a staple of the recent obsession with angelology; and a firmly established part of America's corporate boardroom culture.[25] Rilke's work must of course be filleted pretty carefully to serve in these ways and the rather curious notion of a Rilke of fulfilled love seems to stem more from John Mood's best-selling *Rilke on Love and other Difficulties* (1994) than

Rilke's own fraught love life – or indeed his poetry. Komar traces allusions to Rilke's *Book of Hours*, *Letters to a Young Poet* and the *Duino Elegies*. However, by now the specific references are secondary to the aura of the poet as spiritual guide. There is of course a certain irony in the fact that Rilke can successfully be made to serve the peculiar needs of capitalism (that he so despised) of the late twentieth century in quite this way.

## Rilke in dialogue: poetry as exchange

Although the interest in Rilke has been pretty much a constant in the English-speaking world, the eightieth anniversary of his death in 2007 saw the publication of work by number of high-profile poets – Martyn Crucefix, Sean O'Brien, Patrick McGuinness among a host of others – and the prospect of a new Rilke in English from *Penguin Classics*, to be edited by Michael Hofmann, has almost certainly been the catalyst for other distinguished poets such as Seamus Heaney, Jamie McKendrick, Robin Robertson, Don Paterson and Tom Paulin to try their hand. What is particularly noteworthy about this phase of reception, however, is that poets have been involved not simply in retranslating Rilke for their own historical moment, but also entering into a more profound poetic exchange or conversation with him that also foregrounds their own position within the poem. Thus, for example, Robin Robertson's beautiful 'Fall', a version of Rilke's 'Autumn' (KA I, 282–3), which concludes his spare and anxious 2002 collection *Slow Air*:

> We are all falling now. My hand, my heart,
> stall and drift in darkness, see-sawing down.
>
> And we still believe there is one who sifts and holds
> the leaves, the lives, of all those softly falling.[26]

> Wir alle fallen. Diese Hand da fällt.
> Und sieh dir andre an: es ist in allen.
>
> Und doch ist Einer, welcher dieses Fallen
> unendlich sanft in seinen Händen hält.

Here the shift of perspective is subtle but clear nevertheless. Gone is the absolute faith in a God as compensation for and deliverance from mortality. The introduction of 'we still believe', especially when set against the Rilke poem, foregrounds the fragility of that belief from the perspective of the present day. This is compounded by the contrast between the sound patterns of the poems. Whereas Rilke's poem concludes with the word 'holds' ('hält') and ties up the pattern of rhymes to bring the poem to a secure close, Robertson's version has the hand holding, but also sifting, and concludes on the word 'falling', which underlines the exquisite sound patterns of the strophe but ends on an open and falling cadence – a fitting final word for a collection preoccupied with the landscapes of death. Tom Paulin's 'The Swan', in his *The Road to Inver*, a volume dedicated to characteristically robust responses to European modernism, goes even further.[27] His version (or 'imitation') of Rilke's 'Der Schwan' (KA 1, 473), does away with the straightforward analogy upon which Rilke's poem is based and projects a more uneasy interrelation with human life:

> A drudge on piecework cackfooted he bumbles clumsily
> on the solid ground a plodder – wally– 's a lunkhead
> who wouldn't know a telos if he touched it
> trapped in this adhocery [ ... ]

The tour de force of this version is the comedy of the language which, as in many of the versions in this collection, appears to be a riff on contemporary idiom but slyly underpins the original to great effect ('cackfooted', 'adhocery'). The poem ends with an image of a swan gliding, 'an ark with wings for sails then a sovereign harp', which nets another Rilkean symbol and brings back the poem, like Rilke's, to the business of poetry. If these poems are examples of the way contemporary poets are making Rilke live in the present in a new way, I would like to conclude with two poets who foreground the act of exchange or conversation even further.

Don Paterson's *Orpheus*, billed as a version of Rilke's *The Sonnets to Orpheus*, was published in 2006. In an illuminating 'Afterword' and an 'Appendix' on the business of versioning, Paterson sets out the problem with the 'necessary oracularity' of Rilke's poem: 'It leaves us with poetry that can only be talked around and about, but not *with*.'[28] Paterson attempts to make of Rilke's sonnets something that can exist and be in conversation with our own age. 'Versions', Paterson says, 'are trying to be poems in their own right; while they have the original to serve as detailed ground-plan and elevation, they are trying to build themselves a robust home in a new country, in its vernacular architecture' (p. 73). There is no parallel text and the poems are titled, rather than numbered as they are by Rilke, which usefully names the preoccupations rather than the so-called subject-matter. By calling the book *Orpheus* rather than *The Sonnets to Orpheus*, Paterson keeps the address of the poems open; the book is at once by Orpheus, to Orpheus and about Orpheus, the god of song or, to put it in a more secular framework, the principle of singing itself. And indeed this is the central concern of Paterson in his own poetry and in his work as a professional musician. As the poet Mark Doty puts it in a review: 'Rilke both sings to Orpheus and ventriloquises him, creating, in these 55 sonnets, the remarkable sense that it is song itself, finally, that speaks.'[29] That same precarious double-take and the resulting regression take place once again in Paterson. What Paterson calls 'the near inhuman speed of the sonnet's composition' allows him a certain latitude in delivering the sonnets into English in order to make them comprehensible in the new tongue. Paterson's language is certainly more earthbound than Rilke's and more of the moment, but this does not mean it is in any sense a travesty: rather the metrical authority, taut formal coherence and sonority of the lines in English recreate and answer the German. 'Anemone' (p. 35), the version of Rilke's sonnet II: 5, begins thus:

> In the meadow the anemone
> Is creaking open to the dawn.
> By noon, the sky's polyphony
> Will flood her white lap till she drowns

> Blumenmuskel, der der Anemone
> Wiesenmorgen nach und nach erschließt,
> bis in ihren Schooß das polyphone
> Licht der lauten Himmel sich ergießt
>
> (KA II, 259)

Fittingly this reflection on being open as 'true receivers' in Paterson's English ('Empfänger' in the German) exemplifies the way the dialogue can take place, and the status of these versions as 'open ended enquiry' (p. 78). Paterson even argues for a new life, a potential new relevance, for such a poem.

> The strange anomaly – the fact that the translated poem can undergo conti-
> nuous cultural rebirth, in a way denied to the original – raises the possibility
> that some poems in translation could, theoretically, end up being *more* central
> to a culture than that of the language in which they were first conceived.
>
> (p. 75)

Those things central to *The Sonnets to Orpheus* – the voracity of the ma-chine, the call to confront human nature, the threat to our habitat, the dangers of solipsism, the need to find a way to live in a secular age – all these have a pressing significance in the present day and it is difficult to read the 'till she drowns' of the 'Anemone' poem without feeling (beyond the sexual connotations) some hint of the apocalyptic urgency of the present with which Paterson's versions are invested.

Jo Shapcott's *Tender Taxes*, a collection of versions of Rilke's poems in French, was published in 2001 and also attempts to bring Rilke into the realities of the here and now. The title of the collection refers to 'the tender and taxing conversation' held with Rilke over a decade as Shapcott worked on, and with, his *The Valaisian Quatrains* and the sequences 'Windows' and

'Roses' from the collection *Orchards* in 1926 (each of which furnishes a section of her collection).[30] As Shapcott comments: 'What transpired was not translation: my poems became instead responses, arguments, even dramatisations. I have called them versions here, reluctantly. We don't have the word for this kind of exchange' (p. ix). So Rilke himself is glimpsed 'in a wide-brimmed hat' pacing a vineyard, in the poem 'To Muzot from Gladestry' (p. 33) or 'walking up the lane towards me / with a bouquet of red berries from the hedgerow' ('Rilke spotted above Gilwern', p. 43), and the final section of poems, 'Tender Taxes' (pp. 83–98) is a sustained dialogue with a 'you' that is at once Rilke, a lover, the angel and perhaps poetry itself. The guiding spirit is a Rilkean one: 'transformation' and as in any such exchange everything is open to change.

This is a poetry emphatically rooted in contemporary reality; so the quatrains are translated from the Valais to the Welsh border lands and boast RAF Hawks (p. 30), computers (p. 34), or a garden shed that doubles for Rilke's Muzot bolt-hole and becomes 'a profane tower' (p. 35). But they also give voice to the darker aspects of that political history and landscape: investing Rilke's pastoral idyll with the buried past and the corrosive legacy of mine work, for example (p. 49). Rilke's sequence 'Windows' was originally published the year after Rilke's death in an edition with illustrations by his lover Baladine Klossowka (or Merline as she was known). Besides having a general symbolic resonance for the poet as one of his images of threshold, the subject had a special significance for the pair as instances of transition and absence. Shapcott comments that the challenge to her was 'to make this kind of utterance sound natural, contemporary. I had to invent a modern voice to speak the poems, the voice of someone you could imagine capable of speaking aloud to windows and a woman who is never there' (p. x). The result is a sequence of fifteen poems (each with different times as titles) that respond to rather than directly translate the originals and perform the vigil of a lover / poet whose head is pressed against the window watching the daylight shift and fade and who is seeking a you that is lover, window, poetry.

That sense of dialogue and the intervention by a contemporary sensibility also make themselves felt in the sequence 'Roses' but with a new slant:

> I began to see that in the sequence Rilke's roses were women. And more than that – petal – space – petal – these poems were versions of female genitalia. [...] he speaks to them, tells them what they are like, what makes them up, where their essence is to be found. My roses are given their own voice. They speak. And if you put my poems alongside Rilke's, more often than not you'll

find my roses addressing his, saying, in effect: 'It's not like that it's like this'. [...] Finally though, just as I believe Rilke's roses to be one extended love poem, so mine became the same and, in the end, a love poem to him.

This sense of dialogue with the original poem and poet (elsewhere a 'love letter on the wind' p. 52) means that the poems rarely square one to one with the French originals. Some begin as translations, but others take up motifs from the French poem and combine or vary them. So, for example, 'Dinner with Rilke' (p. 91) starts as a translation of Rilke's third poem from *Orchards* (KA v, 10–12). There are some small additions in the first two strophes: so, for example, where the angel of Rilke's poem is simply 'making up his mind' ('Reste tranquille, si soudain / l'Ange à ta table se décide'), in Shapcott's version the angel 'decides to love you'. However, Shapcott also adds a final strophe, absent in the French:

> You can't help yourself, though
> he's avid for everything, eating,
> kissing, anything to become you,
> to repossess your house.

This captures pretty well the intimacy of the exchange but also threat of loss associated with the transaction. It at once figures as a love affair, but also a literary encounter, thus conjuring the spectre of the 'anxiety of influence'[31] and especially the anxiety of a female poet writing in, but also attempting to write against, a male tradition. It is no chance that the final page of the collection is given over to a single-line quotation from Borges which speaks of intimacy but also loss of possession: 'I do not know which of us has written the page' (p. 100). That Rilke might end up so lost in this translation speaks perhaps of a typical and inevitable arc of literary reception that moves from veneration to identification and finally to critical exchange carried here to unusual extremes. It is clear, however, that the different versions of Rilke to emerge over the last half century or so in the English-speaking world reflect not only the needs of the particular moment but also the protean sensibility of the poet and the unique challenge of his language to stretch our own ways of seeing and saying.

## NOTES

1 From John Bayley's 'Introduction' to Rainer Maria Rilke, *Neue Gedichte / New Poems*, trans. Stephen Cohn (Manchester: Carcanet, revised paperback edition, 1997), p. 18.

KAREN LEEDER

2 Steven Kaplan, *Robert Bly and Randall Jarrell as Translators of Rainer Maria Rilke. A Study of the Translations and their Impact on Bly and Jarrell's own Poetry* (Frankfurt am Main: Lang, 1988), p. 231.

3 Hilde Domin, 'Zur Rilke Rezeption, im Jahre 1975: Rilke, Fragezeichen? Eine Rilke Renaissance im Jahre seines 100. Geburtstags?', in Heinz Ludwig Arnold (ed.), *Rilke? Kleine Hommage zum 100. Geburtstag* (Munich: edition text + kritik, 1975), pp. 60–6 (p. 61).

4 Ernst Jandl, 'Der gewöhnliche Rilke', in Arnold (ed.), *Rilke?*, pp. 7–26.

5 Durs Grünbein, *Ein kleines blaues Mädchen. Zu Rainer Maria Rilkes 'Das Karussell'* (Detmold: Literaturbüro Ostwestfalen-Lippe, 2007).

6 Michael Hofmann, *Behind the Lines: Pieces on Writing and Pictures* (London: Faber and Faber, 2001), p. 60.

7 Eudo C. Mason, *Rilke, Europe and the English-Speaking World* (Cambridge University Press, 1961), p. 42.

8 Ibid., p. 159.

9 W. H. Auden, 'Rilke in English', *The New Republic* 99–100 (6 September 1939), pp. 135–6.

10 Stephen Spender, 'Der Einfluss Rilkes auf die englische Dichtung', *Neue Auslese*, 1/ 10 (1945), 21–5.

11 W. H. Auden, *Collected Poems*, ed. Edward Mendelson (London: Faber and Faber, revised edition 1994), p. 194. Page references in the text are to this edition.

12 In his inaugural lecture as Professor of Poetry at Oxford, 'Making, Knowing and Judging' (1956), in W. H. Auden, *The Dyer's Hand and Other Essays* (New York: Vintage, 1989), p. 51.

13 Sidney Keyes, *Collected Poems* (Manchester: Carcanet, 2002). Page references in the text are to this edition.

14 Compare, for example, the work of the poet soldier Alun Lewis, *In the Green Tree*, with a preface by A. L. Rowse (London: George Allen & Unwin, 1948). In a letter to his wife from hospital in India in early 1943 he writes: 'I think the resultant poems are more morbid than usual – I was reading your Rilke this morning – he says a poet cannot write of joy until he has lamented; and that he has no right to lament unless he has the power of joy. I know I've the power of joy in me: you know it too. So Rilke will authorize my black tone-poems' (p. 32).

15 Archibald MacLeish, *Poetry and Experience* (Boston: Beacon Press, 1961), p. 106.

16 John Berryman, *77 Dream Songs* (New York: Farrar, Strauss and Giroux, 1964), p. 5.

17 Robert Bly, 'A Wrong Turning in American Poetry', reprinted in Bly, *American Poetry: Wildness and Domesticity* (New York: Harper & Row, 1990), pp. 7–35.

18 Robert Lowell, *Imitations* (New York: Farrar, Straus and Giroux, 1961), p. 98.

19 Randall Jarrell, *Complete Poems* (New York: W. W. Norton & Co., 1962), pp. 480 and 483 for the poems. The comment comes from Randall Jarrell, *A Sad Heart at the Supermarket* (New York: Atheneum, 1962), p. 166.

20 Jarrell, *Complete Poems*, p. 215.

21 Robert Bly, *Sleepers Joining Hands* (New York: Harper & Row, 1973), p. 59.

22 Robert Bly, *Selected Poems of Rainer Maria Rilke* (New York: Harper & Row, 1981), p. 3.

23 Robert Bly, *News of the Universe: Poems of a Twofold Consciousness* (San Francisco: Sierra Club Books, 1980), p. 281.
24 Kaplan, *Robert Bly and Randall Jarrell*, p. 238.
25 Kathleen L. Komar, 'Rilke in America: A Poet Re-created', in Hartmut Heep (ed.), *Unreading Rilke: Unorthodox Approaches to a Cultural Myth* (New York: Lang, 2001), pp. 149–70.
26 Robin Robertson, *Slow Air* (London: Picador, 2002), see the section 'From the Jardin des Plantes': 'The Panther', 'The Gazelle', 'The Flamingos' (pp. 32–4) and 'Fall' (p. 62).
27 Tom Paulin, *The Road to Inver: Translations, Versions, Imitations, 1975–2003* (London: Faber and Faber, 2004), 'The Island in the North Sea' (p. 2); 'Piano Practice' (p. 63); 'The Swan' (p. 87).
28 Don Paterson, *Orpheus. A Version of Rilke's 'Die Sonette an Orpheus'* (London: Faber and Faber, 2006), p. 65. Page references in the text are to this edition.
29 Mark Doty, 'The Singer Sung: Don Paterson's *Orpheus*', *The Guardian*, 11 November 2006.
30 Jo Shapcott, *Tender Taxes* (London: Faber and Faber, 2001), p. xi.
31 Harold Bloom, *The Anxiety of Influence: A Theory of Poetry* (Oxford: Oxford University Press, 1973).

Titles of collections, individual works and poems referred to in the text

## Published Works

| | |
|---|---|
| *Advent* | *Advent* |
| *Am Leben hin* | *Alongside Life* |
| *Auguste Rodin* | *Auguste Rodin* |
| *Aus Taschen-Büchern und Merk-Blättern* | *From Pocket Notebooks and Memory Pads* |
| *Briefe an einen jungen Dichter* | *Letters to a Young Poet* |
| *Briefe über Cézanne* | *Letters on Cézanne* |
| *Briefwechsel in Gedichten* | *Correspondence in Poems* |
| *Christus. Elf Visionen* | *Christ. Eleven Visions* |
| *Das Buch der Bilder* | *The Book of Images* |
| *Das Marien-Leben* | *The Life of the Virgin Mary* |
| *Das Stundenbuch* | *The Book of Hours* |
| including: | including: |
| 'Das Buch vom mönchischen Leben' | 'The Book of Monastic Life' |
| 'Das Buch von der Armut und vom Tode' | 'The Book of Poverty and Death' |
| 'Das Buch von der Pilgerschaft' | 'The Book of Pilgrimage' |
| *Das Tägliche Leben* | *Everyday Life* |
| *Die Aufzeichnungen des Malte Laurids Brigge* | *The Notebooks of Malte Laurids Brigge* |
| *Die Frühen Gedichte* | *The Early Poems* |
| *Die Sonette an Orpheus* | *The Sonnets to Orpheus* |
| *Die Weise von Liebe und Tod des Cornets Christoph Rilke* | *The Lay of the Love and Death of the Cornet Christoph Rilke* |

| | |
|---|---|
| *Dir zur Feier* | *To Celebrate You* |
| *Duineser Elegien* | *Duino Elegies* |
| *Geschichten vom lieben Gott* | *Stories of the Dear Lord* |
| *Im Frühfrost* | *Hoar-Frost* |
| *In und nach Worpswede* | *In and After Worpswede* |
| *Larenopfer* | *Offerings to the Lares* |
| *Leben und Lieder* | *Lives and Songs* |
| *Les Vergers* | *Orchards* |
| *Les Quatrains Valaisans* | *The Valaisian Quatrains* |
| *Mir zur Feier* | *To Celebrate Myself* |
| *Mitsou, histoire d'un chat* | *Mitsou, Story of a Cat* |
| *Neue Gedichte* | *New Poems* |
| *Tagebücher aus der Frühzeit* | *Diaries of the Early Years* |
| *Traumgekrönt* | *Dream-Crowned* |
| *Wegwarten* | *Wild Chicory* |
| *Zwei Prager Geschichten* | *Two Tales of Prague* |

## Other works

| | |
|---|---|
| 'Böhmische Schlendertage' | 'Bohemian Walking-Days' |
| 'Das Jahrhundert des Kindes' | 'The Century of the Child' |
| 'Das Testament' | 'The Testament' |
| 'Der Apostel' | 'The Apostle' |
| 'Der Brief des jungen Arbeiters' | 'Letter from the Young Worker' |
| 'Der Wert des Monologs' | 'The Value of Monologue' |
| 'Entwurf einer politischen Rede' | 'Draft of a Political Speech' |
| 'Erlebnis' | 'Experience' |
| 'Florenzer Tagebuch' | 'Florentine Diary' |
| 'Gedichte an die Nacht' | 'Poems to the Night' |
| 'Les Fenêtres' | 'Windows' |
| 'Les Roses' | 'Roses' |
| 'Marginalien zu Friedrich Nietzsche' | 'Marginalia on Friedrich Nietzsche' |
| 'Maurice Maeterlinck' | 'Maurice Maeterlinck' |
| 'Moderne Lyrik' | 'On Modern Lyric Poetry' |
| 'Russische Kunst' | 'On Russian Art' |
| 'Smargendorfer Tagebuch' | 'Schmargendorf Diary' |
| 'Über den jungen Dichter' | 'About the Young Poet' |
| 'Ur-Geräusch' | 'Primal Sound' |
| 'Worpswede Tagebuch' | 'Worpswede Diary' |

(*continued*)

## Poems

| | |
|---|---|
| 'Abend in Skåne' | 'Evening in Skåne' |
| 'Alkestis' | 'Alcestis' |
| 'Alles Gefühl, in Gestalten und Handlungen' | 'All feeling, in figures and actions' |
| 'Alles wird wieder groß sein' | 'All will be great once more' |
| 'Als ich die Universität bezog' | 'When I attended University' |
| 'Am Rande der Nacht' | 'At the Edge of Night' |
| 'An den Dichter: / Vita N:A' | 'To the Poet: / Vita N:A' |
| 'An Jens Peter Jacobsen' | 'To Jens Peter Jacobsen' |
| 'Archaïscher Torso Apollos' | 'Archaic Torso of Apollo' |
| 'Auch du wirst groß sein' | 'You too will be great' |
| 'Auf der Kleinseite' | 'In the Little Quarter' |
| 'Aus dem Nachlaß des Grafen C.W.' | 'From the Literary Remains of Count C.W.' |
| 'Ausgesetzt auf den Bergen des Herzens' | 'Exposed on the Mountains of the Heart' |
| 'Bangnis' | 'Anxiety' |
| 'Begegnung in der Kastanienallee' | 'Encounter in the Avenue of Chestnuts' |
| 'Bei St. Veit' | 'By St Vitus's' |
| 'Blaue Hortensie' | 'Blue Hydrangea' |
| 'Dame vor dem Spiegel' | 'Lady Before the Mirror' |
| 'Das Bett' | 'The Bed' |
| 'Das Kapitäl' | 'The Capital' |
| 'Das Karussell' | 'The Carousel' |
| 'Das Land ist licht' | 'The countryside is bright' |
| 'Das Leben ist gut und licht' | 'Life is good and bright' |
| 'Das letzte Zeichen laß an uns geschehen' | 'The last sign, let it happen to us' |
| 'Das Lied der Witwe' | 'The Widow's Song' |
| 'Das Lied des Trinkers' | 'The Drinker's Song' |
| 'Das Portal' | 'The Portal' |
| 'Das Wappen' | 'The Coat of Arms' |
| 'David singt vor Saul' | 'David Sings Before Saul' |
| 'Denn Armut ist ein groß er Glanz aus Innen' | 'For poverty is a great shining from within' |
| 'Denn, Herr, die groß en Städte sind' | 'For, Lord, the great cities are' |
| 'Denn wir sind nur die Schale und das Blatt' | 'For we are only husk and leaf' |
| 'Der alte Invalid' | 'The Old Invalid' |

| | |
|---|---|
| 'Der Apfelgarten' | 'The Apple-Orchard' |
| 'Der Ball' | 'The Ball' |
| 'Der Berg' | 'The Mountain' |
| 'Der Blinde' | 'The Blind Man' |
| 'Der Dichter' | 'The Poet' |
| 'Der Fahnenträger' | 'The Standard-Bearer' |
| 'Der Geist Ariel' | 'The Spirit Ariel' |
| 'Der Junggeselle' | 'The Bachelor' |
| 'Der Käferstein | 'The Beetle-Stone' |
| 'Der König' | 'The King' |
| 'Der Lesende' | 'The Man Reading' |
| 'Der Leser' | 'The Reader' |
| 'Der letzte Graf von Brederode entzieht sich türkischer Gefangenschaft' | 'The Last Count of Brederode Avoids Capture by the Turks' |
| 'Der Maler' | 'The Painter' |
| 'Der Narr' | 'The Fool' |
| 'Der Pavillon' | 'The Pavilion' |
| 'Der Platz' | 'The Square' |
| 'Der Regen greift mit seinen kühlen Fingern' | 'The rain clutches with its cool fingers' |
| 'Der Schauende' | 'The Man Looking' |
| 'Der Schwan' | 'The Swan' |
| 'Der Turm' | 'The Tower' |
| 'Die Anfahrt' | 'The Arrival' |
| 'Die Braut' | 'The Bride' |
| 'Die Erblindende' | 'Woman Going Blind' |
| 'Die Fensterrose' | 'The Rose Window' |
| 'Die Flamingos' | 'The Flamingos' |
| 'Die Gazelle' | 'The Gazelle' |
| 'Die Genesende' | 'The Convalescent' |
| 'Die Gruppe' | 'The Group' |
| 'Die Heilige' | 'The Saint' |
| 'Die Kathedrale' | 'The Cathedral' |
| 'Die Kinder' | 'The Children' |
| 'Die Kurtisane' | 'The Courtesan' |
| 'Die Parke' | 'The Parks' |
| 'Die Rosenschale' | 'The Bowl of Roses' |
| 'Die roten Rosen waren nie so rot' | 'The red roses were never so red' |
| 'Die spanische Trilogie' | 'The Spanish Trilogy' |

(continued)

'Die Spitze'
'Die Treppe der Orangerie'
'Die Waise'
'Die Zaren'
'Dies ist das schweigende Steigen
    der Phallen'
'Du Berg, der blieb da die Gebirge
    kamen'
'Du kommst und gehst'
'Du lächelst leise'
'Du meine heilige Einsamkeit'
'Du, Nachbar Gott'
'Du siehst, ich will viel'
'Du wirst nur mit der Tat erfaßt'
'Du meine heilige Einsamkeit'
'Ehe'
'Ein Doge'
'Ein Mädchen, weiß und vor der
    Abendstunde. . .'
'Ein Prophet'
'Eine Welke'
'Eingang'
'Engellieder'
'Es war im Mai'
'Es winkt zu Fühlung'
'Fortschritt'
'Fragst du mich: Was war in deinen
    Träumen?'
'Fremde Familie'
'Früher Apollo'
'Funde'
'Fünf Gesänge'
'Für Karl du Prel'
'Gaben'
'Geburt der Venus'
'Geschrieben für Karl Grafen
    Lanckorónski'
'Gewitter, Gewitter'
'Gong'
'Haßzellen, stark im größten
    Liebeskreise'
'Herbst'

'Lace'
'The Steps of the Orangerie'
'The Orphan'
'The Tsars'
'This is the silent rising of the
    phalluses'
'You rock that stayed as the
    mountains came'
'You come and go'
'You smile gently'
'You my sacred solitude'
'You, Neighbour God'
'You see, I want much'
'You are only grasped by an act'
'You my sacred solitude'
'On Marriage'
'A Doge'
'A girl, white and before the
    evening hour. . .'
'A Prophet'
'A Faded Lady'
'Entrance'
'Angel Songs'
'It was in May'
'It beckons us to feeling'
'Progress'
'If you ask: What was in your
    dreams?'
'Family of Strangers'
'Early Apollo'
'Finds'
'Five Songs'
'For Karl du Prel'
'Gifts'
'The Birth of Venus'
'Written for Karl Count
    Lanckorónski'
'Storm, Storm'
'Gong'
'Cells of hatred, strong in the
    greatest circle of love'
'Autumn'

'Herr: Wir sind ärmer denn die
  armen Tiere'
'Hetären-Gräber'
'Hinter Smichov'
'Ich bin, du Ängstlicher'
'Ich bin zuhause zwischen Tag und
  Traum'
'Ich liebe dich, du sanftestes Gesetz'
'Ich möchte dir ein Liebes schenken'
'Ich weiß euch lauschen: eine
  Stimme geht'
'Ich will ihn preisen'
'Im alten Hause'
'Im Saal'
'In einem fremden Park'
'In Karnak wars'
'In tiefen Nächten grab ich dich'
'Jahrmarkt'
'Jugend-Bildnis meines Vaters'

'Kannst du mir sagen, wo das
  Eiland liegt'
'Karl der Zwölfte von Schweden
  reitet in der Ukraine'
'Komm, du, du letzter'
'Kretische Artemis'
'L'Ange du Méridien'
'Leichen-Wäsche'
'Letzter Abend'
'Lieben'
'Lied vom Meer'
'Lieder der Mädchen'
'Man muß sterben, weil man sie
  kennt'
'Mittelböhmische Landschaft'
'Nacht'
'Nächtliche Fahrt'
'Notizen zur Melodie der Dinge'
'O wo ist der, der aus Besitz und
  Zeit'
'Orpheus. Euridike. Hermes'

'Lord: we are poorer than the
  poorest creatures'
'Tombs of the Hetaerae'
'Behind Smichov'
'I am, you fearful one'
'I am at home between day and
  dream'
'I love you, you gentle law'
'I would like to give you a keepsake'
'I know how to listen to you:
  a voice goes'
'I want to praise him'
'In the Old House'
'In the Drawing-Room'
'In a Foreign Park'
'It was in Karnak'
'In deep nights I dig for you'
'Market'
'Portrait of My Father as a Young
  Man'

'Can you tell me where the island
  is?'
'Charles the Twelfth of Sweden
  rides in the Ukraine'
'Come you, you last one'
'Cretan Artemis'
'L'Ange du Méridien'
'Corpse-Washing'
'Last Evening'
'Loves'
'Song of the Sea'
'Songs of the Girls'
'One must die because one knows
  them'
'Landscape in Mid-Bohemia'
'Night'
'Night Ride'
'Notes on the Melody of Things'
'Oh where is he, who from
  possession and time'
'Orpheus. Eurydice. Hermes'

*(continued)*

| | |
|---|---|
| 'Perlen entrollen' | 'Pearls roll away' |
| 'Quai du Rosaire' | 'Quai du Rosaire' |
| 'Requiem' | 'Requiem' |
| 'Requiem für eine Freundin' | 'Requiem for a Friend' |
| 'Requiem für Wolf Graf von Kalckreuth' | 'Requiem for Wolf Count of Kalckreuth' |
| 'Reste tranquille si soudain' | 'Stay calm if suddenly' |
| 'Römische Fontäne' | 'Roman Fountain' |
| 'Römische Sarkophage' | 'Roman Sarcophagi' |
| 'Schrein, schrein!' | 'Cry out, cry out!' |
| 'Schwarze Katze' | 'Black Cat' |
| 'Seele im Raum' | 'Soul in Space' |
| 'Selbstbildnis aus dem Jahre 1906' | 'Self-Portrait 1906' |
| 'Senke dich, du langsames Serale' | 'Sink down, you slow Serale' |
| 'Sieben Gedichte' | 'Seven Poems' |
| 'Sieh, Gott, es kommt ein Neuer an dir bauen' | 'See, God, another comes to build on you' |
| 'Solang du Selbstgeworfenes fängst' | 'So long as you catch the things you throw yourself' |
| | |
| 'Spätherbst in Venedig' | 'Late Autumn in Venice' |
| 'Spaziergang' | 'A Walk' |
| 'Stimmen' | 'Voices' |
| 'Stimmung im Barkenhoff' | 'Atmosphere in the Barkenhoff' |
| 'Sturm' | 'Storm' |
| 'Tanagra' | 'Tanagra' |
| 'Tränen, Tränen, die aus mir brechen' | 'Tears, tears breaking out of me' |
| 'Trotzdem' | 'Nevertheless' |
| 'Und doch, obwohl ein jeder' | 'And yet, although each one of us' |
| 'Und wenn ich rastend dir die Hände gebe' | 'And when I give you my hands in rest' |
| 'Venedig' | 'Venice' |
| 'Venezianischer Morgen' | 'Venetian Morning' |
| 'Vorfrühling' | 'Early Spring' |
| 'Was wirst du tun, Gott, wenn ich sterbe' | 'What will you do, God, when I die' |
| 'Wendung' | 'Turning-Point' |
| 'Wenn ich manchmal in meinem Sinn' | 'When I sometimes in my mind' |
| 'Wie die Natur die Wesen überläßt...' | 'Just as nature leaves its creatures...' |
| 'Wunsch' | 'Wish' |

# GUIDE TO FURTHER READING

*Works used throughout this volume*

Baron, Frank, Ernst S. Dick, and Warren R. Maurer (eds.). *Rilke: The Alchemy of Alienation*. Lawrence: The Regents Press of Kansas, 1980.

Bauschinger, Sigrid and Susan L. Cocalis (eds.). *Rilke-Rezeptionen: Rilke Reconsidered*. Tübingen and Basel: Francke, 1995.

Demetz, Peter, Joachim W. Storck and Hans Dieter Zimmermann (eds.). *Rilke: Ein europäischer Dichter aus Prag*. Würzburg: Königshausen & Neumann, 1998.

Eckel, Winfried. *Wendung: Zum Prozess der Poetischen Reflexion im Werk Rilkes*. Würzburg: Königshausen & Neumann, 1994.

Engel, Manfred and Dieter Lamping (eds.). *Rilke und die Weltliteratur*. Düsseldorf and Zürich: Artemis & Winkler, 1999.

Engel, Manfred (ed.). *Rilke-Handbuch: Leben – Werk – Wirkung*. Stuttgart and Weimar: Metzler, 2004.

Görner, Rüdiger (ed.). *Rainer Maria Rilke*. Darmstadt: Wissenschaftliche Buchgesellschaft, 1987.

Hamburger, Käte. *Rilke in neuer Sicht*. Stuttgart: Kohlhammer, 1971.

Heep, Hartmut. *Unreading Rilke: Unorthodox Approaches to a Cultural Myth*. New York: Peter Lang, 2001.

Metzger, Erika A. and Michael M. Metzger (eds.). *A Companion to the Works of Rainer Maria Rilke*. Rochester: Camden House, 2001.

Mason, Eudo C. *Rilke*. Edinburgh: Oliver & Boyd, 1963.

Ryan, Judith. *Umschlag und Verwandlung: Struktur und Dichtungstheorie in R. M. Rilkes Lyrik*. Munich: Winkler, 1972.

Schnack, Ingeborg. *Rainer Maria Rilke: Chronik seines Lebens und seines Werkes*. 2 vols. Frankfurt am Main: Insel, 1975.

Solbrig, Ingeborg H. and Joachim Storck (eds.). *Rilke heute: Beziehungen und Wirkungen*, 2 vols. Frankfurt am Main: Suhrkamp, 1975–6.

Stahl, August. *Rilke-Kommentar zum lyrischen Werk*. Munich: Winkler, 1978.

Stevens, Adrian and Fred Wagner (eds.). *Rilke und die Moderne: Londoner Symposion*. Munich: iudicium, 2000.

*Biography*

Freedman, Ralph. *Life of a Poet: Rainer Maria Rilke*. New York: Farrar, Straus and Giroux, 1996; and the extended and much improved German version of

Freedman's biography, *Rainer Maria Rilke: Der junge Dichter (1875–1906)* and *Der Meister (1906–1926)*, trans. Curdin Ebneter and Vera Hauschild. Frankfurt am Main and Leipzig: Insel, 2001–3.

Görner, Rüdiger and Duncan Large (eds.). *Nietzsche-Revisionen im 20. Jahrhundert.* Göttingen: Vandenhoeck & Ruprecht, 2003.

Hillebrand, Bruno (ed.). *Nietzsche und die deutsche Literatur*, I: *Texte zur Rezeptionsgeschichte 1873–1963* and II: *Forschungsergebnisse*. Tübingen and Munich: Niemeyer, 1978.

Holthusen, Hans E. *Portrait of Rilke: An Illustrated Biography*, trans. W. H. Hargreaves. New York: Herder and Herder, 1971.

Leppmann, Wolfgang. *Rilke: A Life*, trans. Russell M. Stockman; verse trans. by Richard Exner. Cambridge: Lutterworth, 1984.

Prater, Donald A. *A Ringing Glass: The Life of Rainer Maria Rilke.* Oxford and New York: Oxford University Press, 1986.

Salis, Jean Rodolphe de. *Rainer Maria Rilke: The Years in Switzerland: A Contribution to the Biography of Rilke's Later Life*, trans. N. K. Cruickshank. London: Hogarth, 1964.

Steiner, Jakob (ed.). *Rainer Maria Rilke und die Schweiz.* Zurich: Akademie-Verlag, 1992.

Torgersen, Paul. *Dear Friend: Rainer Maria Rilke and Paula Modersohn-Becker.* Evanston, IL: Northwestern University Press, 1998.

### Rilke as a correspondent

Blankenagel, John C. 'Rainer Maria Rilke's Striving for Inner Harmony'. *Germanic Review*, 11 (1936), 109–21.

Schoolfield, George C. 'Rainer Maria Rilke and Ellen Key: A Review Essay'. *Scandinavian Studies*, 68 (1996), 490–500.

### Early poems

Brodsky, Patricia Pollock. *Russia in the Works of Rainer Maria Rilke.* Detroit: Wayne State University Press, 1984.

Hutchinson, Ben. *Rilke's Poetics of Becoming.* Oxford: Legenda, 2006.

Rolleston, James. *Rilke in Transition: An Exploration of his Earliest Poetry.* New Haven and London: Yale University Press, 1970.

### New Poems

Boa, Elizabeth, 'Asking the Thing for the Form in Rilke's *Neue Gedichte*'. *German Life and Letters*, 27 (1973/4), 285–94.

Phelan, Anthony. *Rilke: Neue Gedichte.* Critical Guides to German Texts, 14. London: Grant and Cutler, 1992.

Sheppard, Richard W. 'From the "Neue Gedichte" to the "Duineser Elegien": Rilke's Chandos-Crisis'. *Modern Language Review*, 68 (1973) 577–92.

Smith, P. C. 'Elements of Rilke's Creativity'. *Oxford German Studies*, 2 (1967) 129–48.

Stewart, Corbet. 'Rilke's *Neue Gedichte*: The Isolation of the Image'. *Publications of the English Goethe Society*, 48 (1978), 81–103.


## The Notebooks of Malte Laurids Brigge

Huyssen, Andreas. 'Paris/Childhood: The Fragmented Body in Rilke's Notebooks of Malte Laurids Brigge', in Andreas Huyssen and David Bathrick (eds.). *Modernity and the Text: Revisions of German Modernism*. New York: Columbia University Press, 1989, pp. 113–41.
Kittler, Friedrich. *Discourse Networks 1800/1900*. Stanford University Press, 1990, pp. 315–36.
Kleinbard, David. *The Beginning of Terror: A Psychological Study of Rainer Maria Rilke's Life and Work*. New York University Press, 1993.


## Duino Elegies

Boney, Elaine. 'Structural Patterns in Rilke's *Duineser Elegien*'. *Modern Austrian Literature*, 15 (1982), 71–90.
Guardini, Romano. *Rainer Maria Rilkes Deutung des Daseins: Eine Interpretation der 'Duineser Elegien'*. Munich: Kösel-Verlag, 1953.
Komar, Kathleen L. *Transcending Angels: Rainer Maria Rilke's 'Duino Elegies'*. Lincoln: University of Nebraska Press, 1987.
Paulin, Roger and Peter Hutchinson (eds.). *Rilke's 'Duino Elegies': Cambridge Readings*. London: Duckworth, 1996.


## The Sonnets to Orpheus

Casey, Timothy J. *A Reader's Guide to Rilke's Sonnets to Orpheus*. Galway: Arlen House, 2001.
Kellenter, Sigrid. *Das Sonett bei Rilke*. Frankfurt: Lang, 1982.
Gerok-Reiter, Annette. *Wink und Wandlung: Komposition und Poetik in Rilkes 'Sonette an Orpheus'*. Tübingen: Niemeyer, 1996.
Peucker, Brigitte. 'The Poetry of Transformation: Rilke's Orpheus and the Fruit of Death', in *Lyric Descent in the German Romantic Tradition*. New Haven: Yale University Press, 1987, pp. 119–65.
Stahl, E. L. 'Rilke's *Sonnets to Orpheus*: Composition and Thematic Structure'. *Oxford German Studies*, 9 (1978), 119–35.
Strauss, Walter A. *Descent and Return: The Orphic Theme in Modern Literature*. Cambridge, MA: Harvard University Press, 1971.
Yates, Edgar W. *Tradition in the German Sonnet*. Bern: Lang, 1981.


## Rilke and modernism

Hauschild, Vera (ed.). *Rilke heute: Der Ort des Dichters in der Moderne*. Frankfurt am Main: Suhrkamp, 1997.
Klieneberger, H. R. 'Romanticism and Modernism in Rilke's Die Aufzeichnungen des Malte Laurids Brigge'. *Modern Language Review* 74, (1979), 360–7.

Nicholls, Peter. *Modernisms: A Literary Guide*. Basingstoke and London: Macmillan, 1995.
Ryan, Judith. *The Vanishing Subject: Early Psychology and Literary Modernism*. University of Chicago Press, 1991.
Ryan, Judith. *Rilke, Modernism and Poetic Tradition*. Cambridge University Press, 1999.
Sheppard, Richard W. *Modernism – Dada – Postmodernism*. Evanston, IL: Northwestern University Press, 2000.

## Rilke the reader

Batterby, K. A. J. *Rilke and France: A Study in Poetic Development*. Oxford University Press, 1966.
Fülleborn, Ulrich. 'Rilkes schwedische Gedichte'. *Blätter der Rilke-Gesellschaft*, 17/18 (1989/90), 156–66.
Jephcott, E. F. N. *Proust and Rilke: The Literature of Expanded Consciousness*. London: Chatto and Windus, 1972.
Mason, Eudo C. *Rilke und Goethe*. Cologne: Böhlau, 1958.
Nalewski, Horst. *Rainer Maria Rilke: Reise nach Ägypten: Briefe, Gedichte, Notizen*. Frankfurt am Main and Leipzig: Insel, 2000.
Singer, Herbert. *Rilke und Hölderlin*. Cologne: Böhlau, 1957.
Tavis, Anna A. *Rilke's Russia: A Cultural Encounter*. Evanston, IL: Northwestern University Press, 1994.

## Rilke and the visual arts

Baron, Frank (ed.). *Rilke and the Visual Arts*. Lawrence, ĸs: Coronado, 1982.
Bridge, Helen. 'Rilke and the Modern Portrait'. *Modern Language Review*, 99 (2004), 694–708.
Bridge, Helen. 'Rilke's *Neue Gedichte* and the Visual Arts', in *Critical Exchange: European Art Criticism of the Eighteenth and Nineteenth Centuries*, ed. Carol Adlam and Juliet Simpson. Oxford: Lang, 2008, pp. 341–58.
Bridgwater, Patrick. 'Rilke and the Modern Way of Seeing', in *Rilke und der Wandel in der Sensibilität*, ed. Herbert Herzmann and Hugh Ridley. Essen: Die Blaue Eule, 1990, pp. 19–41.
Herzogenrath, Wulf and Andreas Kreul (eds.). *Rilke. Worpswede: Eine Ausstellung als Phantasie über ein Buch*. Bremen: Hauschild, 2003.
Pettit, Richard. 'The Poet's Eye for the Arts: Rilke Views the Visual Arts around 1900', in *Imagining Modern German Culture: 1889–1910*, ed. Françoise Forster-Hahn. Hanover and London: University Press of New England, 1996, pp. 251–73.
Stahl, August. 'Rilke und Richard Muther: Ein Beitrag zur Bildungsgeschichte des Dichters', in *Ideengeschichte und Kunstwissenschaft: Philosophie und bildende Kunst im Kaiserreich*, ed. Ekkehard Mai, Stephan Waetzoldt and Gerd Wolandt. Berlin: Mann, 1983, pp. 223–51.
Wilkens, Manja. 'Etappen einer Genieästhetik: Lebensstationen und Kunsterfahrungen Rilkes', in *Rainer Maria Rilke und die bildende Kunst seiner Zeit*, ed. Gisela

Götte and Jo-Anne Birnie Danzker. Munich and New York: Prestel, 1996, pp. 9–29.

### Rilke: thought and mysticism

Detsch, Richard. *Rilke's Connections to Nietzsche*. Lanham, MD, New York, Oxford: University Press of America, 2003.
Gadamer, Hans-Georg. 'Poetry and Punctuation', 'Rainer Maria Rilke's Interpretation of Existence: On the Book by Romano Guardini', 'Mythopoietic Reversal in Rilke's Duino Elegies,' in *Literature and Philosophy in Dialogue: Essays in German Literary Theory*, trans. and ed. Robert H. Paslick. Albany, NY: State University of New York Press, 1994.
Gray, Ronald D. 'Rilke's Poetry' and 'Rilke and Mysticism', in *The German Tradition in Literature, 1871–1945*. Cambridge University Press, 1965.
Heller, Erich. 'Rilke and Nietzsche, with a Discourse on Thought, Belief, and Poetry', in *The Disinherited Mind*. Harmondsworth: Penguin, 1961, pp. 109–55.
Smith, P. C. 'A Poem of Rilke: Evidence for the Later Heidegger', *Philosophy Today*, 21/3–4 (1977), 250–62.
Smith, P. C. 'Heidegger's Misinterpretation of Rilke', *Philosophy and Literature*, 3 (1979), 3–19.

### Rilke and his philosophical critics

Blanchot, Maurice. *L'Espace littéraire*. Paris, Gallimard, 1968; *The Space of Literature*, trans. Ann Stock. Lincoln and London: University of Nebraska Press, 1982.
De Man, Paul. 'Tropes Rilke', in *Allegories of Reading*. New Haven and London: Yale University Press, 1979, pp. 28–56.
Fóti, Véronique. *Heidegger and the Poets*. New Jersey and London: Humanities Press, 1992.
Haar, Michel. *The Song of the Earth*, trans. Reginald Lilly. Bloomington and Indianapolis: Indiana University Press, 1993.
Heidegger, Martin. 'Wozu Dichter?' in *Holzwege*. Frankfurt am Main: Klostermann, 2003, pp. 269–320; *Off the Beaten Track*, trans. and ed. Julian Young and Kenneth Haynes. Cambridge University Press, 2002, pp. 200–41.
Santner, Eric. *On Creaturely Life: Rilke, Benjamin, Sebald*. Chicago and London: University of Chicago Press, 2006.

### Rilke's legacy in the English-speaking world

Benfey, Christoph. 'Rilke in America: How and Why the Work of the Rootless Poet Found Such a Welcome Home Here'. *The New Republic*, 31 (3 January 1994), 31–6.
Enright, D. J. 'Reluctant Admiration. A Note on Auden and Rilke', in *The Apothecary's Shop: Essays on Literature*. London: Secker & Warburg, 1957, pp. 187–205.
Heep, Hartmut. *A Different Poem: Rainer Maria Rilke's American Translators Randall Jarrell, Robert Lowell, and Robert Bly*. New York: Lang, 1996.

McCarthy, Patricia (ed.). *A Reconsideration of Rainer Maria Rilke. Agenda*, 42/3–4 (2007).

Mason, Eudo C. *Rilke, Europe, and the English-Speaking World*. Cambridge University Press, 1961.

Morse, B. J. 'Contemporary English Poets and Rilke'. *German Life and Letters*, 1 (1947/8), 272–85.

Robertson, Ritchie. 'Edwin Muir and Rilke'. *German Life and Letters* 36/1–2 (1982/3), 317–28.

# INDEX

INDEX

# INDEX OF WORKS

# Cambridge Companions to...

## AUTHORS

*Eugene O'Neill* edited by Michael Manheim

*George Orwell* edited by John Rodden

*Ovid* edited by Philip Hardie

*Harold Pinter* edited by Peter Raby (second edition)

*Sylvia Plath* edited by Jo Gill

*Edgar Allan Poe* edited by Kevin J. Hayes

*Alexander Pope* edited by Pat Rogers

*Ezra Pound* edited by Ira B. Nadel

*Proust* edited by Richard Bales

*Pushkin* edited by Andrew Kahn

*Rilke* edited by Karen Leeder and Robert Vilain

*Philip Roth* edited by Timothy Parrish

*Salman Rushdie* edited by Abdulrazak Gurnah

*Shakespeare* edited by Margareta de Grazia and Stanley Wells

*Shakespearean Comedy* edited by Alexander Leggatt

*Shakespeare on Film* edited by Russell Jackson (second edition)

*Shakespeare's History Plays* edited by Michael Hattaway

*Shakespeare's Last Plays* edited by Catherine M. S. Alexander

*Shakespeare's Poetry* edited by Patrick Cheney

*Shakespeare and Popular Culture* edited by Robert Shaughnessy

*Shakespeare on Stage* edited by Stanley Wells and Sarah Stanton

*Shakespearean Tragedy* edited by Claire McEachern

*George Bernard Shaw* edited by Christopher Innes

*Shelley* edited by Timothy Morton

*Mary Shelley* edited by Esther Schor

*Sam Shepard* edited by Matthew C. Roudané

*Spenser* edited by Andrew Hadfield

*Laurence Sterne* edited by Thomas Keymer

*Wallace Stevens* edited by John N. Serio

*Tom Stoppard* edited by Katherine E. Kelly

*Harriet Beecher Stowe* edited by Cindy Weinstein

*August Strindberg* edited by Michael Robinson

*Jonathan Swift* edited by Christopher Fox

*J. M. Synge* edited by P. J. Mathews

*Tacitus* edited by A. J. Woodman

*Henry David Thoreau* edited by Joel Myerson

*Tolstoy* edited by Donna Tussing Orwin

*Mark Twain* edited by Forrest G. Robinson

*Virgil* edited by Charles Martindale

*Voltaire* edited by Nicholas Cronk

*Edith Wharton* edited by Millicent Bell

*Walt Whitman* edited by Ezra Greenspan

*Oscar Wilde* edited by Peter Raby

*Tennessee Williams* edited by Matthew C. Roudané

*August Wilson* edited by Christopher Bigsby

*Mary Wollstonecraft* edited by Claudia L. Johnson

*Virginia Woolf* edited by Sue Roe and Susan Sellers

*Wordsworth* edited by Stephen Gill

*W. B. Yeats* edited by Marjorie Howes and John Kelly

*Zola* edited by Brian Nelson

## TOPICS

*The Actress* edited by Maggie B. Gale and John Stokes

*The African American Novel* edited by Maryemma Graham

*The African American Slave Narrative* edited by Audrey A. Fisch

*American Modernism* edited by Walter Kalaidjian

*American Realism and Naturalism* edited by Donald Pizer

*American Travel Writing* edited by Alfred Bendixen and Judith Hamera

*American Women Playwrights* edited by Brenda Murphy

*Arthurian Legend* edited by Elizabeth Archibald and Ad Putter

*Australian Literature* edited by Elizabeth Webby

*British Romanticism* edited by Stuart Curran

*British Romantic Poetry* edited by James Chandler and Maureen N. McLane

*British Theatre, 1730–1830,* edited by Jane Moody and Daniel O'Quinn

*Canadian Literature* edited by Eva-Marie Kröller

*Children's Literature* edited by M. O. Grenby and Andrea Immel

*The Classic Russian Novel* edited by Malcolm V. Jones and Robin Feuer Miller